BOOKBANNING
IN AMERICA

About the Author

Before taking up writing full time more than twenty years ago, William Noble was a practicing attorney. After graduating from Lehigh University, he received his law degree from the University of Pennsylvania, was a member of the Philadelphia and Pennsylvania bars, and corporate counsel to Armstrong World Industries. He was director of the Model Cities Program of Lancaster, Pennsylvania, consultant to the Pennsylvania Department of Community Affairs and to the international division of the U.S. Department of Housing and Urban Development.

He is the author or co-author of a number of books, including *How to Live with Other People's Children* (a Book-of-the-Month Club Alternate), *"Shut Up!" He Explained* and two other titles for writers (Eriksson) — Main Selections of the Writer's Digest Book Club, and numerous articles and short stories that have appeared in more than thirty magazines and newspapers. He now lives in Cornwall, Vermont.

BOOKBANNING IN AMERICA

Who Bans Books?
— And Why

by

William Noble

Paul S. Eriksson
PUBLISHER
MIDDLEBURY, VT 05753

Manufactured in the United States of America

10 9 8 7 6 5 4 3 2

Library of Congress Cataloging-in-Publication Data

Noble, William.
    Bookbanning in America.

    Includes bibliographical references and index.
    1. Censorship — United States.   2. Prohibited books —
United States.   I. Title.
Z658.U5N6   1990   098'.1'0973   90-3413
ISBN 0-8397-1080-1
ISBN 0-8397-1081-X Paper

The First Amendment

Congress shall make no law, respecting an establishment of religion, or prohibiting the free exercise thereof; or abridging the freedom of speech, or of the press, or the right of the people peaceably to assemble, and to petition the Government for a redress of grievances.

In memory of my grandfather, A.C.,
whose love of books was unsurpassed.

Contents

Foreword

It was 1971, and Richard Nixon sat in the White House.
Salvatore Allende Gossens, an avowed Marxist, had been
elected President of Chile (by a bare plurality — 36 per
cent of the vote), and it was no secret Richard Nixon and
his administration found this a threat. That Allende's
election was lawful and that it continued a centuries-long
tradition of peaceful, democratic change in Chile did not
move the people in the White House.

My wife and I had returned from an extended tour of
Chile, and we planned to write about what we saw.
Perhaps the most intriguing story concerned a Chilean
government program to build low and moderate income
housing using "sweat equity" — a future homeowner
would provide labor (his "sweat") in the construction of
his home, and after he had put in a certain number of
hours, the downpayment would be achieved. Then he
could finance the home through regular payments.

The program appeared to work. Thousands of houses had been built, and many Chilenos could, for the first time, own their own homes. Here was something that might be possible for America.

I called the editor of a U.S. government-sponsored publication and outlined the story.

Delighted to see the manuscript, she said. "We can offer international as well as national coverage, people in the political as well as the housing field are on our mailing list."

We sent the manuscript and waited a month, then another month. No word at all. By the end of the third month I called the editor.

"We're so busy right now," she said, "we'll get to it soon."

"You're still interested?"

"Oh, yes."

Six weeks later the editor called. "We've -ah- had to make some adjustments around here," she said. "We're part of the government, of course."

I knew a turn down when I heard one.

"We liked your piece . . . it was read by a lot of people, comments were positive . . . perhaps if conditions were different . . ."

"The writing didn't work, then?"

"The writing's fine," she said, lowering her voice. "It's just . . . well, I'm not supposed to tell you this, but we've gotten word nothing positive or complimentary about Chile is to be published. Nothing, that's what we've been told."

"Our story isn't political," I argued.

She hesitated. "Your story went all the way to the White House before it was turned down . . . I tried, you see, I really did . . ."

Every writer at some point faces the spectre of censorship because there are no words or combinations of words that can avoid offending the sensibilities of all. For every advocate of free speech there is bound to be someone who sees unforgivable licentiousness. "I do not like that book! . . . I am offended by those references . . . My children may not read such trash! . . ." Emotions such as these are readily translated into value judgments which become a spur to action. In the famous Island Trees case (decided in 1982) a group of Long Island parents felt certain books in the school library were "anti-American, anti-Christian, anti-Semitic . . . or just plain filthy." The fact that some of the authors included Kurt Vonnegut, Bernard Malamud, Langston Hughes and Richard Wright did not deter these parents. They sought control of doing what they considered most effective — they tried to ban the books.

A divided U.S. Supreme Court finally decided the case, and a plurality of the justices subscribed to the comments of Justice Brennan: ". . . the First Amendment rights of students may be directly and sharply implicated by the removal of books from the shelves of a school library; and local school boards may not remove books from school-library shelves simply because they dislike the ideas contained in those books."

"Disliking" ideas is certainly a foundation of censorship, but the reasons for bookbanning are often couched more vividly: *dangerous* is one of the favorites: a book is dangerous to . . . ; another is *offensive:* this book "offends" my . . . ; or *ridicule:* the book "makes fun of, belittles" . . . ; or *ignores:* this book "ignores the importance of" . . .

These are the bookbanner's devils because what the books represent are significant threats to a life of familiar, well-ordered ideas. Anything that creates change carries fallout, and bookbanners see themselves vulnerable in situations they no longer control. The first bookbanning, in fact, reflected this: in 387 B.C. Plato suggested Homer be expurgated "for immature readers" because, of course, there was no way to control how certain information might be received. Four centuries later, in autocratic Rome, Caligula tried to banish Homer's *Odyssey* because he feared the people would be energized by Greek ideals of freedom, and his control would vanish. Censorship has proved to be a mighty foe through the ages, from the burning of the Alexandrian Library in 642 A.D. to the creation of the *Index Liborum Prohibitorum* by Pope Paul IV in 1559 to the operation of vice societies in nineteenth- and twentieth- century America, to the execution order hurled by Iran's Ayatollah Khomeni at Salman Rushdie for *The Satanic Verses*. Bookbanning has been with us for a long time, and its malevolence is every bit as hardy today.

Some of the numbers are startling — more than one thousand bookbanning incidents in America *each year,* and these are only the ones recorded by librarians and educators. There is reason to believe the numbers might be much higher if more informal banning (such as a book conveniently "lost" or quietly burned or not reordered) could be traced. In fact, recent bookbanning incidents in school libraries have increased by nearly two hundred per cent.

Bookbanning is not a closet activity carried out by a misguided soul responding to shouts of fringe-crazies. It is a pervasive ethic that springs from no single socio-economic stratum and resides in no single geographic region. Bookbanning incidents arise in all parts of the country and play themselves out in many forums — school board proceedings, public libraries, legislative hearings, ad hoc parental complaints, governmental committees, private group assessments, open court and even commercial publishing decisions. Bookbanning is as much a part of our lives as the morning newspaper or wake-up television; its cultural influence is strong enough to affect the way we think and the way we communicate.

Years ago the people in the White House decided an article on Chile should not be published because it didn't carry the right political message. The ideas were "disliked," in Justice Brennan's words, and for him this would be enough to violate the First Amendment's guarantee of free expression. Yet there is an even broader lesson: bookbanning is more than the denial of a constitutional right; it establishes an ethic, a system of moral do's and don'ts. To help understand it fully — and to combat it if we wish — this book has been written, examining *why* people ban books, *who* they are and *what* they hope to accomplish.

From the moment of its inception, many offered their help and guidance, and my gratitude is substantial and unwavering. There was immediate encouragement and enthusiasm for a project that proved extraordinarily challenging and satisfying. To list everyone who touched the work would run into hundreds, but among them, I would like to single out a few who provided special assistance:

Thank you to Donna Hulsizer and Arthur Kropp of People For the American Way, Leanne Katz of the National Coalition Against Censorship and Judith Krug of the American Library Association's Intellectual Freedom Committee. My thanks, also, to my editor and friend,

Peggy Eriksson, to Gara LaMarche of PEN's Freedom to Read Committee, to the office of U.S. Senator James Jeffords, and to Mark Lynch, Burton Joseph, Charles Peters, John Swan and Cleo Wilson.

I appreciated the time afforded me by all those I interviewed (some whom appear in the text), but in particular I would like to thank John Ventresco, Gene Garthwaite and Ken McCormick for offering insights that intrigued and worked.

Perhaps most of all, I offer my gratitude to Hans Raum and the Middlebury College Library. Without their unflagging help and interest this book would have been exceedingly more difficult to research and to write.

PART ONE

INCIDENT IN KENTUCKY

1

How It Happens

This was the American Dream: a sanctuary on the earth for individual man: a condition in which he could be free not only of the old established closed-corporation hierarchies of arbitrary power which had oppressed him as a mass, but free of that mass into which the hierarchies of church and state had compressed and held him individually thralled and individually impotent . . .

—William Faulkner, 1955

It was early September, 1986, and on this sultry evening in Graves County, Kentucky, the school board was winding up its regular meeting. Chairman Jeff Howard and the other four board members had disposed of the agenda items, including controversial funding for school construction, and with the clock moving toward ten-thirty it seemed this meeting might adjourn earlier than most could remember.

3

There was nothing remarkable about this school board nor about the school — Graves County High School — that they administered. There was nothing, in fact, remarkable about Graves County, Kentucky, other than that it was home to forty-one Baptist churches and boasted home-town ties to the novelist and short story writer, Bobbi Ann Mason. Graves County sits in western Kentucky, approximately four hours from Louisville, three hours from Nashville, Tennessee and about an hour east of the Missouri border. There was no major hi-tech industry in Graves County, no national or international tourist attraction such as Disneyland or a professional-sports Hall of Fame; there was no major real estate development in Graves County, no pleasure-beckoning "strip," no breathtaking scenic wonder.

Graves County was home to about thirty thousand human beings, a third of whom lived in Mayfield, the county seat. Graves was neither the largest nor the smallest of Kentucky's counties, and Mayfield was neither the largest nor the smallest of the county seats.

Graves County was not a remarkable place in which to live, but its citizens did have strong feelings about their close-in world, and at this school-board meeting these feelings bubbled to the surface.

The school-board meeting room was small, perhaps thirty feet by thirty-five feet. It held the five board members who sat behind a slender table, the superintendent of schools, Billy Watkins, the school board attorney, Dan Sharp, the principal of Graves County High School, Jerald Ellington, several members of the local media and a handful of spectators. It was not a restless group, nor was it confrontational; most eyed the clock as they sensed matters drawing to a close, and their minds focused on the change from air-conditioned comfort in the meeting room to the sticky humidity that awaited them outside. There were times in early September in western Kentucky when no one believed the summer heat would ever go.

Chairman Jeff Howard was about to ask for a motion of adjournment when there was a flutter of movement down the table. "Are there any other items?" he asked.

One of the board members, John Shelton, sought his attention. "Yessir," Shelton said. John Shelton lived in Wingo, a small town about eight miles outside Mayfield, and was the most unpredictable of all the board members because he operated more independently. He was not noted for originating action, but he had the capacity for dominating the plan or agenda of someone else. His education was limited, though he was skilled in his work with heavy machinery. Everyone knew his general nature could be frosty and uncompromising.

On this early September evening in 1986 there was no hint on John Shelton's face of what concerned him. The members of the press groaned because they sensed a delay in their hoped-for early departure. Usually these meetings never ended until after midnight, and most media members dreaded the prospect of attending, knowing that issues were talked to death, not only by board members but by spectators who were allowed to make comments.

In John Shelton's hand there was a book, a paperback, which he slammed onto the table. "I want an explanation why this book is being taught at Graves County High School!"

For the members of the school board, for the members of the media, for staff members of the school administration, it was the first time in memory that such an event had occurred. No one had ever objected to a book being used in local high school in just this way, and there was momentary surprise and confusion.

John Shelton held up the book. The title was easy to read: *As I Lay Dying*. It was by William Faulkner.

> *I got a job in the power plant, on the night shift, from 6 P.M. to 6 A.M., as a coal passer. I shovelled coal from the bunker into a wheel-barrow and wheeled it in and dumped it where the fireman could put it in his boiler. About eleven o'clock the people would be going to bed, and so it did not take so much steam. Then we could rest, the fireman and I. He would sit in a chair and doze. I had invented a table out of a wheelbarrow in the coal bunker, just beyond a wall from where a dynamo ran. It made a deep, constant humming noise, there was no more work to do until about 4 A.M., when we would have to clean the fires and get up steam again. On these nights, between 12 and 4, I wrote* As I Lay Dying *in six weeks, without changing a word . . .*
>
> —William Faulkner, 1932

John Shelton nodded at the book. "I've looked through some of it, and it would not be acceptable to most of you."

There was a hush over the room as he mentioned that LaDone Hills, a friend and neighbor, had brought the book to his attention. Her son was a sophomore at Graves County High School and this book was assigned reading in tenth-grade English. John Shelton could hardly contain his indignation. "This is the kind of book you'd pick up in a backways place and read," he said, opening it and pointing to passages that were highlighted by a yellow marker.

He thrust the volume at Jerald Ellington, the principal of Graves County High School. "I want you to read some of these . . ." indicating the highlighted passages.

"Out loud," he added.

Ellington, a tall, soft-spoken man whose popularity with his students was well known, reacted with surprise. He attempted to demur, but John Shelton was insistent.

You can't escape responsibility, Shelton seemed to be saying, *you must bear the embarrassment* . . .

It was a struggle of wills, and finally Jerald Ellington shrugged and reached for the book. He flipped the pages, stopping at an angry speech of Jewel, a son of the woman whose dying and death consume the book. One line carried the yellow highlighting:

"If there is a God, what the hell is he for?"

Jerald Ellington read it aloud. He flipped to another page and read a highlighted passage, then to still another page — altogether seven separate places in the book where he found some reference to God or abortion, or actual curse words — "bastard," "goddam," "son of a bitch."

The meeting room bristled with tension, and the somnolence of this sultry September evening had evaporated. Jerald Ellington knew his reading had given credence, at least in the minds of the board members, to what John Shelton had charged.

"We have a procedure," he began, "we have a review procedure where administrators and parents are involved. We ask the parents to write their objections to a book, and after we hear the objections and decide, the parents can appeal, if they wish, to the superintendent and then to the board of education . . ."

The board members seemed unmoved by his words.

". . . None of that has been followed in this case," he said. "You are encroaching on First Amendment rights. The ACLU or someone like them is going to jump on this."

Another board member waved the explanation away. He stood up and pointed his finger at Jerald Ellington, his face stern. "Get the damn book off the shelves tomorrow!"

In a moment a vote was taken. The minutes reflect the following:

A motion was made by Johnny C. Shelton, seconded by Robert L. Spaulding, that the William Faulkner book, *As I Lay Dying,* be banned from the Graves County High School. The following voted "Aye":

Johnny C. Shelton

Robert L. Spaulding

Anthony W. Goodman

Charles R. Holmes

Jeffrey D. Howard

Chairman Howard ruled the motion carried.

LONNIE HARP

I was a reporter for the *Mayfield Messenger,* the daily newspaper for Graves County. I covered the school board and I was present at the school-board meeting where the banning of *As I Lay Dying* took place. There was no talk at the meeting of why the book was used in high school English, nor what its purpose was. John Shelton wanted a vote taken right there, at the meeting, and it sounded like he had talked to a couple of others on the school board beforehand, though I never got actual knowledge about this.

The vote was taken so fast we were stunned by the speed, so then they went into closed session [where they could appropriately discuss personnel and pending litigation matters under Kentucky's open-meetings law], and before they did that, I asked John Shelton for his copy of the book, and I took down the passages highlighted in yellow ink. Seven or eight passages were highlighted. It seemed like it was all dialogue, not much exposition. At that point we — the radio reporters and I — said to ourselves, *They've just banned a book!* We knew it would be big news; we were probably the only people in the room who sensed the story possibility here.

After they came out of the closed session, I asked several board members if they had read the book. None said they had, a couple said they had "thumbed" through it. I didn't believe any of them thought they had created a big controversy.

JERALD ELLINGTON

When I had to read those passages at the board meeting, I saw nothing wrong in Faulkner's words, though I hadn't read the book. I did share with the board the fact that what our teachers attempted to do with a book of this nature was not to condone particular language but to try and put in perspective the message the author was trying to get across, using the personality of a particular character based upon his experiences and regardless of whether that character was educated or not.

I also shared with the board the way we chose books at the high school. Our language-arts teachers met with the librarians, and they consulted the recommended list from the American Library Association. Then they all met with the local community college and Murray State University [about 30 miles away] and other nearby colleges to discover what kind of materials these institutions expected our kids to be exposed to. We got recommendations from these various schools and we combined it with the American Library Association list and our people previewing the books; we decided at what grade level students should be exposed to various writings . . . that was the way we came to have *As I Lay Dying* in the school.

They voted, and the meeting was adjourned.

And I got the book off the shelf.

DAN SHARP

I was the school-board attorney, born here in Graves County, a graduate of the high school and Murray State University, and except for three years of law school in Memphis and three years in the service, I have lived here all my life. I have represented the school board the past four years, and they do not always take my advice.

It started one night when a board member mentioned the fact he had gotten some complaints about reading *As I Lay Dying* from a parent. It seemed there was about five minutes of discussion and all of a sudden a motion popped out from this individual that he wanted this book removed from the school library . . . it was almost like cleaning up business at the end of a board meeting. The board member who brought this up very definitely caught everyone by surprise. He said, "I want it banned, I want it out of this school, trash and filth, let's have a vote on it."

Without much discussion at all, the motion was passed unanimously, and I was kind of scratching my head about it. It happened so fast I'm not sure everyone realized the significance. Once the vote was taken, someone made a motion to adjourn, and everyone walked out of there.

The story of *As I Lay Dying* concerns the dying and death of Addie Bundren and the way her husband, Anse, and her sons, Cash, Darl, Jewel, Vardaman and her daughter, Dewey Dell, deal with it. They are poor white Mississippi farming folk, and their reactions to Addie's demise range from surprising empathy to crass self-centeredness. They are the type of family William Faulkner portrayed so well throughout his career.

Addie wishes to be buried at the family cemetery in Jefferson, a full day's ride from the farm, and Anse is determined her wish be fulfilled. After several delays, and some emotional thrashing, Addie finally succumbs, and the family party sets out with Addie laid to rest in a coffin son Cash has just finished constructing.

It takes them nine days to reach their destination because they attempt to ford a river, now swollen by heavy rains, and are met by disaster. A huge log floats downstream, upsets the wagon and breaks Cash's leg so he almost drowns. The wagon and the mules are destroyed, and Addie's coffin slips overboard, barely retrieved at the last moment. But she finally is laid to rest in the family cemetery.

Faulkner told his story from multiple points of view, with each character probing his or her own feelings and reactions to the dying and death of Addie Brundren. The chapters are short and quick-paced, the dialogue true to the regional dialect, the general style stream-of-consciousness and interior monologue. One feels what the characters feel, sees what they see, and tastes, smells and hears along with them.

It is not a long book, nor is it complicated. But it is a sensitive book, portraying a poor family in the throes of crisis, offering unretouched sides of the family personality — from dignified to disgraceful, from pitiable to picturesque.

There are no graphic sex scenes, no strings of four-letter words, no subtle appeal to prurient interest. It does not advocate the overthrow of the government of the United States by force, nor does it attempt to ridicule any minority group or person, nor encourage discrimination by reason of race, religion, color, sex or age. There is occasional use of the epithet, "bitch!," the reference to and the urging of an abortion, the sprinkling of curses or mild-enough blasphemies.

And that is all.

For every writer, the ultimate question is how close to the truth does his work strike. In *As I Lay Dying* William Faulkner seems content that authenticity and believability are the heart of what he has produced.

> *These are people that I have known all my life in the country I was born in. The actions, the separate actions, I may have seen, remembered. It was the imagination probably that tied the whole thing together into a story. It's difficult to say just what part of any story comes specifically from imagination, what part from experience, what part from observation. It's like having . . . three tanks with a collector valve. And you don't know just how much comes from which tank. All you know is a stream of water runs from the valves*

*when you open it from the three tanks — observation, experi-
ence, imagination . . .*
                                        —William Faulkner, 1957

On the outskirts of Mayfield are three important enclaves, each reflective in its own way of the Graves
County personality. Closest in is the Graves County Fairgrounds, its high wooden slats delineating the roadway
from the small grounds and pocket-sized stadium, but
also underscoring the ruralness of the area. Where else, of
course, do fairgrounds abound than as setting for a
county fair? Where else does a county fair arise than on
the porches of rural America?

A bit farther from town, along Kentucky Route 45 on
the road to Paducah, is the sprawling, multi-structured,
highly visible General Tire plant which employs about
2500 people. It is the largest employer in western Kentucky, and the fact that it sits within walking distance of
Mayfield makes its shadow over the community formidable indeed. But it is a benevolent giant, "always good to
the community" as a local political observer describes it,
providing the bulk of donations to local charities such as
the United Way and responding quickly whenever a major emergency has arisen. Many in top-level manage-
ment, however, were neither born nor educated in
Graves County. These are the fast-track executives who
come to Graves County for a while, prove their worth and
then are promoted elsewhere in the many-levelled General Tire corporate structure. But the plant has been at its
present site for more than thirty years, and its union is
strong and active in the community. Some of the General
Tire executives might choose to live outside Graves
County (and endure a thirty to forty-five minute com-

mute), but for the bulk of the employees Mayfield and Graves County are home, and Graves County High School is where many of their children go to school.

A bit farther along Kentucky Route 45 is a group of dark-stained buildings spotted across a hillside. Mostly low and rectangular, these buildings make up Mid-Continent Baptist Bible College, the institution of higher education closest to Mayfield and the forty-one Baptist churches sprinkled across Graves County. Its somber, unpretentious public face belies its importance in Baptist Church affairs because its Baptist missionary training is known the world over, and there are those who come from the farthest corners of the globe to participate. The College now has a four-year accreditation, though its campus, by comparison with Murray State University thirty miles to the south, is barely playground size. Yet it represents a seat of power, and for the Baptists of Graves County it is a source of pride and solidity.

It is to these Baptists that one must look for the religious backbone of Graves County. By far the largest denomination, the Baptists count more than thirteen thousand members in a county-wide population of fewer than three times that number. "People say about this area that it is probably the church-goingest place in the world," says Reverend Charles Simmons, Director of the Graves County Baptist Association. "They used to say about eighty-percent of the population were church-going people." And with forty-one active Baptist churches — as well as Catholic and several Protestant denominations — it is difficult to dispute.

"I think it's a Christian area, and people have been taught and live by that atmosphere, and it's a county way of life," Reverend Simmons continues. "I would hope the Christian influences would cause them to do this. At this particular point the interest in church in Graves County is strong, though it goes up and down, but at this moment it is up. With our group I see a real strong movement all over for people coming back to the basics of Christianity and serving the Lord. I think our church membership is continuing to grow, and Sunday school is primarily the reaching out of our denomination, and this is where we reach the largest numbers of people. We Southern Baptists have millions of members across the country and thousands of churches. What goes on in the schools is important because all of our children are involved — our denomination would be concerned that our schools have a high type of morality."

By seven o'clock the morning after the Graves County school-board vote on *As I Lay Dying,* word began to spray beyond the small group of citizens who listened in silence on that sultry September evening. First to mark the event was the Mayfield radio station whose reporters were part of media coverage at school-board meetings. The seven o'clock local news started off, "At the monthly meeting of the Graves County school board last night a vote was taken to. . . ."

Suddenly the numbers of those who *knew* reached into the thousands. On the eight o'clock local news the story was repeated, and again at nine o'clock. There were many who now wished they had been at the meeting, if only to voice their sentiments.

And what few *could* realize at that moment was that a sparse recitation of the facts had gone out over the AP wire even as the local radio station reported the events to Graves County. The banning of William Faulkner would reach newsrooms across the country in a matter of moments.

Dan Sharp, the school-board lawyer, trudged up the

stairs to his office on this Friday morning, tired and unsettled. Late night meetings were the bane of most school-board attorneys, and Sharp was no exception. His mind was rarely pulsing with energy the morning after the school board met.

He would have no luxurious breather on this morning, certainly. As he reached his outer office, his secretary was waiting, holding a sheaf of telephone messages, more than usually awaited his arrival. She pointed to one from School Superintendent Billy Watkins. "He needs to talk to you right away."

The sense of foreboding Dan Sharp had felt the evening before was stronger now. In a moment he was speaking to the superintendent.

"I've been giving some thought to what went on last night," Dan Sharp said. "There could be problems because of that vote."

"That's why I called you," Watkins said. "It bothers me, too."

"I can see First Amendment questions here, free speech and censorship. It could get embarrassing."

"That little matter wasn't on the agenda, either," Billy Watkins reminded him. "I've been getting phone calls this morning, mainly from the media but a few local citizens, too. I've been referring them to you."

Dan Sharp glanced at the message pile his secretary handed him. Now he understood why there were so many. "I'll deal with them," he said.

When Lonnie Harp arrived for work that morning at the *Mayfield Messenger*, he was met by editor Mike Turley. The story had become big enough to lead the front page. "Get follow-up quotes," Turley told him.

Lonnie Harp went to his desk, remembering that the

major objection to the book at the school-board meeting had been its alleged blasphemy. Religion would play a part in this from now on. Ministers, he knew, were very influential in Graves County. They were opinion leaders, though not in the political sense. But people identified with their churches in western Kentucky, more so than in most regions of the country.

He telephoned Jerald Ellington at Graves County High School. The English Department had taken the school board's action personally. "The board didn't follow appropriate channels in removing the book," Ellington told him. "We're very disappointed."

Lonnie Harp remembered Jerald Ellington reading selected passages aloud from *As I Lay Dying.* That couldn't have set well with professional educators.

"A sentence or paragraph from just about every book in print can be taken out of context," Ellington said, noting that what can be offensive to some readers can also be educational. He emphasized the English Department felt students should be exposed to values and events of other times and places.

Lonnie Harp needed a quote from someone else directly involved. He dialed the high school again and asked for Delora English, who happened to be the teacher in whose class *As I Lay Dying* had been assigned. It didn't take long to realize that pressure from the bookbanning vote was just as strong on her as it had been on Jerald Ellington. "The book," she said, "is a fine example of 'stream of consciousness' literature; it is something I think students should read." Her voice grew firm. "We begin discussions on the book in class next week."

Lonnie Harp couldn't write the story yet — perhaps he never would. But one thing was clear: what Jerald

Ellington referred to as "disappointment" was really outrage, the school board was clamping down on the teachers and they didn't like it a bit. He sensed that in Delora English's clipped tones.

Mike Turley walked over to his desk and showed him the dummy head for the front page:

COUNTY BOARD BANS FAULKNER BOOK

Thirty miles north, the newsroom at the *Paducah Sun* also hummed with the story. A larger paper, situated in a larger city, the *Paducah Sun* nevertheless followed events in Mayfield and Graves County closely. In fact, one of the reporters had been at the school-board meeting, and now the newsroom staff had split up tasks to provide greater dimension for the story. Someone had contacted school-board chairman Jeff Howard.

No, Howard said, he hadn't read the whole book, "only portions," and he didn't know if other board members had read it. But he didn't think the book should be required reading. "God's name is used in vain in several places. A young girl goes to a so-called doctor to get an abortion . . . we hoped the teacher would select a book more appropriate for the sophomore class."

What Jeff Howard saw was a subtle threat to family harmony. "The problem is that many times a student might be so embarrassed by the reading material they may not tell their parents about it. The parents might not know what they are reading."

There was no need to remind the *Paducah Sun* that it was a sixteen-year-old boy who objected to *As I Lay Dying* in the first place. And he did tell his mother about it. In this instance, at least, what Jeff Howard feared did not happen.

The newsroom then contacted Bob Spaulding who had seconded John Shelton's motion to ban the book. "There's a lot better literature for students to read than to learn how to curse," Spaulding said, noting that he was aware students do curse. But that didn't mean schools should require books that had curse words in them.

He mentioned that the year before, his daughter had been assigned to read *As I Lay Dying*. "It just didn't make sense to her why she should have to study it," he said, describing her as uncomfortable with the language and the content. He admitted he had not read the book, though he planned to do so now.

And, oh yes, he said, none of his five children were allowed to have a copy of the book. "Parents need to get involved," he emphasized. "We don't take the time to get involved that we should."

The story was coming together, through eye-witness accounts, interviews, comments and fact-checking. It would run on one of the inside pages of the *Paducah Sun* but it would be multi-columned and multi-paged, and it would bring out the comments of the school board as well as the school administration.

One more side needed to be heard from, though.

Sitting in her small office in Louisville, four hours away, was Suzanne Post, Director of the Kentucky branch of the American Civil Liberties Union. Middle-aged, obviously well-educated and an active participant in prior civil rights struggles, somehow Suzanne Post had heard of the bookbanning. She had no doubt the Graves County School Board had committed a grievous act. "It's certainly an infringement on academic freedom," she told the *Paducah Sun*. "This board is on some thin ice legally. I would hope that a school board would have more respect for issues that involve academic freedom."

What was the ACLU going to do?

She demurred for the moment, but one thing made her press on with uncommon zeal. Years before, she had been in graduate school where her major area of study was William Faulkner, and the subject of her master's thesis was *As I Lay Dying*.

> *If there is a villain in* [As I Lay Dying] *it's the convention in which people have to live, in which they in that case insisted that because this woman had said I want to be buried twenty miles way, that people would go to any trouble and anguish to get her there. The simplest thing would have been to bury her where she was in a pleasant place. If they wanted to be sentimental about it they could have buried her in some place that she would like to go and sit by herself for awhile. Or if they wanted to be practical, they could have taken her out to the back yard and buried her. So if there is a villain, it was the convention which gave them no out except to carry her through fire and flood twenty miles in order to follow the dying wish which by that time meant nothing . . .*
> *— William Faulkner, 1957*

MIKE TURLEY

I've been here at the *Mayfield Messenger* for sixteen years, six years as editor, and the incident caught me by surprise. It was certainly newsworthy, and we had a reporter covering the meetings as we always did, a routine meeting, nothing big on the agenda, late summer. We ran the story on the bookbanning the next day, no larger than a normal school board story would be, but we led with the banning part because it was the most significant thing going on that evening.

I think the headline the next day [*County Bans Faulkner Book*] was a good head and gave it a good start. Once the process got going it generated more interest with parents and got them interested in who could say what goes on the bookshelves. It probably ended up with the situation being better than it had been before.

Jerald Ellington

By the next morning the newspaper and the radio station had the story, and everybody was taken aback by what had happened — you just can't do this sort of thing! — and then the ACLU got involved. When this thing started hitting nationwide, it had a devastating effect on the teacher involved and on the whole department. You're talking about a department of twelve people, and over half of them were Sunday school teachers, and every one of them was a regular church attendee — one of them was a minister. Delora English was in the choir at the First Baptist Church; she was there two or three times a week. She and the others took it all very personally because the chairman of the school board said or implied she should have known better than to teach this stuff. The department felt total abandonment by the school board because no procedures were followed. It was like, "You people are nothing but a den of iniquity."

From that moment I was right in the middle of things because I was trying to hold my faculty together. They were crying, they really felt they had been abandoned.

In the next three days events solidified and feelings grew more outspoken. Where a citizen of Graves County might have harbored private thoughts about the banning, others were coming to see it as an issue that required a public stand. It was not a matter that general school administrative policy could bury, that much was obvious from the first forty-eight hours following the school-board vote. There was a rift in the community, and because it transcended economics and politics, it had no common touchstone, other than what was obscene or not obscene, blasphemous or not blasphemous.

It was, simply, the divide between morality and immorality, free expression and censorship. It was not institutional, nor was it grandly abstract. It was an issue involving a citizen's right — to read or not to read, to write or not to write.

Two days after the school board vote, a dark-haired woman in her forties, soft spoken but determined, sat down and wrote a letter to the *Mayfield Messenger*. "Dear Editor:" she began, "I am the parent who opposed my son reading an assignment in 10th grade literature class at Graves County High . . ."

Her name was LaDone Hills, a resident of Wingo, and it was she who had contacted John Shelton to complain about *As I Lay Dying*. Her son, she wrote, "did not want to read the book because of some of the words written in it."

Most responsible parents would have taken the next logical step, as LaDone Hill did. "Immediately, I began to examine the book." But some would not have reacted as she did. "And [I] was shocked by its contents."

She wrote that she had contacted the school and spoken with Principal Jerald Ellington who explained that if she would send a signed note to her son's teacher, an alternative book would be assigned. She acknowledged that this had been done, but her purpose in writing took on a more somber tone with the next two sentences: "The fact that my son had been excused from reading this book did not extend to others which had or would have this assignment. Normally, I do not get involved in school affairs but because of my concern for other students and to make other parents aware of the contents of the material in this book and perhaps other books, I began to pursue a way to get such materials removed from our educational program."

This letter was not the mark of someone burdened by hate nor bristling for revenge. It was not the undecipherable nonsense of a poorly educated victim of the economic class wars. The conscientiousness, the balanced sense of responsibility LaDone Hills portrayed supported the view her belief was neither rashly acquired nor limited to fringe effect. She considered what she had done to be of vital importance.

"I thank God," she continued, "that we have good moral men sitting in the seats of our county school board who are willing to set 'apart from the multitude' and stand against the use of such books as this one in our educational system. The hand of God working in a few people has accomplished the ban of this particular book and hopefully has alerted us to some of the things we should be aware of in our society."

She offered her priorities: "I had rather my son have a personal knowledge of God than to have the highest formal education or to be chosen as the President of the United States . . ."

She signed herself, "A Concerned Parent."

Mike Turley ran the letter from LaDone Hills in the

Mayfield Messenger, and there were those in the community who found added consolation from her words and from the fact she was willing to speak out publicly. But such public affirmation carried with it the solidifying of values, both pro and con. Simultaneously, more than two hundred miles away, Suzanne Post of the ACLU was composing her own letter, only she did not send it to the local newspaper.

Post directed her words to the Graves County School Board, and the letter opposed what the school board had done, calling it unconstitutional, a violation of the First Amendment guarantees of free expression. In a phone conversation with Lonnie Harp, she amplified her letter. Her tone was indignant, less restrained than the letter would show. "Frankly," she emphasized, "these were improper procedures that were used in throwing Faulkner out of the Graves County schools, it is a pretty extreme situation. We rarely get a Nobel Prize winner thrown out of a public school."

Her feelings might have been even sharper if she could have known there was a meeting of the executive committee of the Graves County Baptist Association going on at that moment. The meeting had not been called specifically to discuss the school board banning of *As I Lay Dying* but, as it happened, the regular executive committee monthly meeting was on this date, and so the bookbanning became part of the agenda. The forty-one Baptist churches in Graves County belonged to the association, and the executive committee consisted of one minister and one lay person from each of those congregations — a total of eighty-two members.

This was the most formidable Baptist committee in Graves County, representing every congregation, every church, as well as secular and religious points of view. For forty percent of the people in Graves County, the executive committee of the Graves County Baptist Association was a moral barometer.

It didn't take long for the school board's bookbanning vote to surface, and it was apparent that the Baptist Association found to its liking what the school board had done. The language, the blasphemies and the cursing in *As I Lay Dying* were enough to mark the book distasteful, and there was strong support for the Graves County School Board.

"We should write a letter," someone suggested.

"It's a moral issue," another said.

"That board was right!" said a third.

A motion was made from the floor. "I move that the Association set forth our support in writing for what the Graves County School Board has done."

"Second!" came quick support.

Discussion followed and then a vote was called. Forty-one Baptist churches, eighty-two representatives. The vote was unanimous.

Reverend Al Cobb, a short, round man, smooth faced, in his early forties was chosen to write the letter. Al Cobb was minister of the High Point Baptist Church, an articulate man, outgoing and friendly. He had read the book and was singularly unimpressed. He found it dull, uninteresting, hardly representative of what a Nobel Prize winner should write.

After the vote Al Cobb drafted the letter. It was shown to the members of the executive committee who gave their approval; then the letter was sent to the school board on Graves County Baptist Association letterhead. Al Cobb portrayed the sentiments of his fellow Baptists precisely:

The executive board of the Graves County Baptist Association by unanimous action on Monday, September 8, 1986 voted to commend the action of the Graves County Board of Education in removing *As I Lay Dying* by William Faulkner from the libraries of the Graves County Schools because of the offensive language content of the book. Realizing that various groups are applying pressure upon the Board of Education to rescind their action, we wish to take this means of communicating our support for the stand you are taking. We urge you to continue to take measures which will safeguard our children from being forced to read and study filthy literature in the classroom.

The furor continued to build as the Graves County School Board prepared for its next public meeting, exactly one week after the vote to ban *As I Lay Dying*. But by now the situation had caught the attention of outsiders. The *Louisville Courier-Journal* called, one of the New York television networks made vague inquiries, letters started to arrive from far away places. Mike Turley's in-box at the *Mayfield Messenger* began to resemble a post office drop. He spoke to Lonnie Harp about getting a statement from the school board before the next meeting.

"Let me try Jeff Howard," Lonnie Harp said, and he dialed the number. Actually, he had been trying to reach the school-board chairman all week. The phone had rung and rung, but no one had answered.

But this time there was success. A woman answered, and Lonnie Harp pictured Jeff Howard's wife, a slender, attractive woman in her early thirties. "Mrs. Howard, I'd like to speak to your husband."

"May I ask who's calling?"

Lonnie Harp identified himself.

She put the phone down and was gone for a long moment. When she returned there was a note of dismissal in her voice. "He can't come to the phone just now, he's sorry."

It was obvious she would say nothing more, and Lonnie Harp pondered another try later. He recalled the other times that week he had called and the phone had kept ringing . . . so he said good-by and hung up.

Thirty miles north, the *Paducah Sun* newsroom was also preparing for the meeting and they tracked down Superintendent Billy Watkins. It was obvious the superintendent and the school board had been consulting.

"The board's going to take some further action on the book banning," Billy Watkins said, adding, "I think that maybe what the board did has been taken out of context. They'll make some clarifications."

Would the ban be modified or lifted?

"I'm not at liberty to say what it will be," the superintendent responded.

Meanwhile, Suzanne Post of the ACLU was in touch with the *Paducah Sun,* and she continued with her frontal challenge. "We are asking that the school board rescind their action which we consider unconstitutional." She said that a number of attorneys across Kentucky had offered their services free-of-charge in order to overturn the banning vote. "People are angry about this. Our fear is that if one school district gets away with it, there will be a ripple effect — it will send a message to other thoughtless people." She mentioned that not only had she sent a copy of the ACLU letter to school board attorney Dan Sharp, but she was in daily telephone contact with him. "He feels the school board is off base, and that's all we need to jump in."

She concluded with a simple assertion: "We're prepared to bring litigation."

On the evening of September 11, 1986, the five members of the Graves County School Board took their seats around the L-shaped table in the first-floor conference room at the board of education offices. The first thing different about this evening was the number of spectators. The meeting room bulged with them. They spilled into the hallway, many of them attending a school board meeting for the first time. The crowd was double or triple its normal size, and for some, attendance was a Christian duty. At least half a dozen Baptist ministers were part of the crowd.

The meeting was called to order by Chairman Jeff Howard. He mentioned letters of support the board had received as a result of its action the prior week. Many letters arrived, he said, and he specifically read the one from the Graves County Baptist Association into the minutes. Other letters came from individual Baptist churches throughout the country, and he mentioned each by name.

"We express our appreciation for all of these letters," he declared, "you don't know how it fills our hearts with joy."

The board moved on to other business for awhile, but the spectators remained in place, waiting . . .

The agenda reached "pending or proposed litigation," and the tension was palpable. Chairman Jeff Howard searched the faces of his fellow board members, caught attorney Dan Sharp's eye, then announced, "We'll go into closed session now." In a moment the meeting room was emptied of all except the five board members, Dan Sharp and school administrators. Without preamble Dan Sharp made reference to the letter he and the board had received from the ACLU. This is serious, he told them, they will bring a lawsuit if we don't change what happened at the last meeting. He explained that in banning *As I Lay Dying* the school board issued a direct challenge to the First Amendment of the Constitution. "You are clamping down on what people can read," he said, "you're interfering with the right to free expression." He picked up a lawbook and flipped to a marked place. "Let me read you some Kentucky school law," he said, and he showed them where other school boards had run afoul of the Constitution and the right to free expression. "Unless you provide due process and right of appeal, it's going to make trouble."

Dan Sharp glanced around the room, measuring the impact of his words. Most of the faces remained stolid, expressionless. In an instant he knew his talk had not taken.

"They're not going to sue us over this," a board member insisted. "It's our opinion against theirs."

"I don't think the ACLU is kidding around," Dan Sharp reiterated. "That book should go back on the shelves. All they need is one parent to come forward and agree to be the plaintiff . . ."

But the board was in no mood to retreat. They won't sue. Period.

In a few moments the closed session ended, and the meeting-room door was reopened. If anything, the crowd outside was bigger now, but they moved back inside in orderly fashion, once again filling every space. The harsh lights made everything stand out starkly.

When the agenda moved to new business, it was Superintendent Billy Watkins who spoke, and it was apparent that he and some of the board members had formulated a plan. He began by justifying the use of a professional staff to choose books in the schools and by recognizing that whatever is selected must be in the best interests of the students and in keeping with the school philosophy of helping every student develop his or her potential. Then he offered a compromise, which he hoped would wipe away the need ever again to ban a book in Graves County High School.

"I recommend," he said, "our teachers in the Language Arts Department review the selections of books that have been made for use as an assigned part of the course of study, that they consider the replacement of any book to be assigned that may not be in the best interest of students . . ."

Lonnie Harp and the other media people looked at one another. Did this mean *As I Lay Dying* would be reviewed again? Under the plan it seemed as if the school itself could actually ban the book before another parent complained.

Superintendent Billy Watkins continued: "I further recommend that a seven-member review committee be established to which any complaints by parents relating to the content of the books or materials in use would be referred . . ." Billy Watkins knew, as did Jerald Ellington and most other educators, that teachers and librarians breathed more easily when decisions dealing with book selection were spread through a committee, even if it was a committee responsible for handling complaints. One person could not — and should not — be a lightning rod for abuse and vituperation.

The superintendent now reached his final point: "It is the intent of the board for this committee to review the Faulkner book, *As I Lay Dying.* The committee will report at the next regular board meeting."

Lonnie Harp and the other reporters had satisfaction only in knowing they had sensed correctly.

Within moments, board member Robert Spaulding had moved that the superintendent's recommendations be accepted. The motion was seconded, and all five members of the Graves County School Board voted "aye."

"Chairman Howard ruled the motion carried," read the minutes.

God didn't merely believe in man. He knew man. He knew that man was competent for a soul because he was capable of saving that soul, and, with it, himself. He knew that man was capable of starting from scratch and coping with the earth and with himself both; capable of teaching himself to be civilized, to live with his fellow man in amity, without anguish to himself or causing anguish and grief to others, and of appreciating the value of security and peace and freedom . . .

— *William Faulkner, 1953*

DAN SHARP

If I had to sum it up about the meeting, I would say the board had backed up a bit but they weren't ready to do anything about rescinding the ban. They had their backs against the wall — this was not an unusual position for them to take. Often we didn't see eye to eye. It was getting to be funny with Suzanne Post. It was to the point where I was looking forward to her calling because it was, "Sharp, I haven't gotten me a plaintiff yet, but I swear to God I'm going to get one if your board doesn't do something!" She wasn't calling for advice or consultation, she was really monitoring the situation to see what the board was doing.

LONNIE HARP

After this decision, the school board became inaccessible. They would say, "I don't know if I can answer your questions because what we did is what we did, and there's no point going into it." After John Shelton saw some local reaction, he wouldn't talk at all — he wouldn't even acknowledge me, just kept walking. They never returned messages, either. But preachers and church types were falling over themselves to talk to me after the meeting, to get on the record and get people to know where they stood on this. One preacher, an associate pastor at a big Baptist church, a moral-majority type, was the most vocal; in his thirties, fire in his eyes, it was fair to say he and some of the others saw this as a way to step into the limelight and get in front on the march for decency. He and a couple of others came to me and wanted to say things, and he was critical of our newspaper coverage . . .

REVEREND CHARLES SIMMONS

The major objections seemed to be that the book and the language were distasteful, and you know there are better words to be used. I think Christianity is against this kind of language, there are a lot better expressive words that can be used. I think that's where the problem was and that's where we took our stand. If you hear that type of language, you would associate it with a rough, unruly group that is involved in a more worldly type of life than living a Christian life with the Lord. What goes on in the schools is important because all of our children are involved. Our denomination is concerned that our schools have a high type of morality. Not only the Baptists but most all the religious groups would be against the blasphemy in the book where they take the name of the Lard in vain.

JERALD ELLINGTON

I met with the faculty two or three times, and I told them I supported them one hundred percent, that I was not going to side with the board, that they had my full support. The superintendent came over and shared that the board's action was not his feeling either, that he supported our regular process. It was just that when you're accused of something, people looked at you a little differently. These things were being said about the book, and here were all these people in church on Sunday asking, "What's going on?" I had very little, if any, contact with the board members about the book once the banning decision had been made. My relationship with the board was very strained. I didn't feel I had any backing on the board for my position about the book, but the superintendent and the faculty gave me much support. The faculty, in fact, was in total support of what the teachers were doing here.

The next morning the battle was joined again. It was now eight days after the banning vote, and even though the board had agreed to a procedure for examining library books, acknowledging by implication that its action eight days earlier might have been hasty, there was little softening or wavering.

"It's my vote and I have to live with it," board member Robert Spaulding said to Lonnie Harp.

"It's tough to do a job and to do what we know is right," Chairman Jeff Howard told the *Paducah Sun*. "I've had no second thoughts about this, at all."

But then, board member Andrew Goodman offered the first break in the school-board monolith. "I expect we will go along with whatever the review committee suggests," he told Lonnie Harp. "They'll provide a balanced view of the book."

It isn't hard to picture the soft sweep of relief that now touched the Graves County School Board. If there was a committee, they would do the voting, *we* won't have to stand naked as jaybirds and take whatever is thrown, dropped or shoved on us.

"The committee's recommendations," Chairman Jeff Howard said to Lonnie Harp, "will weigh heavily."

A-men! That was the collective emphasis from the Baptist churchmen who had rallied to the board's side. It wasn't that they liked trouble in their community, but there were certain things a good Christian had to stand for. This book was unfit for impressionable, teenage minds, and it should not have been on the school library shelves. "I'll tell you one thing," Reverend Al Cobb, the author of the letter from the Graves County Baptist Association, said, "If this was the only book that Faulkner ever wrote, nobody would have heard of him."

Al Cobb was not the only Baptist minister with something to say about the book. Terry Sims, whose church was on the western side of the county, called it pornography. "As a parent, I wouldn't want my daughter reading this book," he said. "I feel like somewhere along the line people have to make a stand against this kind of thing."

Ronnie Stinson, another Baptist minister, echoed Sims, in fact went one step further. "It's something that if

I caught my kid reading out of literature class, I would have to discipline him for," he insisted.

But the pressure was building for the Graves County School Board to step back from the legal precipice. No matter what the board's supporters or detractors were saying, this school board had voted — and voted unanimously — to ban a book, and the book had never had a chance to defend itself.

"I recommended that the board set up this committee," Dan Sharp told the *Paducah Sun*. "I also recommended the book be placed back in the library."

But that wasn't done. The book remained out of reach for the students of Graves County High School.

"The school board is constitutionally vulnerable because of what they have done," Dan Sharp added. The banning of *As I Lay Dying* had opened the Graves County School Board to the possibility of a lawsuit because they appeared to have violated the First Amendment to the United States Constitution.

Congress [or the state of Kentucky or any school district therein] shall make no law . . . abridging the freedom of speech or of the press . . .

Dan Sharp knew, as did any first-year law student, that these freedoms included freedom to read, freedom to write. It is the freedom of expression that is protected.

"Constitutionally vulnerable," was the way he described the Graves County School Board after it had refused to return the book to the school library. And his words had a touch of prophecy because the ACLU's Suzanne Post was now determined to take the school board into court.

"This book is a minor classic," she said, her dark eyes gleaming with indignation. "What this school board has done is censorship at its worst." Once word reached her that after the second school board meeting *As I Lay Dying* would remain off the high school shelves, she called her general counsel.

"I want to find a plaintiff!"

"It's our kind of case," he acknowledged.

Quietly, they began to search for someone in whose name they could file suit, someone who felt sufficiently aggrieved by what the Graves County School Board had done. Someone who was willing to carry the standard of the First Amendment.

In the meantime, and not so quietly, an indignant Suzanne Post went public with her views on what was going on in Graves County. The school board's action at the second meeting and the policy they imposed was "illegitimate, mindless, anti-intellectual, authoritarian and extremely dangerous." What the board had shown was nothing more than a "pre-fascist mind-set — the kind of mind-set that led to what the Nazis did in Germany."

Her words and characterizations were picked up and quoted by the *Paducah Sun*, and suddenly the unremark- able, steady citizens of Graves County found themselves paired with another unseeing society that had set the stage for the most heinous free-expression killers in the twen- tieth century.

"A pre-fascist mind set . . ." she had said. Were the people unaware of what a bookbanning could lead to?

"When you're dealing with a man of Faulkner's stature, I think it's such a ringing indictment of the collective intelligence of that school board that it makes me very sad for the children in those schools," she said. "We're horrified!"

Her comments took on added weight because she was suddenly awash in volunteer lawyers. Members from five prominent Kentucky law firms had been in touch. "We'll do it *pro bono,*" they had offered.

At the *Mayfield Messenger* during this week after the second school-board meeting, more letters came in. Mike Turley was especially interested in one from Bob Carrico, a recent honors graduate of Graves County High School, still in his teens. Young Carrico declared that he was morally opposed to the bookbanning and to the philosophy underlying it. "In the first place," he wrote, "no one can be corrupted by the ideas in a book without his own consent. Man is a being of free will. His mind is capable of rational examination of any ideas he may encounter, and of the decision to embrace or reject these ideas . . ."

Mike Turley hesitated not at all. He published Bob Carrico's letter, seeing it as vivid testimony from the precise age-group that was affected by the Graves County School Board's decision. The penultimate paragraph stuck to his mind: *Book banning is wrong at any time, at any place, for any reason, for any work . . .*

Mike Turley liked the way that was phrased.

Yet there were other Graves County citizens who wrote to the newspaper from the opposite perspective, and their comments, too, found a place in the *Mayfield Messenger.* It was not Mike Turley's role to filter this news. "Our children will learn fast enough (without teaching them in school) about using God's name in vain," wrote one citizen. "I think that the people who want to put that book back on the shelves are wrong."

Another ended her lengthy criticism of liberals, the ACLU and People For the American Way with the following: "Someone is sick and I submit to you — it is *not* the members of the school board."

Mike Turley added up the number of letters he received. There were at least ten times more than for any story in his sixteen years with the newspaper. And there appeared to be a definite majority opposed to the banning — about two out of three, in fact.

Toward the end of the second week Mike Turley began to get responses from outside the country. A former Mayfield resident living in Paris sent a clip on the banning from the *International Herald Tribune,* along with a terse observation: "you've got to be kidding!". A letter arrived from South America, clipping the story to a single sheet of paper containing a large exclamation point (!). A letter came from Canada, also sending a clip from an English-language newspaper.

Then there were the phone calls. Some came directly to Mike Turley, from people outside Graves County, calling to see if the story were true. Calls also came to the Graves County School Board or to Mayfield city government. Lonnie Harp told Mike Turley that a few calls were from outside Kentucky. One, in fact, was from Florida, another from Indiana.

Hard to miss, also, was the television crew that had arrived from Louisville. ABC intended to highlight the story on its network nightly news, and the crew was setting up at the school-board office and at the high school.

In the days following the second meeting Lonnie Harp had been trying to talk with members of the school board but without success. He knew *they* had been talking with one another and with Superintendent Billy Watkins. He suspected they had been seeking advice from people out-side Graves County.

But he knew nothing for sure. He decided to contact Chairman Jeff Howard one more time. He sensed Howard had an inclination to talk about what was happening and to try to explain why the school board had done what they did.

He dialed the familiar number, and the rings numbered six before the phone was answered. It was Mrs. Howard, and Lonnie Harp asked to speak to her husband.

"Is this the newspaper?" Then, without waiting for an answer, she said, "I'll see if he wants to speak with you."

In a moment she was back. Jeff Howard had nothing to say to the newspaper.

As Lonnie Harp replaced the phone, Mike Turley, standing by his desk, said, "Superintendent's office just called." He handed Harp a note. A special board meeting, Thursday evening, September 18th, 6 P.M. The only agenda item, a superintendent's report.

"You have any idea what this is about?" Mike Turley asked.

Lonnie Harp shrugged.

I took this family and subjected them to the two greatest catastrophes which man can suffer — flood and fire . . . I took whatever I needed wherever I could find it, without any compunction and with no sense of violating any ethics or hurting anyone's feelings because any writer feels that anyone after him is perfectly welcome to take any trick he has learned or any plot he has used . . .
— *William Faulkner, 1957*

There was still good daylight at 6:30 on this mid-September evening in Graves County, and the sultry Indian summer weather continued. The meeting room of the Graves County School Board was filling fast and it was certain the crowd would be larger than the room could accommodate. Strips of sunlight made it appear the meeting room had a fuzzy glow, but old hands knew this would fade as the overhead lights came on.

Silently, quickly, the members of the school board filed to their seats around the L-shaped table. The school administration, led by Superintendent Billy Watkins, were already in their places, and off to the side in their accustomed location were Lonnie Harp and other members of the media.

Some of the spectators searched the room, wondering if one of the television networks might be taping (no, they weren't), picking out supporters and non-supporters of the bookbanning (plenty of both), hoping they would be interviewed after the meeting (probably not), noticing set, somber expressions on school-board members' faces (as usual).

Chairman Jeff Howard acknowledged the superintendent, who began to read a prepared statement. His words fell with a flatness of under-emphasis, as if the sentiments were customary and, hence, undramatic. "Since there is a board-approved school policy relating to the selection of material . . ." he said, and for an instant, most expected a rehash of the past two weeks.

But then: "I recommend . . ." and everyone's attention was alerted. "I recommend," said Superintendent Billy Watkins, "that the Board action #63 of September 4, 1986, relating to banning of the Faulkner book, *As I Lay Dying,* be rescinded . . ."

Rescinded!

The faces of the school-board members showed no surprise, no sudden gathering of emotion. It would seem they were aware of the superintendent's recommendation before he made it. They had to understand the conflicts that had been swirling about their community; they had to sense the ridicule and the passion and the confrontations bound to come.

Hadn't their attorney spelled out their precarious legal position the week before? Hadn't their local newspaper editorialized against them? Hadn't school officials showed their displeasure and their anger?

No sooner had Superintendent Billy Watkins read through his recommendation than board member Andrew Goodman moved that the recommendation be accepted.

"Second!" said Robert Spaulding, and he offered a statement of explanation. The responsibility for his switch of viewpoint lay with Dan Sharp and Billy Watkins, he said. They had advised that this was what he should do, so he was doing it. But . . . "this second in no way endorses my acceptance of books with foul language being assigned to our students." His sentiments were resolute. "It seems strange to me that in our society they would ban the hanging of the Ten Commandments on a school wall, yet will endorse books for students which contain such matters."

In quick order a vote was taken. It was four to one to rescind the ban of *As I Lay Dying.*

Only John Shelton was unmoved.

The minutes reflected reality: "Chairman Howard ruled the motion carried."

Jeff Howard was not quite finished, though. He, also,

had a statement to make, and he spoke not only to the members of the school administration who sat in quiet relief on the side, but to his neighbors and constituents who were now a part of this history. It was apparent some things were and always would be non-negotiable: "We believe . . . that books containing abusive language [should] not be taught in our school system. We believe there must be some standard concerning what books our children study."

He mentioned the severe criticism the school board had received, and he acknowledged that, procedurally, the board was vulnerable because of the way it went about its bookbanning. "For this reason we have serious doubts as to successful litigation," and he concluded that to push the matter further would be a waste of the taxpayers' money.

But he continued to feel that some books don't belong in the schools. "Certainly we want our children exposed to the opinions and ideas of great writers. Neither are we so naive as to believe that our children aren't exposed to profanity, both in our community and among their peers. We do believe that literature can be found which passes to our children all the ideas of Western Civilization that do not border on obscenity or in fact are obscene . . ."

Appropriate literature was what he and the school board sought, a standard that the citizens of Graves County could certainly understand.

Or could they?

Before the sun disappeared in western Kentucky on this Indian summer evening, the Graves County School Board adjourned, and the meeting room, which had seen such drama these past two weeks, emptied quietly and quickly.

The next day *As I Lay Dying* returned to the shelves of the Graves County High School.

What threatens us today is fear. Not the atom bomb, nor even fear of it, because if the bomb fell on Oxford [Mississippi] tonight, all it could do would be to kill us, which is nothing, since in doing that, it will have robbed itself of its only power over us; which is fear of it, the being afraid of it. Our danger is not that. Our danger is the forces in the world today which are trying to use man's fear to rob him of his individuality, his soul, trying to reduce him to an unthinking mass by fear . . .
                                        — William Faulkner, 1951

PART TWO

PROFILES AND PORTRAITS

2

Colonial Beginnings

The elderly man stepped through an open door of the second-floor courtroom in New York's City Hall. He made for a seat along the aisle, thankful he had arrived early before all the spaces would be taken.

His name was Andrew Hamilton. He was from Philadelphia, and his presence in the courtroom this day would become legend.

He was a lawyer, highly respected, even if not from New York. In fact, in this year 1735, to be from Philadelphia was akin to living at the edge of most New Yorkers' concept of civilization. Philadelphia was three days' journey, beyond the dense, barely charted forests of New Jersey and across the gray, treacherous waters of the Delaware River.

He saw that seats had been taken by two of those who had asked him to New York: James Alexander and William Smith, both New York lawyers, but neither permit-

46

ted to practice their craft in this courtroom because of a dispute with the chief justice, James DeLancey, and the governor, William Cosby.

Movement in the front of the courtroom caught Hamilton's eye. A short, round-headed man came through a side door, followed by another man, dressed in waistcoat and wig. Obviously the defendant and John Chambers, his court-appointed attorney.

Hamilton examined the round-headed man. His name was John Peter Zenger, and he had been in prison for almost nine months awaiting trial. Thirty-eight years old, Zenger was not a native New Yorker. He had emigrated from Germany at thirteen. Now married and the father of a son, Zenger was a printer in New York colony.

Andrew Hamilton noted the arrival of Chief Justice DeLancey and his assistant judge, Frederick Philpse, both attired in dark red robes and impressive wigs. De-Lancey, Hamilton knew, had prohibited James Alexander and William Smith from practicing in this courtroom because they had had the temerity to question his impartiality at an earlier hearing for John Peter Zenger.

"All rise!" intoned the bailiff, striking the hardwood floor with his staff: "Hear ye, hear ye, this honorable court is now in session . . ."

From the moment of his arrival from England to assume the post of Governor in New York in August, 1732, William Cosby alienated substantial segments of the population. He had a farmer whipped for not moving a team and wagon out of the way of his carriage fast enough; he demanded a salary that included a special unearned gratuity. He appointed his son to a high government post, and he offered to sell various local political jobs.

For James Alexander and William Smith the practice of law seemed an ineffective weapon to combat the increasing arbitrariness and greed that Cosby appeared to show. What they wanted was something to rally the anti-Cosby sentiment, to keep the seeds of dissent growing, to attack Cosby regularly, week in, week out. They needed a steady, unwavering opposition.

They knew a printer, John Peter Zenger, who had been in business near Maiden Lane for seven years. A newspaper would be born. Zenger would be printer and publisher, James Alexander and William Smith — under assumed names or no names at all — to write much of the political commentary.

On November 5, 1733, the first issue of *The New-York Weekly Journal* appeared, bearing Zenger's printing stamp. On its front page it announced it contained "the freshest advices, foreign and domestic," and it began with an open letter to the publisher detailing the political issues to be joined. A week later in its second issue, and a week after that in the third issue, the newspaper extolled the value of free criticism of government officials. A disreputable minister was an "impudent monster in iniquity . . . let him receive the lash of Satyr . . . sting him with the dread of punishment, cover him with shame . . . render his actions odious to all honest minds. . . ."

Without mentioning anyone by name, *The New-York Weekly Journal* concluded: "Very few ministers can be hurt by falsehood, but many wicked ones by seasonable truth."

Andrew Hamilton listened intently as the jury was chosen for the trial. With his long mane of white hair and rugged complexion, he was the source of curiosity among spectators.

Chief Justice DeLancey indicated to Attorney General Richard Bradley that he should read the charges. On this stuffy, mid-summer morning in early August, the prosecutor spoke with coolness and confidence. "May it please your Honors, and you, gentlemen of the jury," he began, "the information now before the court, and to which the Defendant Zenger has pleaded *not guilty,* is an information for printing and publishing *a false, scandalous and seditious libel* in which His Excellency the Governor of this Province, who is the King's immediate representative here, is greatly and unjustly scandalized as a person that has no regard to law nor justice."

Andrew Hamilton knew that the prosecution was especially inflamed over two separate issues of *The New-York Weekly Journal,* those of January 28th and April 8th, 1734. Zenger had written that the people of New York ". . . think, as matters now stand, that their liberties and properties are precarious, and that slavery is like to be entailed on them and their posterity, if some past things be not amended." Adding emphasis by using capital letters, Zenger wrote: "WE SEE MEN'S DEEDS DESTROYED, JUDGES ARBITRARILY DISPLACED, NEW COURTS ERECTED WITHOUT CONSENT OF THE LEGISLATURE . . . BY WHICH, IT SEEMS TO ME, TRIALS BY JURIES ARE TAKEN AWAY WHEN A GOVERNOR PLEASES."

In a moment the prosecutor finished and John Chambers responded. He made a mild statement, briefly explaining that seditious libel was an acknowledged crime because in calling into question the decisions and the personality of governing authorities, it had the power to disrupt both established order and general peace. If there was doubt about whom John Peter Zenger referred to in his newspaper, there could be no conviction. No doubt must remain, John Chambers emphasized.

Quietly, almost apologetically, he sat down, and Andrew Hamilton slowly pushed himself to his feet. If one looked closely there were laugh lines about his eyes, indicating a bright sense of humor, but on this day his tone and his demeanor were grave indeed.

"May it please Your Honor," he declared as a wave of surprise flowed through the courtroom. "I am concerned in this cause on the part of Mr. Zenger, the Defendant. The information against my client was sent me a few days before I left home . . ."

The courtroom was astir as Hamilton made his way to the front. He had, he said, no quarrel with the argument that John Chambers had offered on Zenger's behalf. "Yet I cannot think it proper for me (without doing violence to my own principles) to deny the publication of a complaint which I think is the right of every free-born subject to make when the matters so published can be supported with truth."

For Andrew Hamilton the matter was simple and clear. A person should be able to publish what he wished, so long as it is true. Even if it was critical of the government.

Then there was a surprise. Andrew Hamilton admitted, on his client's behalf, that the newspapers in question had been printed and published by the accused.

To which Attorney General Bradley replied: "Then if your honor please, since Mr. Hamilton has confessed the fact, I think our witnesses may be discharged."

Andrew Hamilton agreed, and the witnesses made their way from the courtroom.

Smug with the admission that Zenger had printed and published, as charged, Richard Bradley now argued that the case was over: "Indeed sir, as Mr. Hamilton has confessed the printing and publishing of these libels, I think the jury must find a verdict for the King; for supposing they were true, the law says that they are not the less libelous for that."

Andrew Hamilton responded quickly. "You will have something more to do before you make my client a libeler," he said. "For the words themselves must be libelous, that is, *false, scandalous and seditious,* or else we are not guilty."

From the moment of its first publication *The New-York Weekly Journal* had had the attention of Governor Cosby's supporters. Seditious libel had been a prickly irritant in the long history between citizens and their government; the Chief Justice of England had defined the crime as criticism that tended "to beget an ill opinion" of the government and its officers.

Cosby's supporters finally had had enough after the newspaper called him a "rogue Governor," "an overgrown criminal," "a monkey," an "impudent monster." They sought to have a grand jury indict Zenger. But to their surprise the grand jury took no action. They pressured the general assembly to legislate Zenger's guilt, but here again, no action was taken. Finally, out of frustration and growing anger, Governor Cosby himself ordered the attorney general to have Zenger arrested and tried. Keep him in jail until his trial, the governor insisted. That will stop the libels.

But it didn't. Each week John Peter Zenger's wife and sons came to visit him in jail. Each week they listened to him speak through a hole in the door of his cell, giving them instructions and suggestions for the next issue of *The*

New York Weekly Journal, messages for James Alexander and William Smith, ideas for succeeding issues. They had questions and he answered them, and somehow the authorities didn't know.

The New-York Weekly Journal never missed an issue!

Attorney General Richard Bradley sprang to his feet as Andrew Hamilton finished his argument that John Peter Zenger could be guilty of seditious libel only if what he printed and published was false.

Richard Bradley repeated his earlier contention, this time with added emphasis. "Mr. Hamilton has confessed the printing and publishing, and I think nothing is plainer, than that the words in the Information are *scandalous, and tend to sedition, and to disquiet the minds of the People of this Province.* And if such papers are not libels, I think it may be said, there can be no such thing as libel."

Andrew Hamilton, however, did not back away. "I freely acknowledge," he said, "that there are such things as libels, yet I insist at the same time that what my client is charged with is not a libel; and I observed just now that Mr. Attorney in defining a libel made use of the words *scandalous, seditious, and tend to disquiet the people,* but, whether by design or not, he omitted the word *false.*"

Richard Bradley dismissed what Andrew Hamilton said on the ground that a libel is a libel no matter its truth or falsity. He appealed to Chief Justice DeLancey who had been observing the by-play with growing impatience. Finally, the chief justice decided: he refused to hear anything more about the truth and falsity of the charges.

In exasperation Hamilton muttered that the hearing resembled an infamous Star Chamber proceeding.

"Mr. Hamilton!" DeLancey glared at him. "The Court

has delivered its opinion, and we expect you will use us with good manners; you are not to be permitted to argue against the opinion of the Court."

There was a moment's quiet as the elderly Philadelphian allowed his ruddy countenance to focus on the jury. With bare civility Andrew Hamilton acknowledged the position held by the chief justice and the attorney general. He would not dispute their argument any longer — at least not in this case. Instead, his eyes continuing to stay with the jury, he expanded his conception, and for the first time the courtroom was treated to a ringing plea that transcended the narrow confines of truth and falsehood.

"All the high things that are said in favor of rulers and of dignities and upon the side of power will not be able to stop people's mouths when they feel themselves oppressed," he declared. "People will speak out, people will demand changes when they are treated unfairly. It is a right which all free men have. They have a right publicly to remonstrate the abuses of power in the strongest terms, to put their neighbors upon their guard against the craft or open violence of men in authority, and to assert with courage the sense they have of the Blessings of Liberty."

Andrew Hamilton warmed to his words. His voice calm, purposeful, he continued speaking directly to the jury, as if they, and they only, were the important people in the courtroom. He reached back into Roman history for episodes in which free speech could not be repressed, and he tied them to more recent British incidents. All of this, he implied, showed that when men felt oppressed, they would speak out. They *must* speak out.

He mentioned that two centuries before, those who challenged the established church were burned at the stake, but that now, in 1735, the church could be criticized without penalty. Sardonically, he added, "It is pretty clear that in New York a man may make very free with his God, but he must take special care what he says of his Governor."

On and on Andrew Hamilton argued, enticing the jury to think for themselves, not to be bound or swayed by what the Court thought or expected them to decide. "Jurymen are to see with their own eyes, to hear with their own ears, and to make use of their own consciences and understandings in judging the lives, liberties or estates of their fellow subjects." You have the *right,* he told them, to decide for yourselves.

Then, suddenly, he came to the end of his argument. "You see," he said, "I labor under the weight of many years and am borne down with great infirmities of body." The strain of his courtroom appearance, coupled with the effects of his arduous journey from Philadelphia, was all too clear to the jury. What was remarkable was that a man near eighty years of age could have continued to expound in such a lucid manner. "Yet old and weak as I am," he went on, "I should think it my duty, if required, to go to the utmost part of the land where my service could be of any use in assisting to quench the flame of prosecutions upon informations set on foot by the government to deprive a people of the right of remonstrating (and complaining too) of the arbitrary attempts of men in power."

Andrew Hamilton was no longer a simple advocate. Now he offered to martyr himself, to challenge an essentially unfair, corrupt system. He identified himself with the right to free expression, the right to criticize, com-

plain and cry out in the face of oppression and prosecution. "The question before the Court and you gentlemen
of the jury is not of small nor private concern, it is not the
cause of a poor printer, nor of New York alone, which
you are now trying; No! It may in consequence affect
every freeman that lives under a British government on
the main of America. It is the best cause. It is the cause of
liberty."

For only when free men write and speak truth will the exercise of
arbitrary power be exposed and opposed.

The Philadelphian moved away from the bench, his
white crown of hair still a centerpiece of attention. As he
seated himself he heard Attorney General Richard
Bradley provide a modest rebuttal. And this was followed
by Chief Justice DeLancey moving quickly to charge the
jury, saying, in effect, they should disregard most of what
Andrew Hamilton had said because it was not the law of
New York.

The chief justice tried his own brand of forceful certainty on the jury. "The only thing that can come in
question before you is whether the words as set forth in
the Information make a libel."

Within moments the jury withdrew to consider their
verdict, and among the trial participants there was a
collective sigh of relief. It had been a long hot day, with
much courtroom tension.

Here and there in the courtroom and outside, in the
second-floor hallway and along the stairs, small groups
gathered, but this was not unusual. The period of waiting
for a jury always brought a rush of anticipation, and some
didn't wish to be far away from the locus of jury
deliberation.

Then — surprise! Word filtered through the courtroom and out into the hallway. The jury had reached a verdict. It had taken them but ten minutes.

They filed back to the jury box, and most of the spectators resumed their seats. The chief justice ascended to the bench, and Andrew Hamilton took his aisle seat.

"Is John Peter Zenger guilty of printing and publishing seditious libel?" the court clerk asked the jury.

At a later date, John Peter Zenger himself recorded the jury's response. "They answered by Thomas Hunt, their foreman, *Not Guilty,* upon which there were three huzzas in the hall which was crowded with people and the next day I was discharged from my imprisonment."

Many believe this case represented the first strike for freedom of the press — and, hence, freedom of expression, freedom to write and criticize a government and its leaders — in the life of the infant United States. Certainly there was no such right in the common law, and even though the founding of the country was more than forty-five years in the future, the tribulation of John Peter Zenger was a landmark on the road to our First Amendment. In fact, Gouverneur Morris, one of the Founding Fathers, said in 1776: "The trial of Zenger in 1735 was the germ of American freedom, the morning star of that liberty which subsequently revolutionized America."

Seditious libel, however, did not die away with this jury verdict. In fact, less than ten years after George Washington's inauguration, the Congress of the United States passed the Alien and Sedition Acts, which, among other things, gave legislative life to the idea of seditious libel. When John Adams and his Federalists came to power, they wasted little time in using the Acts against their political enemies who had written caustic, critical comments about them. More than 20 editors, one congressman and a host of private citizens were prosecuted, but gradually the Acts felt the sting of popular disapproval, and after a few years they were rarely enforced, though they were never actually repealed or declared unconstitutional. Justice William Brennan wrote in 1964: "Although the Sedition Act was never tested in this court, the attack upon its validity has carried the day in the court of history."

To this day, John Peter Zenger is remembered. A prize has been given each year since 1954 by the University of Arizona, for distinguished service in promoting freedom of the press and the people's right to know. It's called the John Peter Zenger Freedom of Information Award.

3

"Truth!
stark, naked truth . . ."

Peter Holmes was a nervous man on this day in 1821. The Supreme Judicial Court of Massachusetts was about to decide his appeal from a conviction that he published and circulated a lewd and obscene book. Peter Holmes understood his livelihood depended on what the court said today.

As he made his way up Boston's Boylston Street, he couldn't help noticing the liveries and pedestrians filling the narrow streets leading to the Common and the general bustle of the marketplace down towards Constitution Wharf. Boston was not the largest city in the still-young United States, but it was among the busiest, and Peter Holmes knew its citizens thirsted for more than what hard-shell Puritanism would allow. The growing trade with continental Europe, and especially with England, had brought flavorful contact with new ideas and thoughts, new experiences. The Puritan world of Massachusetts could not suppress these things forever; not everyone felt content with a rigid code of morality where "decency" was measured by religious scruples.

Peter Holmes might have thought back to his trial in Suffolk County Common Pleas Court. A *criminal* trial? He hadn't killed anyone, he hadn't robbed or raped anyone, he hadn't tried to burn down buildings, he had only published and circulated a book.

The coarse, unnerving words of the charges stuck with him: ". . . being a scandalous and evil-disposed person . . . to debauch and corrupt . . . create . . . inordinate and lustful desires . . . publish and deliver . . . a certain lewd, wicked, scandalous, infamous and obscene printed book . . . to the manifest corruption and subversion of the youth and other good citizens. . . ." He remembered six counts in the indictment, as well as the air of righteousness that pervaded the courtroom the day of his trial. Three people to whom he had circulated the book were the chief witnesses against him, each leaving no doubt Peter Holmes had been responsible for publishing the book.

One thing puzzled him — one thing brought up at his trial and reiterated by Mr. Mills, his attorney, when the case was argued on appeal. The indictment did not mention the exact words or passages in the book that were considered lewd and obscene. He remembered his attorney asking, "How can a person be guilty of anything when the indictment makes no detailed showing of it?" Surely, our law required a defendant to be told specifically what crime he is said to have committed.

Peter Holmes remembered the way the indictment read: "a certain lewd, wicked, scandalous, infamous and obscene printed book, entitled etc., which said printed book is so lewd, wicked and obscene, that the same would be offensive to the court here, and improper to be placed on the records thereof . . ."

The indictment didn't even mention the title!

Peter Holmes approached the courthouse now. In a moment he would join his attorney and together they would hear the judgment of the appeals court. He knew the book in question was a good book:

Memoirs of A Woman of Pleasure, by John Cleland

The prisoner gazed at the barred window high on the damp dark-stoned wall, hoping the light would last long enough for him to complete writing one more page. He was a strange one, this slender Englishman with the look of travel and education. He was not as slatternly as others in this large, stinking prison ward. He dressed no differently — filthy clothes, tattered shoes, unshaven, unbathed, but there was *something* about him that allowed him privacy among the remnants of humanity in this hellhole people called the Fleet.

He bent once again to the paper on his knee, scrawling in the fading light, oblivious to the squawks and shouts and arguments that swept around the cavernous, smelly, unsanitary space. It was a jungle-life in this prison and he had been careful to shield himself from its most inhumane conditions. Cruelty piled upon cruelty — prisoners bashing one another for sport or for profit, warders bashing prisoners for control and for example, attorneys and bailiffs preying upon those with a little money put by, sexstarved inmates raping and pillaging within sight and sound of anyone in the common ward.

John Cleland was this prisoner's name, and the year was 1747. He was almost forty years old, and this was his first prison experience, but it would not be his last. His crime was simple and conclusive: he owed a debt he could not pay, and his creditor insisted upon a familiar remedy—debtor's prison.

Cleland was down to the last line of the page when a loud clatter caused him to look up. One of the prisoners was staring at a pile of earthen shards on the slick, fetid rock floor. Another prisoner stood alongside, laughing uproariously. The first prisoner's daily beer ration bubbled around their feet.

It wasn't only beer, it was gin, too, that was permitted here, and the result was a continuous surge of riotous drunkenness with prisoners falling into slop made by other prisoners, vomiting and peeing and defecating without concern for elementary sanitation. John Cleland stifled an urge to show displeasure at the interruption; it might only make him a new victim. But he would remember these conditions, and one day he would write that the Fleet was one of "those burial places of our fellow creatures alive."

There seemed no avenue Cleland could take to leave the Fleet; his sentence had no term, only a condition, and he had little hope of satisfying that condition while behind bars. If he did nothing, he could spend the remainder of his days in this devilish place, and for a man not yet forty that was a forlorn prospect.

Especially since he had travelled widely—to India and the continent of Europe among other places—and he understood how much there was to the outside world. Two things were clear to John Cleland: his family had abandoned him, leaving him completely on his own, and he must find a way to pay off his debt. Otherwise there would be no outside world for him ever.

He folded the pages he had been working on, stuffing them under his tattered shirt. *This* might be the way, he told himself for the hundredth time, but whom should I contact? The parchment felt stiff against his skin, and he lay his head against the slimy, stony prison wall, willing his mind to remember how he had opened his tale:

> Madam . . . Hating, as I mortally do, all long un-necessary preface, I shall give you good quarter in this, and use no farther apology, than to prepare you for seeing the loose part of my life, wrote with the same liberty that I led it.
>
> Truth! stark, naked truth, is the word; and I will not so much as take the pains to bestow the strip of a gauze wrapper on it . . .

Not bad, he thought, not bad, at all.

Cleland would feel the effects of his 376 days in the Fleet for years to come, his memory a jumble of the grisly reality that allowed him to withdraw and immerse himself within the pages of his book. Prison was no place to keep a secret, of course, and somehow word of what he was doing filtered from within the gray walls out to the book-sellers' marketplace. Soon, a London publisher named Fenton Griffiths visited Cleland and asked about what he was writing.

"Read it," Cleland urged Griffiths. "Notice I use no four–letter words, that my narrator is no brassy Moll Flanders or vile creature from the streets. My Fanny Hill is a nice, agreeable girl-woman, a bit naive, perhaps, but adventurous, too. She is kind and she is generous."

Fenton Griffiths showed the manuscript to his partners, one of whom was his brother, Ralph, who also happened to be a bookshop owner. They saw merit in its publication, though another partner wondered if the book was "safe" to publish. They agreed, however, that its unusual style, with its breathless, suggestive adventuring, made it different from anything written before. But first, of course, the author had to be released from confinement; he must be allowed to go free.

"You may publish my book," John Cleland told them, "*if* you help me pay my debt."

On November 21, 1748, the following advertisement appeared in a major London newspaper, the *General Advertiser:*

This Day is Published, (Price 3s)
MEMOIRS OF A WOMAN OF PLEASURE
written by a PERSON OF QUALITY
printed for G. FENTON, in the Strand.

It was John Cleland's long-awaited book, and the story of its writing flew around literary and not-so-literary London.

Soon, John Cleland walked out of the Fleet a free man.

But the book's success was elusive. The initial printing was 750 copies, and sales were slow. Ralph Griffiths wondered why there had been concern that the book could be accused of "corrupting the King's subjects," as the Common Law at the time might have charged. The book was simply sinking from view, and no one cared!

Or so it seemed. But a year after the notice appeared in

the *General Advertiser,* it was apparent there *was* attention
being paid to the book. Several high officials of the
Church of England had contacted Lord Newcastle, the
secretary of state, and demanded the arrest of the author,
printer, and publisher.

On November 10, 1749, John Cleland was back in
prison, and from that day forward, he and his book
remained the centerpiece of a bookbanning struggle that
was to last for many years, on both sides of the Atlantic.

Peter Holmes and his attorney found themselves a
small space near the bailiff's table. It was crowded in the
courtroom and for good reason: the Massachusetts Supreme Judicial Court would render a series of opinions,
and those who would be affected by them were all present. It was not only Peter Holmes's day of judgment.

But Peter Holmes's fate this day would far outlive
anything that happened to the other defendants. His
attorney, Mr. Mills, understood the weaknesses in his
client's case, even as he supported Peter Holmes.

There was a comparison to make with the *Sharpless*
case, decided in Pennsylvania six years earlier, in 1815. A
reading of the indictments in both cases showed remarkable similarity of language: in *Sharpless* the defendants
were "evil disposed persons," while Peter Holmes was "a
scandalous and evil disposed person"; in *Sharpless* the
defendants intended "to debauch and corrupt, and to
raise and create . . . inordinate and lustful desires . . ."
and the very same words appeared against Peter Holmes.
It was obvious the prosecutors had been in touch with one
another.

Of course, there was a difference: in *Sharpless* the item
under scrutiny was a painting, while here it was a book.

But Peter Holmes and his attorney had to ask themselves in full candor: did it really make a difference? If a Pennsylvania court was offended by a painting, could not a Massachusetts court be offended by a book?

Peter Holmes knew something of the history of *The Memoirs of A Woman of Pleasure* — that within eighteen months of its publication it had been banned in England. The bishop of London had written to the secretary of state to "give proper orders, to stop the progress of this vile Book, which is an open insult upon Religion and good manners, and a reproach to the Honour of the Government, and the Law of the Country."

Within twenty-four hours, the banning had taken place, *and the book remained banned in England right up to the moment of Peter Holmes's judgment*!

Peter Holmes and his attorney knew this history would not add to their credibility, but they also knew that a Massachusetts court might regard anything the British did as an example of what *not* to follow. It was, after all, only seven years since the British had torched the White House during the War of 1812 and only six years since they had been finally defeated.

Then, too, there was the fact the indictment did not mention those parts of the book considered obscene, nor did it even allow the title of the book to be included! How could one defend against a phantom like this?

A hush fell over the courtroom as the members of the Supreme Judicial Court filed into their seats. On the other side of the courtroom Peter Holmes saw Solicitor General Davis, familiar now from when he argued the Commonwealth's case against him. Alongside Davis was the county attorney, Newton, who had been Peter Holmes's chief tormentor at the trial

The spectators leaned forward as Chief Justice Isaac Parker nodded toward Holmes and his attorneys. It was apparent that judgment in the case of Commonwealth versus Peter Holmes would be rendered first.

"The second and fifth counts in this indictment are certainly good . . ." began the Chief Justice.

Peter Holmes listened carefully as the words of Chief Justice Isaac Parker descended upon him. The first thing he heard destroyed the argument he and Mills had developed so adroitly (and had convinced themselves could prevail) that the indictment was faulty because it contained no passages from the book, not even mentioning the book's title. Chief Justice Isaac Parker was singularly unimpressd . . . *The second and fifth counts in this indictment are certainly good. . .*

Probably, it would not have impressed Peter Holmes had his attorney—with the benefit of hindsight years later—told him: "This is the first obscenity case for a book in United States history. You are the first defendant to be convicted for publishing and circulating a so-called obscene book."

Small comfort, Peter Holmes would most likely have responded, especially as he might have recalled the words of Chief Justice Isaac Parker: "It can never be required that an obscene book and picture should be displayed upon the records of the court . . . this would be to require that the public itself should give permanency and notoriety to indecency, in order to punish it . . ."

Peter Holmes had fallen victim to an unfair circumstance: the book's obscenity had already been decided before he was arrested, yet he had to defend himself without knowing what the obscenity was; his accusers offered nothing but generalized conclusions, calling *Mem-*

oirs of A Woman of Pleasure "lewd, wicked, scandalous, infamous and obscene," citing no specific chapters, no passages, no words.

This would be to require that the public itself should give permanency and notoriety to indecency, in order to punish it.

In a matter of moments Peter Holmes's appeal was denied, and he stood convicted of publishing and circulating a lewd and obscene book.

Chief Justice Isaac Parker concluded that it was a misdemeanor, but a crime, nevertheless. For Peter Holmes a solemn epitaph might come from the final page of this heroine's tale:

> If you do me then justice, you will esteem me perfectly consistent in the incense I burn to Virtue. If I have painted Vice in all its gayest colors, if I have decked it with flowers, it has been solely in order to make the worthier, the solemner sacrifice of it, to Virtue.

It took one hundred and forty-five years before *Memoirs of a Woman of Pleasure* could breach the wall of obscenity and be legally available for reading by the general public in the United States. Appropriately enough the test case arose in Massachusetts in 1963 with the attorney general declaring the book to be obscene and prosecuting those who would sell it. As in 1821, the trial court and the Massachusetts Supreme Judicial Court agreed that the book was obscene, but now there was a difference—the United States Supreme Court. It was here that *Memoirs of A Woman of Pleasure* finally had an effective champion. Unless a book is "utterly without redeeming social value" said the court, it may not be banned, and the court majority clearly saw something here of value. Suddenly the whimsical, erotic adventures of this eighteenth-century maiden who was determined to tell "Truth! stark, naked truth" became available to all.

Though Peter Holmes was the first person convicted of obscenity in the United States, it was more than seventy years before another obscenity conviction occurred anywhere in the country. Some states passed laws criminalizing the publishing, printing or selling of obscenity, without attempting to define it (Vermont was the first, in 1821, followed by Connecticut and Massachusetts, in the 1830s), but there was little concerted effort to follow it through.

Until the 1890s when spurred by the vice societies, especially in New York and Boston, and a changing urban landscape, the ogre of obscenity loomed larger and larger in the American consciousness. Soon, the courts were dealing with obscenity cases regularly, legislatures were grappling with ever-changing demands for reform, and books continued to appear presenting new, more varied, more graphic, more challenging forms of erotic portrayal. It was a struggle that would last through the first three-quarters of the twentieth century.

4

The Most Dangerous Book in America

It was shortly after noon on a late fall day in 1859. The mood in Washington D.C. was emotionally charged, and many felt the fate of the country rested with those who at that moment struggled in debate on the floor of the House of Representatives.

Perched atop a gentle rise, the Capitol building seemed placid enough, seen from Pennsylvania Avenue. Not so the atmosphere inside nor the human beings who occupied the Hall of the House of Representatives. On this December 5th, 1859, the Thirty-sixth Congress was to convene, and the first order of business was to choose a Speaker. Old rivalries sparked through the chamber. It was the next-to-last year in the term of President James Buchanan, and tensions between North and South had been building. The Republicans, most of whom were from the East and Midwest, had more members than the

Democrats, most of whom were from the South. But regional allegiances were bound to play a strong role and party loyalties were not secure.

Within minutes after the proceedings began, the old antagonisms flared. John Clark, a Democrat from Missouri, offered a resolution:

> Resolved that the doctrines and sentiments of a certain book . . . called *The Impending Crisis in the South — How to Meet It* written by one Hinton R. Helper, are insurrectionary and hostile to the domestic peace and tranquility of the country, that no member of this House who has endorsed and recommended it, or the compendium from it, is fit to be Speaker of the House.

Applause erupted from the jammed galleries.

John Clark turned up the emotional volume. The people who support this book were urging insurrection, treason, even murder, he declared, ridiculing those Republicans who had signed a circular endorsing the book. Now they wanted to elect one of those book supporters as Speaker. It was "the perpetuity of the Union, itself!" that was at stake.

David Farnsworth, a Republican from Illinois, sought the floor. "Excuse me, if you please," responded Clark, obviously annoyed.

Farnsworth, however ignored him. "We can act more understandingly on the resolution," he announced to the entire chamber, "if the gentleman from Missouri will have the book read. I wish to suggest that it be read."

"I will have everything read," John Clark insisted.

"I have never read the book," admitted Farnsworth, "and I presume the gentleman from Missouri never read it. I think it would be well, therefore, to have it read."

"It would be well if the gentleman could also say he had never signed the recommendation," John Clark answered, referring to the circular endorsing the book.

"I recommend the literature to the gentleman from Missouri, that is all," said an obviously pleased David Farnsworth. "I think it would do him a world of good."

What was this book some members of Congress wanted to condemn so adamantly? Its roots had taken hold in the early life of the author, Hinton Rowan Helper, who was born in 1829 in the Yadkin Valley of North Carolina. His family were farming people—poor, struggling, hard working—but Hinton Helper showed little interest in the land. He had a bookish turn, and was more interested in reading and studying than in sweating through the day behind a team of horses or digging and plowing and harvesting. In school he excelled in literature and history, but instead of going to college, he did what most poor white farm boys in North Carolina did in their late teens—he sought a job. In this case it was as apprentice to a storekeeper, who hired him and with whom he stayed for three years (and helped himself to small sums from the storekeeper's accounts, regularly and surreptitiously). By the time he was twenty-one years old Hinton Helper was over six feet tall, and athletic-looking, with jet-black hair and piercing blue eyes. His commanding presence was not what poor white farm boys from rural North Carolina usually developed.

In 1850, with his purloined funds and some savings,

Hinton Helper struck out for New York City looking for fame and money. But within a year he was off again, this time to California, San Francisco and the gold fields. His mind soaked up facts, his antennae sought money figures and tables of statistics. He listened and learned, and became a huge well of information.

And he never lost his storekeeper's account-book ways: adding, subtracting, income versus expenditures, costs versus benefits. He was not able to shuck the neat, mathematical certainty of figures and tables. It was here that he looked for answers to demanding questions of social science. Human behavior could be reduced to mathematical certainties, good and bad could be plucked from the account book.

Within four years he was back in New York, and he wrote his first book, *The Land of Gold Versus Fiction*, which spotlighted the negative side to California, its unkept promises of employment, its discomforts, its squalor, its misery, its corruption, its crime. He had travelled the state, he had seen the future.

The future was not California!

He used statistics and tables, citing figures about how much gold had been actually produced, then applying the costs and expenditures of extraction and transportation. He concluded that the gold rush in California, with all the people, businesses and capital coming in, actually created a state deficit of one hundred million dollars. "It is a greater sacrifice of moral and physical wealth than a single exchange of it afterwards can possibly restore," he wrote.

Such sentiments created the attention he craved, but by the time the book was published he was already hard at work on another. The disagreeable concept of slavery had consumed him for years, ever since his early North Carolina days. But his feelings were not based on natural rights or civil libertarian concerns. He had no use for slavery because it acted as a drug on the economy; it limited growth and it narrowed business opportunity. As he went about his days in New York he saw how a free society bubbled with exciting challenge, how capital and talent were encouraged. If only slavery could be abolished in his native South!

By 1856 he finished his new book, calling it *The Impending Crisis in the South — How to Meet It*. It embodied his strongest hopes and his most vituperative criticisms. On the title page he dedicated it to "THE NON-SLAVEHOLDING WHITES OF THE SOUTH," all in capital letters, a stentorian declaration. His book blossomed along intertwining paths: an economic comparison of life in the North with life in the South set off by almost sixty tables and numerous statistics (those storekeeper habits again) and a rousing call for abolition of slavery, even if it might mean bloodshed.

"Of you, the introducers, aiders and abettors of slavery, we demand indemnification for the damage our lands have sustained," he wrote, calculating that seven and one half billion dollars would be acceptable compensation for the centuries of slaveholding exploitation. "Our claim is just and overdue. We have already indulged you too long. Your criminal extravagance has almost ruined us."

He reminded the slaveholding South of his iron purpose: "We are firmly resolved never to degrade ourselves by becoming the mercenary purchasers or proprietors of human beings." *You owe us.*

His attack on slaveholders was personal and harsh. Slaveholders, he wrote, "Bring disgrace on themselves, their neighbors, and their country, depreciate the value of their own and others' lands, degrade labor, discourage energy and progress, prevent non-slaveholders from accumulating wealth, curtail their natural rights and privileges, doom their children to ignorance . . ."

Hinton Rowan Helper offered an eleven-point agenda for doing away with slavery and slaveholders. It included cutting all contact with slaveholders, stripping them of political and religious power, boycotting them economically, and levying a tax on them for each slave they owned. Those professing pro-slavery sentiments hereafter should be labeled "Ruffians, outlaws and Criminals."

He quoted George Washington, the Marquis de Lafayette, James Madison, and Henry Clay as well as John Locke, Dr. Samuel Johnson, William Burke, Jean Jacques Rousseau and Hugo Grotius for support of his contention that slavery flew in the face of natural law and human dignity. "Our motto," he directed to the slaveholders, "and we would have you understand it, is *the abolition of slavery, and the perpetuation of the American Union.* If, by any means, you do succeed in your treasonable attempts to take the South out of the Union today, we will bring her back tomorrow — if she goes away with you, she will return without you."

By spring, 1857, the book was being readied for publication. Hinton Rowan Helper had allowed some friends to look at the manuscript, and to his surprise they didn't like it. He showed copies to people in North Carolina, and the reaction was even more negative. The book would sell few copies, they predicted. No one would want to read it.

But then Hinton Rowan Helper met the editor of the *New York Daily and Weekly Tribune.* Horace Greeley was a staunch Republican supporter, and when he read the book, he saw something others didn't see. It would aid the Republican cause, he realized. It had credibility because it was by a southerner castigating his own, and it painted southern slaveholding Democrats in the harshest way.

On June 26, 1857, the book was published and the *Daily Tribune* offered an unqualified endorsement, predicting it would be a best seller. Less than three weeks later the newspaper provided a spectacular review, calling Hinton Helper a spokesman for the southern white masses, "one who utters no stammering, hesitating nor uncertain sound, who possesses a perfect mastery of his mother tongue, who speaks as well from a long study and full knowledge of his subject as from profound convictions." The statistics and tables in the book? Anything but boring, they were "interspersed with rolling volleys and dashing charges of argument and rhetoric." Horace Greeley rejoiced in the publication of Hinton Rowan Helper's book.

In the weeks to follow there were other reviews across the North, laudatory and congratulatory. *The New York Evening Post,* for example, called the book "the most compact and irresistible array of facts and arguments to the impolity of slavery." Newspaper after newspaper, magazine after magazine, fell into line as the book took on the character of abolitionist symbol. It was not just a book, it was becoming THE book against slavery.

In the South, of course, Hinton Helper's book got bare mention. Most local editors and columnists chose to ignore it, and its circulation was limited at best. When reference to the book was made, it was couched in derogatory asides, skewering Helper more for his character than his words, and offering the explanation that the book was

merely a sop to the fanatic urgings of the New England–
New York Abolitionist axis.

In spite of Horace Greeley's rousing support, however,
sales for *The Impending Crisis* were not what Hinton
Helper hoped them to be. He had expected national
attention, and that had not seemed to happen. He had
hoped his book would change the nature of American life,
but in the months since publication it had only made
believers more certain and disbelievers more angry.

Once again Hinton Helper turned to Horace Greeley.
The book is probably too long, Helper said. He was
thinking of a shorter version, a compendium of the most
important points. The editor arranged for Hinton Rowan
Helper to meet with influential Republicans and seek
funds. Within a few weeks the money began to come in
and a printing of 100,000 was agreed upon.

The compendium was to run about 200 pages, and
Helper decided to forgo royalties. The important thing
now was to get the book *out!* Never mind profit or income.
People must read this book, they must understand!

During the next few months Helper encouraged the
Republican Party to adopt the book, and by the early
spring of 1859 many prominent Republicans—including
Horace Greeley—did so. In order to help sales and distribution a circular-letter was prepared, dramatizing the
book's contents and showing the signatures of many well-
known Republicans.

Within a year it was apparent that the compendium
had worked. By the fall of 1859 many copies of *The
Impending Crisis in the South — How to Meet It* were in the
public's hands, and suddenly the *New York Herald,* ar-
dently pro-Democratic, unleashed an attack. The compendium, it said, was the most dangerous disclosure

"brought to light in this country since the treason of Benedict Arnold was detected at Tarrytown." The newspaper saw the book as a severe threat to Democratic victory in the 1860 elections because of its anti-slavery, abolitionist pronouncements.

Attention like this added to the book's allure, and by early December, 1859, more than five hundred copies a day were being ordered. Many copies were going to border states such as Illinois and Indiana, though some also found their way into the South.

Enough, in fact, to stir local resentment and bring flagrant reaction. Stories began to find their way back North about southerners who had been discovered with copies of *The Impending Crisis in the South — How to Meet It.* Private citizens, mostly, certainly without a hair's breadth of treason on their minds.

There was Charles Dixon of Maryland who had been arrested for distributing the book and held for $10,000 bail because he violated a state law concerning possession and circulation of incendiary documents.

There was Thomas Crua who had distributed the book in Virginia to slaveholders and non-slaveholders, and was arrested because he was "interfering with the colored population." He was released only after paying $2500 bail.

In North Carolina six men were arrested for circulating the book, three more were driven from their homes by mobs, and the Reverend Daniel Worthy was tried on the grounds that he preached to make the slaves dissatisfied. His defense contended he sold the book only to white persons so how could slaves have become dissatisfied when they weren't aware of what the book said? But the prosecution read portions aloud during the trial to show that the book was incendiary literature regardless of who was exposed to it. The jury deliberated little more than four hours and returned a guilty verdict.

In South Carolina, Harrold Wyllis was in jail because he had had seven copies of the book in his possession, and his local Congressman went on the floor of the U.S. Congress to state that Wyllis would hang.

In Arkansas three men *were* hanged for having the book in their possession.

And in New York City plans were being made to publish another printing of *The Impending Crisis in the South — How to Meet It* because per-day sales were expected to double by the end of December.

It was now the second day of the first session of the Thirty-Sixth Congress, December 6th, 1859, and in the Chamber of the House of Representatives the election of a Speaker continued unresolved.

John Clark, the Missouri Democrat, retained the floor and waved a document at his fellow congressmen. It was a circular-letter dated March 9, 1859, and it contained numerous Republican members' signatures.

A moment later he read it into the record:

"Dear Sir: If you have read and critically examined the work, you will probably agree with us that no course of argument so successfully controverting the practice of slavery in the United States, and enforc- ing a precise and adequate view of its prostrating effects, material and moral, has equaled that of the volume entitled 'The Impending Crisis of the South — How to Meet It' by Hinton Rowan Helper of North Carolina."

When John Clark finished reading, his words echoed across the House chamber. The book, he said, contains passages which demand "The North must seize the riches of the South," urging "nonslaveholders to strike for Treason," promising "Revolution — Peacefully if we can, Violently if we must."

John Clark's voice rose with indignation. "How would they like us to say to the North that their forests — which they say are so profitable — their work shops, their mines and their branches of industry, are not well managed, and that we could use them more profitably than they?" Why *should* the wealth of the South be dedicated to the North? Yet, "that is the sentiment in the book which these gentlemen recommend to have circulated gratuitously all over the South."

He ended with a question. "Are such men fit to preside over the destinies of our common country?"

In a few moments, John Sherman from Ohio rose to respond. He was a Republican and one of the signers of the circular-letter John Clark had so viciously criticized. He was a candidate for the Speaker's position; in fact he was the leading candidate, but his signature on the circular-letter was proving a source of embarrassment. As he addressed his fellow House members, John Sherman held up a letter he had received from F.P. Blair, a well-known Maryland Republican. Slowly, he then read the letter into the record, emphasizing that Blair had informed Hinton Rowan Helper he would have to remove the more inflammatory passages in his book if he wanted Republican support.

"I understand that it was in consequence of his assurance to me that the obnoxious matter in the original publication would be expurgated, that members of Congress and other influential men among the Republicans were induced to give their countenance to the circulation of the edition so to be expurgated."

But, of course, the book had not been expurgated, and John Sherman implied that he and other Republicans had been mislead.

That, and only that, was the reason his name appeared on the circular for a book that inflamed as it defied. "I do not recollect signing the paper referred to," John Sherman went on, "but I presume from my name appearing in the printed list, that I did sign it. I therefore make no excuse of that kind." And now a rather startling admission: "I have never read Mr. Helper's book, or the compendium founded upon it. I have never seen a copy either."

And he resumed his seat to bursts of applause from the galleries and his fellow Republicans.

Now Shelton F. Leake from Virginia took the floor. He addressed Samuel Curtis of Iowa, one of John Sherman's defenders: "Sir, upon the 9th day of March last, this publication in relation to Helper's book was written with that gentleman's signature affixed to it, in which he is pledged to revolution in the South, to throttle slavery and to abolish the institution — peaceably if he can, forcibly if he must . . . now, I want to know whether he disavows the document to which he has placed his signature? He has not said it, and he will not say it."

Samuel Curtis jumped up to take issue but Albert Rust of Arkansas was quicker. "What portion of the pamphlet do you indorse?" he demanded of Curtis. "You signed the recommendation."

"I say I never read that pamphlet," Samuel Curtis answered. "I indorsed the preparation of a compendium containing tabular statements and historical extracts for general use."

"What was their design?" Albert Rust demanded.

"They were designed to be circulated for the benefit of the human race."

Laughter pealed from the galleries and the Republican benches. One could imagine Samuel Curtis wearing a pixyish smile as he savored his riposte.

A few moments later, all was serious again. Shelton Leake resumed and his words carried an unsettling certainty: "Now let us come back to the only point which the gentleman from Iowa is making upon us. We may as well meet them as they arise, for I warn the Gentlemen on the other side that . . ." and here he mispronounced the title . . . " *The Impending Crisis at the South* has got to be met, and we of the South are going to settle it as we go . . ."

The Speakership battle roiled through the House of Representatives in December and January with no candidate receiving a majority of votes. Ballot after ballot showed John Sherman leading but unable to muster enough support to win the prize. The main sore point continued to be his endorsement of Hinton Rowan Helper's book. Finally, on February 1st, 1860, almost two months after the session began, a compromise candidate emerged — William Pennington from New Jersey. On the forty-fourth ballot Pennington gained the minimum number of votes and became Speaker of the House of Representatives. It was — and remains — the longest election battle for this post in the history of the United States.

The legacy of Hinton Rowan Helper's book had left its imprint. A Pennsylvania Senator wrote to a friend, "Nothing has made so much bad blood as the endorsement of the Helper book. . . ." And a year or so later, after Republican Abraham Lincoln had been elected, the

"New-York Herald" — that staunchly Democratic voice — blamed presidential-election defeat on the book. "For weeks and months," the newspaper claimed, " express loads of the vile production were forwarded into every nook and locality of the Union, disseminating views which soon became deeply rooted in the rural districts and against which the anti-constitutional newspapers did not pretend to utter a protest."

5

Frolicking in Ford Hall

Early spring in Boston is a creature of the calendar rather than a provider of gentle weather. April days tend to bite, and the sun is more notable for its absence. It's the last flick of winter's tail.

So it was on a mid-April evening in 1929. In this early spring of a decade whose catastrophic final months would sear the American consciousness, the mood — at least in one Boston location — was both optimistic and unrestrained. Financial disaster was months away, and a party was in progress.

The revels took place at Ford Hall, a spacious Boston meeting place often used for large gatherings. More than 700 people were there, and the atmosphere pulsated with excitement. The party, which included a reception and dinner, was put on to lampoon Boston censorship, to ridicule "Banned in Boston" which had become a national sobriquet.

At the head table was a group of authors whom Boston had banned: Percy Marks, Arthur Garfield Hays, Morris L. Ernst, Mrs. Glendower Evans and Reuban L. Luise. In the middle slouched the beefy frame and tousled countenance of Chicago trial lawyer, Clarence Darrow. From time to time he would grin down the table at a woman in her mid-forties, who sat quietly with a huge gag over her mouth.

This was birth-control advocate Margaret Sanger, whom Boston had forbidden to speak in any public forum. Clarence Darrow leaned across and said, loud enough so the press could hear, "What we need is a Watch and Ward Society for liberty." He referred to the Boston book-censorship organization, now in its fifty-first year.

Around the hall placards stood out, each one containing the title of a book that had been banned in Boston: *The Plastic Age, Oil, Bad Girl, Hard-Boiled, Virgin, Nigger Heaven.* Lettered on each placard was "suppressed," large enough to be seen across Ford Hall.

Earlier in the evening young students, dressed in costume to resemble characters in banned works of fiction, had paraded among the guests. They wore signs showing the books they portrayed, and they sought signatures on a petition to ban the latest book by Percy Marks, *A Dead Man Dies.* "We want this book suppressed in Boston," the students urged, "it'll guarantee a large sale all over the country!"

It was a fun-loving group of partygoers that listened to "Chief Roastmaster" Arthur Schlesinger as he read aloud words that Margaret Sanger had written but was unable to speak. Nodding along with the gag over her mouth she seemed to punctuate each sentence, even with her silence.

Then Clarence Darrow rose, this rumpled man now in his early seventies. He underscored what he had just heard. "Who," he asked, "is opposed to birth control? Preachers and the rich. Why? Somebody has to have children so they can keep on being rich. They want to have a monopoly of the good things in life."

Deftly, he turned the birth-control debate to books censorship. "Who," he asked, "censors the books of Boston? A policeman. Who tells the policeman it is bad?" By now he had every eye in Ford Hall, every mind. In ringing certainty, he answered his own question: "The real censor is in some obscure corner of Boston, a super-annuated preacher who is too old to be influenced by literature."

Modern book-censorship in Boston probably owes its push to a New Yorker, Anthony Comstock, whose zeal in pursuing what he considered "offensive" literature led him to create the New York Society for the Suppression of Vice in 1873. Comstock, whose determination was boundless, maneuvered himself an appointment as a special agent of the U.S. Post Office Department with responsibility for seeking out and destroying any and all forms of "obscene literature." It was a time of urban upheaval in the major U.S. cities with many young men, following the end of the Civil War, gravitating to a rootless anonymity, away from their families and moral control. Unrestrained now, they sought greater sensual pleasure and found it in relatively graphic depictions in newer books and magazines such as the *Police Gazette*. This seriously alarmed those who had heretofore exercised moral leadership — the churches and the conservative politicians

— and Anthony Comstock saw himself as the protector of this traditional morality.

In this capacity he went to Boston in 1878 and met with a group of ministers at historic Park Street Church. He spoke of the evils of "impure literature," and he had a receptive audience. Within a short time the New England Watch and Ward Society was born, modeled on Comstock's Society for the Suppression of Vice but with a more genteel flavor. It eschewed the confrontational style that Comstock favored; instead, the Watch and Ward Society relied on quiet persuasion and an appeal to reason and sensitivity. Its board was a mix of wealthy Boston Brahmins devoted to social reform and liberal Protestant church leaders, most of whom saw themselves less as censors and more as community thought-leaders. Theirs was a gentlemanly world in which others — booksellers, book publishers, book distributors — could be encouraged to act in the same manner, when their "best instincts" could be appealed to.

For the first thirty years or so, there is little record of formal action taken by the Watch and Ward to control what Bostonians read, though there is little doubt that such control — informal as it may have been — was exerted. For example, Walt Whitman's *Leaves of Grass* was banned in 1882, quickly and decisively. Then, ten years later, another controversy erupted. In 1892, a public-school principal by the name of Mortimer Warren wrote a modest book of sex instruction, *Almost Fourteen,* and submitted it to Dodd, Mead and Company. The publisher asked his wife to read it and also showed it to the pastor of the Broadway Tabernacle and the Church of the Heavenly Rest and to a Dr. Lyman Abbott. All three saw no problem with the book and so it was published.

For five years the book enjoyed modest success, even becoming a part of several Sunday-school libraries. No complaints, no protests were heard, and according to some it was on its way to becoming a minor classic. But then it sparked special attention from a reformer who saw the book as an important support for liberal policy change. He gave it a strong push and woke up the censorship dragons. The Watch and Ward purchased a copy from a bookseller and filed a complaint with the police about it. The bookseller was arrested and convicted for selling obscene literature. And the author lost his job as principal in the public school.

By the time the twentieth century was less than a decade old, the tide of social change was sweeping through Boston. Immigrants flooded the city, new political alliances were being formed, organized labor was flexing its muscles and the Brahmins were not so sure of the social control they once exercised. Advances in transportation and communication made exposure to other thoughts, other concepts available, and the idea that a small homogeneous group of self-appointed censors could exert moral control without challenge lost support. The Watch and Ward Society was not getting the respect it thought it deserved, and something needed to be done.

In 1915 the Watch and Ward joined forces with Boston booksellers to form the Boston Booksellers Committee, composed of three members from the Watch and Ward Society and three local booksellers. They read and evaluated current fiction, providing a stamp of approval on those books that passed muster, notifying the bookselling community on those that didn't. The standard was *clean books,* and woe to the bookseller who ignored the committee recommendations. If a bookseller sold a book that was on the list of the disapproved, the Watch and Ward would descend swiftly and wrathfully, bringing a prosecution for violation of Massachusetts's obscenity statute with maximum public opprobrium. Little support could be expected from other booksellers; it was, after all, *their* committee that disapproved the book. And, if that wasn't enough, Boston newspapers refused advertising for any book condemned by the committee, and book reviewers would refuse to review it.

It was a grand literary conspiracy, almost airtight in its control by censorship and thorough in its financial penalties. "[I]f the bookseller won't sell and the reviewer won't review," boasted Richard Fuller, a bookseller member of the committee, "the book might as well never have been written."

Or, if the bookseller tried to sell a condemned book, and the reviewer wouldn't review, the book's chances of success were greatly reduced. It would be the bookseller, as well as the author and publisher, who would suffer.

For a decade or so the committee worked quite well (insofar as censorship committees go), probably because benevolence and reasonableness were uppermost. The committee tried to do its work in a socially responsible way: "We consider the book as a whole," said Richard Fuller, "and we consider the author's motive in writing the story, and the probable effect it will have on the public."

The most immediate effect on the public was easily measured: by the middle 1920s the Boston Booksellers Committee had suppressed between sixty and seventy titles.

At Ford Hall on that April evening in 1929 the party grew less restrained as the evening moved along. While

the 700 guests applauded and cheered head-table statements reviling Boston book-censorship, it soon became
apparent that the organizers had a special treat ready — a
live skit that would portray the censorship dragon with
dramatic satire.

Quickly, a makeshift stage was set up and a few props
scattered. The guests leaned forward in anticipation.

On a stand was a simple sign: "The Suppressed Book
Shop," and next to it was a desk with another sign:
"Today's Suppressions." Reuben Lurie, one of the censored authors at the head table, entered with a traveling
bag and stood by the desk, cradling a telephone which
connected him to police headquarters — whose number,
Lurie advised, was *LI*berty 1776.

A woman entered, seeking to purchase a book.

"But why do you want to buy a book?" Lurie asked with
mock surprise.

"Because I want to be intelligent, even if I do live in
Boston!" There were howls of laughter, and she waited for
them to subside. "I want a copy of *Mother Goose,*" she said.

"Why goodness gracious!" exclaimed Lurie, "Do you
realize the things that are in that book? Take Jack and
Jill. Did you ever consider that Jack went up the hill
ostensibly to get a pail of water and then tumbled down?
Think of the conclusions that can be drawn." He reached
in his traveling bag and removed a thermometer which he
place in her mouth . . . and in a moment he took it out
and it glowed red hot.

So he was forced to sell her the telephone book. "I
recommend it highly," he said, as she walked off to rip-
pling laughter.

Mrs. Glendower Evans, another of those at the head
table, entered. "I'd like *Grimm's Fairy Tales,*" she said.

Lurie registered abject horror. "Don't you know that

book contains Bolshevik material?" he exclaimed. "Little *Red* Riding Hood and the Three Little *Bears!*" He recommended something else: copies of the Republican and Democratic-party platforms. "These," he told her, "are guaranteed to be pure."

Then author Gardner Jackson entered in a policeman's uniform and began searching around the desk and stand. He informed Lurie and the audience that he was looking for an "obscene" book; he knew there had to be one here.

Sure enough he found it: a plane geometry text containing triangles, that erotically suggestive symbol. "You're under arrest," he told Lurie and began dragging him away. But not before Lurie could place a sign, "Moved to Cambridge," on the front of his "shop."

And the audience hooted and laughed and cheered.

With the success of the Boston Booksellers Committee came the realization in the mid 1920s that the Brahmins of the Watch and Ward Society had formed a subtle though effective alliance with the fast emerging Irish Catholic majority in Boston. The Catholic Church was as adamantly opposed to "sinful" books as the Watch and Ward, and their common interests led them to support one another in censoring and controlling what people in Boston read. But they had to contend with a decade in which change was part of the landscape, in social relationships, in science, in art, in peoples' ability to mold their own environment. The old rules were being challenged, and the moral bases for book censorship were in the front lines. The genteel approach of reasonable people seeking to do reasonable, socially responsible work hardened into urgent demands: *we must do something or else!* . . . , and the result was stepped-up, militant censorship by the Watch and Ward, the Catholic Church and the local authorities. In 1927, for instance, more than sixty titles were banned in a single year.

But a year before that, it became apparent that authors themselves were going to take the offensive against Boston book-censorship. In the April, 1926, issue of the *American Mercury,* Herbert Asbury told the story of "Hatrack," a prostitute in Farmington, Missouri. She was locally shunned, even when she went to church to repent, but every Sunday evening, after fiery pentecostal meetings, her customer list would boom. Asbury did not detail any graphic sex, other than to report she entertained her Protestant customers in the Catholic graveyard and vice-versa, and that she rarely received more than a dollar for her services.

The Watch and Ward was incensed by the intertwining of religion and sex and succeeded in getting the *American Mercury* issue banned in Boston. But H.L. Mencken, editor of the magazine, took up the fight and travelled to Boston with his lawyer, Arthur Garfield Hays (one of those who sat at the head table in Ford Hall, three years later). Together they walked to Boston Common and set up at "Brimstone Corner," as the press came to call it. Mencken publicly hawked the magazine while the press stood by. By pre-arrangement a member of the Watch and Ward bought a copy and immediately had Mencken arrested.

No doubt most expected the courts to follow through with a conviction because it was rare for the Watch and Ward to lose. But, somehow, Municipal Judge James D. Parmenter saw it differently, castigating the Watch and Ward because of its practice of intimidation, and the ban on *American Mercury* magazine was lifted.

The reaction of Boston censorship was to redouble efforts, and by 1928 the list of banned books had grown to upwards of a hundred, including Sinclair Lewis's *Elmer Gantry*, Ernest Hemingway's *The Sun Also Rises*, William Faulkner's *Mosquitos*, John Dos Passos's *Manhattan Transfer* and Theodore Dreiser's *An American Tragedy*. Authors such as Upton Sinclair (whose book, *Oil*, about political scandals in the recent Harding Administration, had been banned because it contained references to birth control) took to the streets in a display of public theatre. Sinclair resented the implication he had written an indecent book, and one June day, wearing only a sandwich board which resembled a fig leaf, he paraded through downtown Boston selling his book with the offending passages cut out. "We authors are using America as our sales territory," he shouted, "and Boston is our advertising department!"

But he was left untouched. No judge would issue a warrant.

Then, in the spring of 1929, a hearing was held in Cambridge on an appeal in the *American Tragedy* banning. The defendant was Donald Friede who had published the book, and there was good reason to believe the anti-censorship forces would prevail for public opinion seemed to be turning against the Watch and Ward and the more militant censorship advocates. Boston had acquired international notoriety for its bookbanning. In many places it was scored and satirized, and more and more citizens were finding that a source of embarrassment. There were moves in the state legislature to amend the obscenity statutes and make them more liberal, and the defense had the renowned attorney, Clarence Darrow, in its corner.

In the middle of April, 1929, the appeal was heard, though Darrow confined himself to reading portions of *An*

American Tragedy to the jury. It was a dramatic performance, and it was followed by the appearance of author Theodore Dreiser who, the defense expected, would show that he never intended to write an indecent or obscene book.

But Dreiser never had a chance to tell the jury.

"Was [your book] founded on an actual incident?" asked defense attorney Arthur Garfield Hays.

Excluded.

"Did you do any studying in connection with writing the book? What material did you study?"

Excluded.

"In order to get the background, would it not be necessary to read the whole book?"

Excluded.

"Can one get an idea of the background of the book by reading less than the entire book?"

Excluded.

"Mr. Dreiser, will you tell the whole story of *An American Tragedy* so we may know the theme?"

Excluded.

That evening the "Ford Hall Frolics," as they came to be known, took place in Boston, and the next day the jury in Cambridge began debating the decision in the *American Tragedy* bookbanning case.

Twenty-four hours later, civic reaction to what had taken place at Ford Hall began to surface, and suddenly there was deep-seated anger at the intellectual put-downs that were reported. Those attending should be "deported," said veterans' organizations. It was "too unworthy and too contemptible," said the minister of the Park Street Church. "These people are promoting discord in this country," said the Massachusetts adjutant general. "I hope someone will charter a ship and send that crowd to Russia where they will be right at home in their own element," added another high state official.

And in Cambridge, the jury came back and affirmed the conviction of Donald Friede for publishing an obscene book — Theodore Dreiser's *An American Tragedy*.

Boston's bookbanning resurgence lasted for only a few months, however. In October, 1929, John Tait Slaymaker, a Watch and Ward agent, went to the Dunster House Bookshop in Cambridge after receiving word that D.H. Lawrence's *Lady Chatterley's Lover* was for sale. The bookshop owner was a well-respected bibliophile and former Yale librarian, James DeLacey, who had little use for graphic sexual matter. He was well known for his modest tastes.

Slaymaker went to the bookshop under a false name and tried to buy the book. But DeLacey wouldn't sell it to him. Slaymaker returned two more times, and finally, DeLacey relented. As soon as money and book changed hands, he was arrested on a complaint by the Watch and Ward. A few weeks later he was convicted, fined $800 and sentenced to four months in prison.

But it turned out to be a pyrrhic victory because on appeal the Watch and Ward was attacked for its brazen use of undercover agents, especially when they used false names.

Nevertheless, the court affirmed the conviction, though wiping away the jail sentence, and making plain its distaste for what the Watch and Ward had done. Even the prosecutor considered the society a composite of "falsifiers" and "procurers," and bitterness over what had happened to highly respected James DeLacey spread across the literary landscape.

Its methods questioned, its judgments criticized, its purpose no longer so respectable, the Watch and Ward Society slowly declined into obscurity after the Dunster Bookshop case. Within two years financial contributions had dried up by forty percent and many of its board members and supporters had resigned or moved on. By 1931, it was clear that Watch and Ward was never again to be a major force in Boston literary circles.

But *Banned in Boston* had left its mark.

6

The Leer of the Sensualist?

Through the early years of its published life, the book carried the plainest cover — dark blue without markings of any sort. The title, in fact, wasn't on the cover, nor was the author's name. It was a blank wrapping, yet it was what most book buyers expected when they bought it far from home.

It had taken the author more than six years to write this book, and even before it was finished, word had spread that something special was in progress. It would be a very long book, and it offered an extraordinary variety of insights, characterizations, aesthetic releases — and erotic depictions. The author wrote not only for the eye but for the ear, and his words had the ringing cadence of the poet wrapped in the solidifying frame of the novelist. It was, to be sure, a work of fiction, but it carried the art form higher and further than most could have imagined.

While the author was writing this book, excitement and anticipation were such that the *Little Review* wrote him and suggested printing an excerpt.

That would be fine, said the author. It was 1918; after all, the terrible war was almost over, and modern civilization had somehow survived. A new world seemed to beckon. The author showed the editor of the periodical some completed sections, and she chose what came to be called the "eleventh episode."

Eventually the eleventh episode appeared in the literary magazine, and for a brief period the author and the editor felt the glow of praise.

But then the United States Post Office informed them it was confiscating all copies of the magazine.

Why? they demanded.

Obscene. It violated United States law. The Post Office took the magazine copies and burned them. Every last one.

The author, who had not finished his book, was distraught, but he saw himself more victim than perpetrator, and he never stopped writing. Finally, in 1920, he was finished, and then the literary magazine was in touch with him again. He reminded the editor of what had happened two years before, but he also felt a surge of anger that his extraordinary book had been so crassly judged. Publish away! he finally told the editor. Perhaps Americans will understand better this time.

An excerpt appeared, but the author, who was neither an American citizen nor an American resident, had seriously misread the American tolerance level. This time it wasn't the Post Office that intervened.

Instead, it was a large, rotund man with mutton-chop

whiskers and steely blue eyes — the secretary of the New York Society for the Suppression of Vice. His name was John Sumner, a lawyer by training and education, but a censorship vigilante by choice. Sumner read the excerpt and immediately brought suit in Federal District Court to prevent further printing and sale. He even sought the arrest of the editor of the literary journal.

The author, who lived in Paris, was dumbfounded. His book had been praised in reviews on both sides of the Atlantic, and he didn't know what to make of American culture.

Then he heard that his book had been burned by English customs authorities, and he amended his viewpoint: he didn't know what to make of English culture, either.

In New York, John Sumner and his lawsuit prevailed, and copies of the excerpt were confiscated once again (no one had even tried to publish the entire book in the United States). By 1922, two years after he finished his book, the author had reason to wonder whether it would ever be read in an English-speaking country. Yet he did have patience, and he would persevere, and in ensuing years his book would become the most important breakthough in the censorship wall.

His name: James Joyce.

His book: *Ulysses.*

The New York Society for the Prevention of Vice was founded in 1873 by the notorious Anthony Comstock, a forbidding figure who dominated the book-censorship scene for more than forty years. He was a deeply religious man, who by the age of eighteen, was already crusading against alcohol. He saw in certain books the embodiment of sin, and he directed his singleminded obsession against all depictions of obscenity. He lobbied Congress for a law which would allow the Post Office Department to seize, confiscate and destroy any form of obscenity that came through the mails, and in 1873, after a short debate, passed such a law. It barred the mailing of any "obscene, lewd, or lascivious, indecent, filthy or vile . . . book. . . ."

Then Anthony Comstock had himself appointed a special agent of the Post Office Department and set about enforcing this law. At age twenty-eight he had become the most powerful censor in the United States.

In his first six months Comstock bragged he had seized 134,000 pounds of books, and he operated with an impunity and an independence we can only gasp at. He conducted raids on literary classics and non-classics alike, backed by his vice society who saw him as a hero and a staunch defender of Victorian morality. Comstock operated with the general consent of the authorities. He and the New York Society for the Suppression of Vice would bring a prosecution under the law, and when a conviction resulted — as it often did — one-half the fine would go to the Society.

Comstock targeted hundreds of books, and he was particularly interested in foreign authors whose works were slated for delivery in the United States. Among those he went after were Honoré de Balzac (a dealer who sold *Droll Stories* and the *Heptameron* to Comstock was fined and jailed for two years), Gustav Flaubert (whose *Madame Bovary* was burned by Customs agents) and Nicolai Tolstoy (whose *Kreutzer Sonata* was barred by the postmaster general).

By the early twentieth century Comstock could crow

that he had been responsible for 3600 prosecutions and had destroyed more than 160 tons of "obscene" material. In 1905, however, his crusade hit a bump: he ran afoul of George Bernard Shaw when he had *Man and Superman* relegated to the reserve shelf at the New York Public Library. Shaw was incensed and coined a designation, "Comstockery," which skewered what had been a serious obsession. Most of the English-speaking world was able to grin as Shaw declared "Comstockery" to be "the world's standing joke at the expense of the United States. . . . It confirms [Europe's] deep-seated conviction of the Old World that America is a provincial place, a second rate country. . . ."

Less than ten years later Comstock came face to face with a highly popular novel, *Hagar Revelly,* the story of two poverty-level young girls trying to survive in New York. *Obscene*! Comstock shouted, and he seized all copies at the publisher's office as well as 2000 copies at the bindery. The publisher was arrested, and the case went to trial. But the jury, disregarding the judge's warnings that a not-guilty verdict would establish a dangerous precedent, had read the book. They liked it and they refused to convict.

It was a body blow to Anthony Comstock.

A year later, Comstock was dead, but the New York Society for the Suppression of Vice did not go away. John Sumner succeeded Comstock, and the prosecutions and the censorship continued. The Society still considered it had a mandate on what the public should read, so Sumner was as zealous as Comstock had been. Obscenity was "an offense against society"; it was "detrimental to the public well-being."

Sumner took office just as the liberalizing hints of the 1920s surfaced. New York was not Boston with its carefully controlled culture and manageable population enclaves. New York was a vibrant mix of immigrants, commerce and constantly evolving values, a thriving, bustling place which was the artistic and the financial center of the United States, a crossroads for millions of people. The Society found itself struggling with a judiciary and a population that saw its purpose more limited, less important than at any time. For John Sumner the reality struck a year or so after he succeeded Anthony Comstock. He singled out Theophile Gautier's *Mademoiselle de Maupin,* a French classic written in 1836, swooped down on a local bookstore and arrested the clerk who was selling it. But the judge was not sympathetic. The book may have had "indecent paragraphs" the judge said, but that didn't make it obscene.

Case dismissed.

As the 1920s went along, the Society found its victories fewer and fewer, its defeats more galling. Occasionally, there would be success, such as the prosecution of the *Little Review* for publishing the excerpt from *Ulysses,* but mostly there were defeats. By 1930 the Society was not the formidable presence it had been a quarter of a century earlier. Now it had little more than its solid mid-town brownstone to remind it of past glories. A visitor to the offices reported the atmosphere gloomy, "the golden-oak furnishings dark and massive. A large portrait of Anthony Comstock dominated the cluttered office and a dusty cuspidor provided a further reminder of the founder's brooding presence. In the bare yard a scrawny ailanthus tree struggled towards the sun." In a somber office worked John Sumner, jowly and paunchy, his heavy frame bent over his roll-top desk.

Never again was the New York Society for the Suppression of Vice to rise to any position of power and influence. It was on the threshold of becoming an anachronism. Yet its legacy was much alive, particularly with *Ulysses*, because the prosecution of 1922 still held. It was forbidden to sell the book in the United States, and the only way it circulated this side of the Atlantic was by travelers returning from Europe and smuggling the dark blue paperbound work past sharp-eyed Customs and the Post Office.

One day in the summer of 1933 a young actor, traveling from France, disembarked at the Port of New York and approached the customs shed. Willingly, he opened his bags for inspection and waited for the inspectors to find their bounty.

He was sure they would find the contraband.

But he was waved on. No one bothered to look in his bags.

"Just a moment," he said.

"Move along, please."

"What about this?" He reached into his bags. "*This!*"

"It's a book," one of the customs inspectors said.

"It's *Ulysses,*" the actor said.

"Oh!" they said, and arrested him, commencing a series of events which forever changed the obscenity laws in the United States.

The comic-opera attempt to smuggle *Ulysses* was a tableau designed by publisher Bennett Cerf and his Random House publishing company in order to test the then-current obscenity laws. The scheme had actually begun more than a year earlier when Cerf had contacted James Joyce in Paris and sought permission to publish *Ulysses* in the United States. He wanted this permission so he could produce an "authenticated" edition of the book which, by now, had already reached the minor classic level in Europe. Pirated, uncopyrighted editions had been circulating for years in America because of John Sumner's earlier attack. "Obscene" was the label the book carried, so it could not be published here and it was uncopyrightable.

Joyce wrote to Bennett Cerf in April, 1932, and wished him well with his plan, noting that finally he might get some royalties on book sales in America. "It will permit American readers who have always proved very kind to me to obtain the authenticated text of my book without running the risk of helping some unscrupulous person in his purpose of making a profit for himself alone out of the work of another."

The copy of *Ulysses*, confiscated in the customs shed in 1933, was the French edition, and Random House editors had pasted inside the book favorable comments about it by well-known literary figures, so the reviews would become part of the evidence in a trial.

The story of *Ulysses* itself takes place during one day, June 16, 1904, and involves the thoughts, feelings, words and actions of a number of characters, including Leopold Bloom and his wife Molly (who many feel is the incarnation of Joyce's wife, Nora), and Stephen Dedalus, a young writer. Joyce delves into physical and sensual pleasures, describing them in overt terms. He provides emetic references and offers intimate sexual depictions in the frankest language. The book is a journey of the spirit in which the interrelationship of all men is reinforced by the minor steps of daily living. The past and the present join to develop impressions which affect life and behavior. Joyce uses the stream of consciousness technique and his characters flow back and forth between the external world and their internal reactions. The book, in short, is different from anything that preceded it.

In the Fall of 1933 the trial of *Ulysses* began in New York's Federal District Court before Judge John M. Woolsey, without a jury. Representing Random House was Morris Ernst, a well-known civil liberties lawyer and First Amendment advocate. The United States Attorney sat in for the government. At issue, a simple point: was *Ulysses* obscene, pornographic? What concerned the government was the proliferation of four-letter words and genital references such as *fuck, scrotum, hymen, penis, vagina,* as well as some obvious genital euphemisms. Ernst portrayed the historical roots for some of these words, seeking to remove the notion of shame.

"Judge," he argued, "as to the word 'fuck,' one etymological dictionary gives its derivation as from *facere* — to make — the farmer fucked the seed into the soil. This, your honor, has more integrity than a euphemism used every day in every modern novel to describe precisely the same event."

"For example?" the judge wondered.

"Oh — They 'slept' together. It means the same thing."

The judge smiled. "But Counselor, that isn't even usually the truth!"

Later, the judge indicated he had read the book, but that it had been hard going. Morris Ernst agreed but pointed out that even as he stood before Judge Woolsey and tried this case, his mind had been clicking to other things. "I was thinking of the gold ring around your tie, the picture of George Washington behind your bench and the fact that your black judicial robe is slipping off your shoulder. This double stream of the mind is the contribution of *Ulysses.*"

Judge Woolsey acknowledged the argument. "Now for the first time I appreciate the significance of this book," he said, mentioning that the dream sequences at the end disturbed him because of their erotic nature. But then he confessed that while listening to Ernst, "I have been thinking at the same time about the Hepplewhite furniture behind you."

And so Judge Woolsey understood how external and internal reality could be bound up together, how they could interact. Why, for example, couldn't someone fantasize erotically while functioning mundanely? If it happened in life, why couldn't it appear in a book?

In late December, 1933, Judge Woolsey rendered his verdict. James Joyce, he said, "sought to make a serious experiment in a new, if not wholly novel, literary genre." The book was not "dirt for dirt's sake," nor was it "written for the purpose of exploiting obscenity."

Some of the language, and the sexual, emetic references bothered Judge Woolsey, but not to the point of offensiveness. "In spite of its unusual frankness," he wrote, "I do not detect anywhere the *leer of the sensualist.*"

Ulysses was not an obscene book.

The most significant result of Judge Woolsey's decision was to force judges and prosecutors to examine a book in its entirety before concluding it was obscene. Until this time one page or even one paragraph could taint the entire book. But no longer, Now the entire work had to be judged as a whole.

There were those, of course, who had trouble accepting

the idea that *Ulysses* was not obscene. Such feelings even burst forth on the floor of the United States Senate where Senator Reed Smoot of Utah couldn't contain his disgust: a ten-minute review of the book, he insisted, indicated 'that it is written by a man with a diseased mind and a soul so black that he would even obscure the darkness of Hell. Nobody would write a book like that unless his heart was just as rotten as it could possibly be.'

No longer does the book invite such discomforting reactions, but it remains a source of intense interest to scholars who continue to strive to unravel the mysteries in the text. Spelling, punctuation and syntax have been argued about for decades, with one "definitive" *Ulysses* edition after another being published. Recently, a highly respected Joycean scholar produced his own "corrected" version of the book, only to find himself challenged by other scholars who claimed that he had made hundreds of errors. The dispute even reached the level of how many periods the scholar added and how many he deleted.

More than one hundred thousand copies of *Ulysses* are sold annually, so there's no danger the book's influence will fade. Perhaps the most perceptive comment of all was made by James Joyce himself when he said, shortly before his book was published, "I've put in so many enigmas and puzzles that it will keep the professors busy for centuries arguing over what I meant."

7

A Casualty of War

The NBC television studios at New York's Rockefeller Center hummed with subdued tension on this cold November morning in 1977. Another edition of "The Today Show" was flowing across America. According to the program log the next segment was an interview, and it promised to be controversial. Sitting quietly under the lights was the host, Tom Brokaw, who had recently come to "The Today Show" after a career in broadcast news. This type of interview fit well with his newsman's background.

Facing Brokaw was a thirty-three-year-old author, dark haired, square-faced, earnest-looking. The author, a former CIA agent, had written a book about the CIA and the last days in Vietnam. What made the situation dramatic was that the author's book had been published without CIA approval, even though he had agreed he wouldn't do this.

And the CIA was very angry.

Tom Brokaw, his notes discreetly available, began asking about the book. The author answered without guile or uncertainty. Brokaw came to a key point:

"In publishing this book, you've broken an oath you took. . . ."

"That's right," the author acknowledged.

". . . "when you became a member of the CIA. . . ."

"That's right."

". . . not to publish."

"That's right."

"And when you met with Stansfield Turner, who is the head of the CIA now, earlier this year," Brokaw continued, "you deliberately misled him about your plans to publish this book."

"That's right," admitted the author.

The author was Frank W. Snepp III, a graduate of Columbia College in New York, a native of North Carolina and a former CIA employee. For four and one-half years he had been the CIA's chief strategy analyst in Vietnam. He resigned from the agency shortly after his return to the United States, and his book was highly critical of the CIA's uncaring attitude towards its Vietnam allies in the final days of the war.

But when he joined up and when he left, he signed agreements he would publish nothing about his CIA experiences unless the agency could see it first.

Only he didn't show his book manuscript to the agency. The first time they read it, in fact, was after it had been published by Random House in 1977.

While he had been writing his book, Frank Snepp had requested a meeting with Stansfield Turner, the new director of the CIA. He wanted to talk about CIA conduct in Vietnam, even though he was no longer in the agency. The meeting took place in May, 1977, and Turner had John Morrison, the CIA's Deputy General Counsel, there, taking notes. It was not a fruitful meeting. Snepp's manuscript came up; but that's about all the participants could agree on later. According to Frank Snepp, he never agreed to let the CIA have a copy of his work before publication; according to Turner and Morrison, he did agree.

A few days later, however, a letter came for Frank Snepp from John Morrison. "They demanded a copy of the manuscript and along with it was a copy of my original secrecy agreement," Snepp recalled. "I hadn't seen it since 1968, hadn't even thought of it."

Morrison's letter said, in part, "We were pleased that you acknowledged your obligations under your Secrecy Agreement and your understanding that you may not submit an outline, manuscript or any other material or information you propose to publish to a publisher, agent or any unauthorized person prior to a review by the Agency to determine if it contains classified information."

But Frank Snepp had been very careful in what he had written — his book, to be titled *Decent Interval* — would contain no classified information. None whatsoever.

John Morrison asked Snepp to confirm, in writing, that he understood his obligations under the secrecy agreement, and that he intended to comply with it. Doing this, Morrison wrote "will make it unnecessary for us to take any further action at this time."

Frank Snepp, however, found the veiled threat more annoying than fearful, and he contacted his editor at Random House. As they had done for months when they wished to discuss sensitive matters, Snepp and his editor met in a quiet park a few blocks from the publisher's office. He pulled out the letter and let the editor read it.

"They're trying to trap you," the editor said and asked if he could show a copy to the Random House lawyers.

A few days later the lawyers' response came back to Frank Snepp. "This is a Book-of-the-Month Club-type letter," they told him, and he understood right away. You don't respond, you keep silent, you've bought the package.

So he wrote to the CIA saying he didn't agree with their understanding. After this, things began to turn mean. An agency friend told him the CIA was going to trap him, and others passed on information that Stansfield Turner felt Snepp had lied to him in their meeting. "I never concealed from CIA I was writing a book," Frank Snepp said, "they knew I was and they knew what it was about. My feeling was always this: I'm not a CIA-baiter or -hater, I had a typical 'we vs. them' attitude, and I had this while I was writing." He couldn't, however, shake his initial reaction to Stansfield Turner at that May, 1977, meeting. "I found him very condescending and arrogant."

Events, however, were closing in on Frank Snepp, even as his book was making its appearance. In October, 1977, Stansfield Turner decided to clean house at CIA, and this meant wholesale firings. More than 800 veteran agents were dismissed in what came to be called the "Halloween Massacre." With Frank Snepp and his unapproved book staring him down, few could blame Stansfield Turner for wondering how many other ideas—perhaps as critical of the agency—bubbled in the minds of the dismissed agents. Frank Snepp had not shown his manuscript ahead of time, even though he had been requested to do so, even though his secrecy agreement had required it — and nothing had been done.

What if the word got out, as it surely would. Might other former agents decide to take the plunge?

A deluge of books criticizing the agency?

Only a strong example would stop things.

A few weeks later Frank Snepp was invited to testify before the Senate Intelligence Committee. He came prepared to expand on why he had written his book; he thought the senators would be interested in what went wrong in Vietnam.

He asked if any had read his book. None had. He tried to explain what needed to be done to improve the agency, but he was met with stony dismissal. The senators did not care to hear his views.

He heard himself called a "squealer." There were suggestions he was a traitor. We don't care why you wrote the book or what you said. . . .

As Frank Snepp remembered it, "I was excoriated. No one wanted to know about the fall of Vietnam."

A few weeks later he was handed official-looking papers. It was a lawsuit, *United States v. Frank W. Snepp III.* The Department of Justice wanted all his royalties for *Decent Interval* — forever.

Because he had not abided by his contract to show the manuscript to CIA first. Even though he hadn't revealed a scintilla of classified information.

It was early December, 1977, now, and the first signs of winter were making their unwelcome appearance in Washington. The television season was in high gear, and politics and government occupied the talk-show circuit.

Frank Snepp was being interviewed by Pat Mitchell on a local Washington television station. The name of the show was "Panorama," and once again the questioning got around to what he lied about and what he didn't lie about.

"You did interview people, though, throughout — in a chapter of the book," Pat Mitchell stated.

"That's correct. That's correct." Snepp said.

"And you told them or at least you're reported as telling them, that you were going to have the book reviewed by the CIA."

"I told them various tales in order to get their cooperation," Frank Snepp said. "I did not tell them that I was going to work for the CIA and that I was going to cover classified information. In fact, I told them specifically don't give me classified information."

A short time after he was sued by the Department of Justice, Frank Snepp heard from the American Civil Liberties Union. They would defend him, if he wished them to do so. There was a strong First Amendment Issue at stake here. Offering his services was Mark Lynch, a tall, slender young attorney whose laconic manner covered a fierceness in his support of free expression. Frank Snepp's reaction was mixed. "At first I felt uncomfortable because Mark was a liberal and I wasn't." He also realized something else, and it did nothing to ease his discomfort. "Years before, Mark Lynch had come to Vietnam with a pacifist group, and we used to spy on them. Now he was going to be my lawyer."

But Frank Snepp had few choices, and he knew the lawsuit was at the very heart of his economic survival. He had already received an advance of more than twenty thousand dollars from Random House, and he also knew the book had been selling well in the weeks it had been out. But he stood to lose thousands of dollars unless he could mount a vigorous — and expensive — defense.

As he could not afford that kind of defense, he teamed up with Mark Lynch.

The trial was held several months later, in federal district court in Alexandria, Virginia, before Judge Oren Lewis, an elderly conservative, sitting without a jury. Mark Lynch and the government attorneys had agreed to most of the facts, so there would be only a minimum of evidence presented. The rest of the trial would consist of oral argument by the attorneys. But even before matters got going, the tone appeared set; the Judge peered down at Mark Lynch and Frank Snepp and said, "You'll want to know where the appeals court sits: you take I-95 and follow it to Richmond."

As the trial progressed, Mark Lynch offered argument on the First Amendment and how the secrecy agreement was a violation of the Constitutional right to free expression. He suggested that Frank Snepp had not lied or misled the CIA on whether he would turn over his manuscript before publication; he had simply been unresponsive. He emphasized that no classified information had appeared and that the government's primary motive for bringing suit was that the book took the agency to task. In short, Mark Lynch wondered how the United States could possibly be harmed by Frank Snepp.

The government, however, found fertile ground as it regaled Judge Lewis on Snepp's clandestine public-park meetings with his New York editor in order to show his sneaky intentions right along, on the precedent it would establish in the event Snepp could get away with ignoring his secrecy agreement, on the fact that Snepp had, indeed, lied to and misled his superiors at CIA.

At one point in the trial, Stansfield Turner appeared as a witness for the government. He was asked if there had been any adverse consequences from what Frank Snepp had done.

He left no doubt. "There clearly has. Over the last six to nine months we have had a number of sources discontinue work with us. We have had more sources tell us that they are very nervous about continuing work with us."

A little later he embellished: "If [Frank Snepp] is able to get away with this, it will appear to all those other people that we have no control, we have no way of enforcing the guarantee which we attempt to give them when we go to work with them."

It was more than enough for Judge Lewis even though Turner had not said Snepp had let out classified information. Judge Lewis found for the government and placed a constructive trust in favor of the government on all proceeds Snepp had or might get from *Decent Interval*. Snepp had "willfully, deliberately and surreptitiously breached his position of trust with the CIA and the secrecy agreement."

Two years later the case found its way to the Supreme Court because the court of appeals, to whom Mark Lynch and Frank Snepp appealed Judge Lewis's decision, said that as long as there was no classified information published, the First Amendment prevented any restriction on what could be written. Frank Snepp had achieved a minor victory.

But in the Supreme Court, things were different. No briefs were allowed, no oral argument. The Court would decide on the written record.

And they did so — six to three *against* Frank Snepp because he had "irreparably harmed the United States government." No one signed the opinion — it was a collective judgment.

But Frank Snepp lost his royalties for the last time.

In 1980, a select committee on intelligence of the House of Representatives took testimony on procedures used to insure no classified material would be published by former employees. Frank Snepp's name came up and the committee had the chance to consider a television interview he had given in December, 1977.

In sunny Los Angeles, Frank Snepp faced an experienced broadcast journalist named Jess Marlow on a show called "Newscenter 4," on KNBC, a major affiliate of the National Broadcasting Company.

Jess Marlow didn't waste any time. After thanking Frank Snepp for appearing, he dove into the secrecy agreement and spelled out where Snepp had agreed to show the CIA anything containing classified information. "Clearly," Marlow charged, "you've violated that oath."

"I surely have," Frank Snepp admitted. "As a matter of fact, I published the book without any agency clearance whatsoever because I felt that the agency had to learn from its mistakes."

Marlow's next question extracted more damaging information. "You made an additional agreement in promising Director Turner last May that you'd submit the manuscript of your book to him."

"Yes, I did," Snepp said, arguing that he did so because Stansfield Turner had been trying to discover what would be between the book's covers, even to ordering an FBI surveillance of him. "So I turned the agency's tactics against them and really fooled them into believing that I was doing nothing at all."

Representative Les Aspin of the House Select Committee on Intelligence now faced Herbert Hetu, Chairman of CIA's Publications Review Board. What Frank Snepp had said, what Frank Snepp had done, was hung up on the question of whether there was classified information in *Decent Interval.*

"Do you know specifically which portions were classified?" asked Les Aspin. "Has there been a post mortem review of that? There must have been a damage assessment of some sort."

Hetu acknowledged the agency had looked the book over.

"What kind of things were in there, and what were the kinds of things bothering you?"

"I don't remember specifically," Hetu said. "There weren't that many. I don't even remember the number."

Herbert Hetu was certain about one thing, however. If Frank Snepp had submitted the book to the CIA *ahead of time,* "he could have been published with a few changes and would not have been censored, as he said."

Then, a final assurance: *"We would not have hurt the sense of the book at all."*

But that was precisely Frank Snepp's point. He knew that if CIA had seen his manuscript ahead of time, they would have demanded changes, and he feared these changes would sanitize the book. More than any other thing, Frank Snepp wanted to tell his story fully; he knew CIA would never let him do that.

In the end, of course, Frank Snepp had little to savor except his published book. His story — the way he wanted to tell it — had been told; what he never anticipated was that he would become a part of American legal history. The *Snepp* decision would thereafter become a shadow on the right to free expression for all Americans.

In the spring of 1980 Frank Snepp and Mark Lynch, attired in three-piece suits, well groomed and carrying attaché cases, walked out the oversized front door of the Department of Justice onto Pennsylvania Avenue. They had just handed over, as the Supreme Court had required, a cashier's check for one hundred sixty thousand dollars, Snepp's up-to-the-moment royalties for *Decent Interval* (ultimately they would reach over two hundred thousand dollars).

A cab pulled to the curb, and they got in. The cabdriver turned and looked them over, then he put the cab in gear, shaking his head.

"You guys," he said, "you lawyers, I bet you're rich as Croesus!"

In the years since his Supreme Court defeat, Frank Snepp has continued to write. Eighteen times he submitted his work to CIA and eighteen times he was allowed to publish after some minor changes. But in 1985 he submitted a proposed treatment for a television mini-series based on his experiences in Vietnam. He had signed an agreement with a television production company, and he would receive $22,500 once it was completed and submitted to CBS, who expected it by January, 1986.

CIA's first response was to ask whether the work would be fact or fiction; if fact, a number of changes would be required; if fiction, only one change was needed. Frank Snepp could not speak for the production company, and so he could not answer the question.

We'll treat it as fact, said CIA.

About two months later, CIA gave Snepp a list of eleven specific deletions it wanted. If he complied, his television treatment could move forward.

When he read what CIA wanted changed, Snepp felt perverse vindication: this was clear evidence of why he had not wanted to show the agency his book before it had been published. They would have disagreed on almost everything.

Now he saw the same thing with the television treatment. Eleven objections, and Snepp agreed with none of them.

"You can appeal our decision, of course," said CIA.

"My deadline for submission of the treatment has already passed," Frank Snepp told them. But appeal, he did, because he had little choice if he hoped to stay with the mini-series and get it produced without major change.

In March, 1987, Frank Snepp's appeal was upheld by the Director of CIA. In all but one instance what the CIA censors wanted deleted was overturned. Frank Snepp could now follow through on the television treatment.

Except for one thing.

The January, 1986, submission deadline had passed fourteen months earlier. In the television business one season's enthusiasms rarely live to the next, and what Frank Snepp prepared in 1985 was a relic by 1987.

And the $22,500 he hoped to receive for this work?

A casualty of the secrecy wars.

8

A Book is Easier to Burn Than to Explain

One day in 1980 Gene Lanier was sitting at his desk in Joyner Library at East Carolina University in Greenville, North Carolina. In his late forties and quiet-spoken, he had been a teacher and professional librarian for more than twenty years, and was the Chairman of his university's Department of Library Science.

Within the past few days he had relinquished another chairmanship—that of the North Carolina Library Association. He was looking forward to more time with his family, and he basked in the respect other North Carolina librarians felt for him.

Perhaps it was because of that respect—though Gene Lanier could never be certain—that he decided to maintain a role with his state library association. When someone mentioned how pleasant it would be to walk away, Gene Lanier was quick to respond: "Hey! I want to

119

be involved somewhere; I just don't want anything strenuous."

Someone suggested the state library association's Intellectual Freedom Committee. "They need a chairman."

He could see a good fit. It was his area of concern. The committee galvanized whenever a North Carolina library was struck by demand to ban a book.

"How active are they?" he wondered. There was no point in exchanging one strenuous post for another.

"Only two complaints in the past two years," he was told.

Perfect! He could pursue his interest, but without doing overtime.

So he accepted.

On this day, sitting at his desk, he felt comfortable in his new position. He would serve the North Carolina Library Association well.

Though he had no idea at that moment *how* well.

His phone rang. It was Judith Krug, Director of the American Library Association's Intellectual Freedom Committee. She kept track of bookbanning in all the states.

"Congratulations on your new appointment," she said, "your timing is impeccable."

"I'm looking forward to the work," he responded.

"Gene, you should know the Moral Majority has just targeted three states. One of them is North Carolina."

In the next two years Gene Lanier responded to more than 100 calls for help from librarians across North Carolina. The censors were out in force, and they saw libraries and librarians as vulnerable targets.

In Iredell County, Aldlous Huxley's *Brave New World* was temporarily removed from the classroom because a parent complained: "It's completely anti-family, and anti-Christian."

In Sampson County, Peter Benchley's *Jaws* was removed from the county library because it contained profanity.

In Columbus County, Judy Blume's *Wifey* stirred an uproar because of its sexually explicit passages.

In April, 1981, Gene Lanier became aware of a Moral Majority literary "hit list," a compilation of titles that would be challenged, particularly in the North Carolina schools. Among them was J.D. Salinger's *Catcher in the Rye,* a book about adolescence, reflecting the adolescent point of view and devoured by adolescents through two generations.

So Gene Lanier began to speak out: "There have been more attempts at censorship since the 1980 election," he told an interviewer. "It seems that overnight we have all these self-appointed advocates of clean literature." He hit upon a theme which he would use with great effect: *A book is easier to burn than to explain.*

The Moral Majority's H. Lamarr Mooneyham, a Baptist preacher from Durham, responded: "We have never advocated book censorship or book removal. We have tried to stress the positive side."

Gene Lanier rejected this. "Imagine the thoughts, the philosophies that will never reach the printed page," he said, "if these groups are successful in censoring what appears in our textbooks. How can our students make reasonable and rational choices if they do not have all the options presented to them?"

Reverend Mooneyham pressed on: "Public libraries are strictly voluntary," he insisted, "but in a sense, public schools have a captive audience." It was this that concerned the Moral Majority. Parents should have a greater say in their children's education, they should have more control. "A good parent who has good lines of communication with his child's teacher won't have many of these problems," Reverend Mooneyham declared.

But Gene Lanier saw the issue differently: no parent should be able to control what other parents' children can or can't read. To him, what the Moral Majority advocated was, indeed, simple censorship, and he responded as vehemently as he could.

So much so, in fact, that one day in 1982 he was informed he had won a First Amendment Award from the Hugh Heffner Foundation. The citation read:

> For his contributions and dedication to the fight for First Amendment rights at the grass roots level, by working to defeat censorship legislation and by responding to hundreds of librarians who have been threatened by would-be censors.

Lanier and his wife traveled to Chicago where they were feted at a reception, along with the other award winners. They toured the Playboy mansion, they lingered in the grotto and they met Christie Heffner, who by this time had assumed most of her father's day-to-day duties with the Playboy Corporation. They had a chance to talk with many on the Foundation staff, and Gene Lanier felt comfortable with himself, with his point of view and with this award. What he supported, the Playboy Foundation seemed to support.

"I have no regrets in accepting this award," he announced, "no regrets at all."

What is it in a man's background that breaks down the urge to censor and instills a basic faith in the integrity of free expression? Certainly the reasons can be many and varied, but somewhere along the way there must be some *thing,* some event, which triggers natural inclinations and learned thought processes. Perhaps a particular conversation, or a vivid event or series of events, perhaps a book or major article. *This* is what I felt all along, *this* is what I must strive to protect.

For Gene Lanier this secular epiphany came during his days with the U.S. Army in and around Stuttgart, Germany, in the 1950s, following his early training as a librarian. He was in counter-intelligence, and his job was to identify double agents (hardly an easy task). He wore civilian clothes, and he befriended a number of Germans who invited him into their homes. While he remained the implacable double-agent tracker, he also found himself learning of German regrets — even *mea culpas* — about the Hitler catastrophe, and he heard stories of German book-burnings. He was shown photos of grinning SS men throwing books on smoking pyres, books by world-renowned authors, some German, some not, but all in disfavor.

"We did nothing to stop it," he heard.

"We didn't realize. . . . Hitler was offering us stability, pride, a strong economy. . . ."

Gene Lanier listened and listened. "We didn't understand what was happening; it didn't seem so important."

It was these conversations that propelled him towards a deep-seated feeling for free expression. He began to sense

that this could happen anywhere; people could be apa-
thetic about voting and other rights, a trade-off for something else. How simple it could be to give it all up.

How difficult it would be to gain it back.

He reflected on the often-used allegory about life in
Nazi Germany: "When they came and took away the
Jews, I was unconcerned because I wasn't a Jew. Then
they came for the union leaders, and I felt the same way.
Next they took the farmer and the merchant, but this
didn't bother me either, because I was neither of these.
Then they came for the intellectual, the scholar, and I
cried STOP, but I looked around and there was no one
left to hear me."

*We've always had these rights. We assume we will always have
them. We take them for granted.* It was this which pierced
whatever lethargy he might have felt about supporting a
right to free expression. Because now he knew there were
always individuals and groups who sought implacably to
usurp one's rights, and, unless it was called to their attention over and over, most quiet citizens would never realize, until too late, it was happening.

And when he left Germany in 1957, he was a committed First Amendment supporter.

Now it was more than a quarter of a century later, and
Gene Lanier continued his struggle. His stands on bookbanning and censorship kept him in the public eye, and
librarians across North Carolina continued to seek his
assistance as one challenge after another hurtled at
schools, public libraries and major bookstores But while
this case-by-case effort was being waged, another challenge, much broader and far ranging, appeared. It was in
the state legislature, and a resolution had been introduced

to examine the state obscenity laws. Such a review rarely ended without changes being made, and the danger was that the law could be tightened and made more stringent.

Gene Lanier was asked to sit on the commission that would examine the obscenity laws, and he agreed, knowing the battle would not be gentle. When the names of others on the commission were made public, he groaned inwardly. He would have to share table-space with John Cavanagh, a state senator from Winston Salem.

It was John Cavanagh who had introduced legislation a year or so earlier that would have eliminated a hearing in front of a judge on an obscenity question before any prosecution could take place. It meant that the prosecution could proceed solely on the opinion of the arresting police officer. If he thought something was obscene, he'd make the arrest and the case would be tried before a judge who would decide everything: obscenity, guilt or innocence, as well as the penalty.

What Gene Lanier feared was that John Cavanagh would once again try to rewrite the legislation. Gene Lanier saw only danger here because there was no adversarial safeguard against what the policeman decided *at the time he inspected the allegedly obscene material.* No one said: Wait a minute! A policeman is not the right person to pick up a book, inspect it and decide it is obscene. Or: We need a hearing in front of a judge *before* anyone is arrested. Someone had to argue it was not obscene, so the judge could hear both sides.

Deeply rooted in all of this were tales — and fears — from two, three and four generations earlier, when policeman, and their allies from the vice societies, made unilateral obscenity decisions about books. Arrests of bookstore owners, authors, publishers, from Boston to Los Angeles, occurred on such one-sided opinion, and the trials that came later often resembled mini-inquisitions rather than fair, innocent-until-proven-guilty hearings.

Gene Lanier asked to testify before his commission about the importance of retaining the adversary hearing prior to any arrest for obscenity. It would avoid harassment by the censors, he wanted to say; it would keep them from acting unilaterally, embarrassing people and bringing punitive action. While the commission considered whether to allow him to testify, a college professor took the witness stand and offered a possible — and dangerous — scenario: "If you don't have an adversary-hearing process, you could get a sheriff running for re-election, or a prosecutor running for re-election, and what better issue could he get than sweeping into a Piggly-Wiggly or convenience store and start taking up all the *Playboy* magazines?"

It was precisely for this reason that Gene Lanier wished to go on the record. Shortly, his request was granted. He would be allowed to testify.

As he seated himself, he glanced at John Cavanagh, a round-faced man with thinning hair, in his forties, a born-again Christian. Lanier could feel the solid disapproval from the Winston-Salem Republican, but he concentrated on his text and began to speak.

There was commotion at the back of the room. A dozen children crowded through the door — young children, adolescents, even younger, a phalanx of them followed by television cameras. The children marched to empty seats that now appeared to have been saved for them, and as the room quieted down, the television cameras whirring steadily and there was another commotion at the door. This time, in marched a group of mothers, and these mothers carried brown paper bags which they held aloft and then opened, displaying magazines and books.

"Pornography!" someone said. "Only fit to carry in a brown paper bag." The mothers milled across the hearing room, and a few surrounded Gene Lanier, pointing at him, wagging their fingers.

"Pornographer!" someone shouted. There was more pointing, and Gene Lanier sensed that matters were growing ugly. He could see angry red faces, and he determined not to provoke anyone further. He tried to sit quietly, even as the group around him continued its condemnations. He searched the faces of other commission members, and his spirits sank. The demonstration was having its effect. He saw concern and sympathy—even some intimidation. Who could vote against mothers and children?

Eventually, the hearing room was quieted, as the mothers took whatever seats were available. The atmosphere, however, remained tense, and Gene Lanier resumed testifying. When he finished, John Cavanagh prodded him, gently at first, then with some vehemence:

—Didn't you receive an award from *Playboy* magazine?

Gene Lanier acknowledged he had received the Hugh Heffner First Amendment Award.

—Doesn't Hugh Heffner publish *Playboy* magazine?

The award was from the foundation, Gene Lanier said.

—Doesn't Hugh Heffner own *Playboy* magazine?

Gene Lanier acknowledged that he did.

—How do you feel about receiving an award from a known pornographer? John Cavanagh demanded.

And before all these mothers and children and television cameras and spectators Gene Lanier knew that hereafter he would carry this burden — accurate or not — for as long as he spoke out in support of free expression.

His award was from an *alleged* pornographer. Some would never forgive him for that, but he was philosophical. He reminded himself that by climbing out on this limb, he had to be prepared to accept what was out there.

"I've become a First Amendment purist," he said with feeling. "When the Constitution says, 'Congress shall pass no law . . . abridging freedom of speech,' that means *no* law. None!"

In the end, his opposition to John Cavanagh's legislation on allowing a policeman to make a street decision about obscenity did have some effect. The responsibility for the obscenity decision was given to the prosecuting attorney. It was a step better than allowing the local policeman to become a pornography vigilante.

But it did remove the judge and the adversary hearing from the picture, and in this Gene Lanier saw the continuing danger that a self-righteous prosecutor could be even more dangerous than a vigilante-minded policeman. "The disturbing thing," he said, "is that several other states have come here to model their new state statutes on what we have passed." If the states could interlock their procedures so they presented a phalanx of disapproval, what would prevent overzealousness from becoming the norm? The vivid record of the vice-societies from two, three, four generations ago could be re-energized. *That* would be a disaster.

"A book," Gene Lanier emphasized, "is easier to burn than to explain."

In mid-1987 the American Library Association found out that librarians were targeted by the FBI in something called "The Library Awareness Program." The FBI wanted librarians at certain university libraries to keep track of those — particularly foreigners — who read or checked out math, technical, and scientific books and journals. Name, address, affiliation, if possible; any "suspicious" activities encountered.

Then, a story on the Library Awareness Program appeared in the *New York Times*. It was the first time anything about the project had appeared in public.

The librarians complained about the program. They were being enlisted as "unofficial spies." It was an unwarranted intrusion on personal privacy and confidentiality. A few librarians even told of FBI coercion, if they didn't acquiesce.

Nonsense, said the FBI. The program is "narrowly focused"; we're sensitive to the Constitutional rights of all persons.

The American Library Association asked for a meeting. It was held in late 1988 and Gene Lanier was there. We'll meet at the J. Edgar Hoover building — headquarters — said the FBI.

No we won't, said the American Library Association. The District of Columbia Public Library is only a block away. That's where we'll go.

The meeting lasted three hours, and the atmosphere was anything but tranquil. "Evidently," remembered Gene Lanier, "the FBI took this thing seriously because the head of their KGB Division, the heads of their Eastern European Division, their Counter-Intelligence Divisions — five people in all — showed up." On the other side of the table were the members of the American Library Association's Intellectual Freedom Committee.

"We weren't able to get much information that day

because they'd answer our questions with 'we'd love to tell you that but it's classified' or 'we're sorry but we can't get into that.' Most of us were not pleased." Earlier, a Freedom of Information Act request to the FBI had been returned with seventy-five percent of the material blacked out. The FBI was obviously playing hardball with the librarians.

"The FBI told us they intended to continue the program because it was a major source of their counter-intelligence effort. They admitted they didn't like the story in the *New York Times,* though they felt it did make librarians aware of the Communist threat."

Near the end of the meeting, Gene Lanier responded: "Well," he said, "if you want awareness, you give us a statement on your program, and we'll put it in the library press and then 50,000 librarians will be aware of it."

The FBI agreed.

But Gene Lanier and the librarians have never seen the statement.

9

UnGodly Humanism

The federal judge peered at the covey of lawyers and litigants in his courtroom. It was mid-morning of an October day in 1986, and he was ready to start.

Some had already labeled the trial, even before the first argument or the first witness, the secular humanism case.

Some, also, had wondered if this judge had urged the litigation, actually encouraged it, because of his beliefs on church-state separation, the existence of a Supreme Being and the "nature" of religion.

On this mid-morning in October, however, few were willing to voice such sentiments openly; on the surface all appeared proper and sedate, a fitting perspective for the languid atmosphere of Mobile, Alabama, where the trial would take place. In the second-floor courtroom of the John Archibald Campbell Courthouse, the air was gentle and the lighting good. Not many spectators had shown up, even though word had circulated in local and state-wide newspapers. The ample courtroom could hold many more people, but the participants knew the importance of the case transcended a body count.

The federal judge, W. Brevard Hand, was sixty-one years old, and had been appointed by Richard Nixon fifteen years earlier. Silver-haired, with glasses, a sturdy chin and a mellow baritone, Judge Hand was unmistakably patrician, and carefully intellectual. He was courtly yet firm, analytical yet humane.

Above him, underscoring the fact he was a *federal* judge, hung a three-foot-wide circular bronze seal of the United States.

Arrayed before Judge Hand were attorneys representing 624 plaintiffs, and defendants, mainly the Mobile County Board of School Commissioners. Other organizations and individuals had been granted permission to intervene on one side or the other. The essential dispute, however, lay between the 624 plaintiffs and the Mobile County School Commissioners.

"As I understand," Judge Hand said, opening the trial, "one of the basic issues that this court is going to have to address is, what is secular humanism? Is it a religion and is it being taught?"

As he spoke, lawyers and litigants could survey the courtroom and note stacks of books piled on tables. They resembled neatly arranged cordwood, and before this trial was over they would be thumbed through repeatedly.

Because it was these books, forty-five in all, that the case was about. Should they be banned from the public school system? Did they or did they not encourage secular humanism which might or might not be a religion?

"And if the parties do not provide to this court an adequate discussion of [the secular humanism] issue," Judge Hand continued, "then this court will be forced to call its own witnesses in an effort to ascertain, by expert testimony, what is that definition."

Included were history and home economics texts, and the plaintiffs felt the books advanced the idea that man and his values, rather than God, were at the center of things. Secular humanism stood for views like:

> Just as you make mistakes, so do parents. . . . They are only human.
>
> What can stop the spread of cheating? The foundation of integrity has to come from within a person . . .

The plaintiffs saw the hand of God resolutely removed from these and many other value judgments which surfaced on the pages of the books their children had to read.

It was a determined Judge Hand who set the parameters of the trial. And from the first moments of public testimony it was clear that secular humanism would be on trial.

"I pass no judgment on it," the Judge announced, but there were many who felt he had already made up his mind.

The lawsuit grew out of an earlier case in which Judge Hand was also involved. In 1982 Ishmael Jaffree, who lived in Mobile, objected to an Alabama law which allowed a minute of silence for "meditation or voluntary prayer" in public schools. Among other things he claimed this violated the "establishment of religion" clause of the First Amendment. Judge Hand heard the case and decided against Jaffree, but Jaffree appealed to the U.S. Supreme Court.

In 1985 the Supreme Court decided 6–3 in Jaffree's

favor. The Alabama "meditation or voluntary prayer" in the public schools was declared unconstitutional.

But Judge Hand had foreseen this possibility, and he had taken steps to prevent the dispute from withering. In a footnote to his decision against Jaffree, Judge Hand had written: "If this court is compelled (by higher courts) to purge 'God is great, God is good, we thank Him for our daily food,' then this court must also purge from the classroom these things that serve to teach that salvation is through one's self rather than through a deity."

After the Supreme Court decision, he contacted the attorneys for the defendants in the Jaffree case, and he suggested they might wish to bring their own lawsuit— this time against those who controlled what the school children of Alabama, or Mobile at least, might read. It didn't take long to fashion a legal theory. Secular humanism was the culprit, it oozed from the textbooks, it tainted those who were exposed.

As an attorney defending the Mobile School Commission put it, the complaining parents felt secular humanism was "a godless religion which rejects any notion of the supernatural or a divine purpose for the world. They also claim that secular humanism rejects any objective or absolute moral standards and embraces a subjective 'anything goes' approach to morals based on personal needs and desires."

But of course there were those who disagreed.

In Judge Hand's courtroom that October morning, the attorney for the plaintiffs had concluded his opening statement. The 624 people he represented, he had said, were teachers and parents, and they were asking that the "public school system, which they are forced to support as taxpayers, not be used against them." This would happen, he had argued, if their children were exposed to the religion of secular humanism at the expense of any other belief.

William Bradford, one of the defendant's attorneys, rose to speak. He was a member of a prestigious Washington D.C. law firm, and a descendant of one of those who crafted the Mayflower Compact, America's first venture into self-government. An experienced trial attorney, Bradford understood the importance of getting sharply defined views on the record as early as possible. "Secular humanism," he told Judge Hand, "is not a religion. It does not have the spiritual or supernatural or transcendent qualities that the law requires of a religion." Sure, he added, there are some passages in the textbooks consistent with what secular humanists believe, but there are many more consistent with what Christians believe. It was not selected passages from these forty-five textbooks that might have caused a problem for the children, he maintained. You can't blame the books. It was "the almost inevitable clash between the views of biblical literalists, which these plaintiffs are, and our modern society."

Up jumped Barber Sherling, one of plaintiff's attorneys. A local lawyer, he was a Presbyterian church elder whose own children attended church schools. "Judge," he interrupted, "we object to his characterization of plaintiffs. This is supposed to be an opening argument of what he expects the evidence to show."

Judge Hand peered down at William Bradford, "Do not," he instructed, "classify or make a speech to the press about what the plaintiffs are. Let them establish that themselves."

"Your honor," William Bradford responded, "I am simply referring to deposition testimony in which these facts were established."

Barber Sherling would not be put off. "We will submit that that is his characterization still, Your Honor."

Judge Hand brought the flare-up to a close with a quiet admonition to William Bradford. "I would prefer to have the facts presented to me, and I will draw my own conclusions," he said.

But the lines were now tightly drawn.

Over the next few days plaintiffs called several academic experts to show that references to religion were significantly absent from the forty-five textbooks. A professor of American history from Johns Hopkins University was asked:

"Can one teach American history without distortion if there is no mention of religion or the role of religion?"

"I think it's impossible," said the professor.

And later: "Do you believe that these textbooks discriminate against students who are Christians?"

"Yes," was the answer.

"In what fashion?"

"In the fashion that they give students the experience of learning about their country's history in complete absence of major understandings of the role of their religion."

And finally: "In your opinion is humanism a religion?"

"Most scholars, most thoughtful and educated people now regard it as such."

On the third day of the trial Douglas Smith took the stand. He was the parent in whose name the lawsuit had been brought. He had taught eighth-grade science for nine years and had been reprimanded for questioning the textbook portrayal of man as a descendant of the apes.

"What do you understand humanism to be?" asked Barber Sherling.

"It is a nontheistic religion that states that man is the center of all importance," Smith answered.

"Do you subscribe to that view?"

"No sir."

"What belief do you have?"

"That God is the center of everything that is important. He is the Creator and our value comes from what He says about who we are, rather than anything that we might determine just within ourselves."

Shortly, the plaintiffs rested their case.

To anyone noticing, it was clear that months before the lawsuit, these 624 parents had received high-powered support for their views. On a March day seven months earlier, genial, tanned Pat Robertson stood before a live audience in the sunshine of Fort Worth, Texas. He was hosting an alfresco session of his 700 Club on the Christian Broadcasting Network, and in his spiffy blue suit and yellow print tie he was full of good fellowship.

Pat Robertson, law-school graduate, minister, talk-show host, soon to be a candidate for president, was in Texas to celebrate the state's one hundred fiftieth anniversary.

A woman from Arlington, Texas, caught his attention.

"Do you think Christians are making any inroads against the humanism that has permeated our public-school system?" she asked.

Pat Robertson laughed and nodded. "Yes, emphatically." He told her he had founded an organization whose primary purpose was to oppose the American Civil Liberties Union, and he claimed he had more than 700 lawyers working with him. "We were the prime counsel in Alabama in a lawsuit that was a continuation of the Alabama prayer case. We represented 600 students, teachers and parents, and we said, 'You are teaching humanism in the schools of Alabama.' "

His manner continued genial; the smile never left. "The governor of Alabama, George Wallace, said, 'I don't want to teach ungodly humanism in the schools where I'm governor,' " and Pat Robertson laughed.

Ungodly humanism! It was good, it was perfect.

" 'Let's get 'em out of here,' " Pat Robertson remembered George Wallace saying. Meaning the books of course.

Still smiling, still genial, Pat Robertson described how the local school board in Mobile had agreed to remove references to humanism in the school texts, even though it was the state board of education which had to set policy. Give us a fair shake, he asked, don't delete references to contemporary Christian experience from these textbooks. "*We* are being discriminated against, you are expunging important material."

With the sun continuing to shine from the Texas sky, Pat Robertson beamed at his live audience. "Alabama is a landmark move for religious freedom for Christian people," he said. "We are going to see that followed up in state after state because we can challenge those people in every single state they're doing it. It's unconstitutional, and it's wrong."

Judge W. Brevard Hand had given much thought to the next step in the trial. The plaintiffs had rested and now he must make a decision. Would he call his own expert or should he allow the defendants to proceed? Sitting behind his bench, fingertips pressed in deliberation, Judge Hand knew his own expert might help clear the issues, but would it be necessary?

Then again, here was a witness that he, Judge Hand, could control. Somehow, that seemed important.

For those who wished to trace them, Judge Hand had never hidden his religious beliefs. A Methodist, he had spoken to a group of more than 100 people on "Why I Worship" not long before the trial. Having grown up in rural Mississippi, he said that the church had been the center of community life. He knew "beyond a shadow of doubt" there was a Supreme Being. "And I was never permitted the luxury of not being in Sunday School on Sunday morning. They instilled in me the basic knowledge and love of the church."

God and religion, he said, "You have to be taught, carefully taught. And there is nothing wrong with that."

On the morning of October 15th, Judge Hand informed the attorneys that he would call his own witness, Dr. Russell Kirk, a writer, textbook editor, professor of history, politics and journalism. For William Bradford there would be little surprise in Dr. Kirk's testimony. Judge hand, after all, would hardly call a witness who disagreed with his underlying beliefs.

The witness was led through his qualifications by Judge Hand, including his many publications and teaching accomplishments. There was little doubt he would qualify as an expert in the areas he would testify about. Then Judge Hand got down to business.

Had Dr. Kirk studied or researched literature used in the school system where the "tenants" of secular humanism were promoted?

"Yes, Your Honor, I have," Kirk responded, not surprisingly. "Particularly as a textbook editor one encounters such problems continually. In short, there prevails in textbook publishing circles an attitude which is uneasy with traditional religious doctrines or creeds, but which readily accepts views which might be labelled those of secular humanism."

Judge Hand continued the questions, but he had what he sought—an expert's opinion, more unbiased than any other because the witness did not belong to plaintiff or defendant. He had more credibility.

And the judge liked what he heard.

In a while it was William Bradford's turn to cross-examine Russell Kirk. After establishing that one of Kirk's main objections to secular humanism was its failure to recognize the soul ("there is only the human animal, the naked ape, if you will"), Bradford displayed why the human side of this controversy could never be discounted.

Did the witness recently edit and write an introduction for a book, *The Assault on Religion?*

Yes, Russell Kirk said, that was true.

"And is it fair to say that that work—well—it has an article on this very case, doesn't it? An article on the Jaffree case, the school prayer case?"

"Yes."

"Is it fair to say," William Bradford continued, "that article was laudatory of Judge Hand's opinion in that case and fairly critical of the United States Supreme Court's opinion in that case?"

"Yes. Quite."

"Do you recall who the book was dedicated to?" William Bradford asked.

"I think it was dedicated to Judge Hand, is it not?"

"Yes, it is. The dedication is to Judge W. Brevard Hand, defender of the Constitution and religious liberty."

Did it matter that, a few moments later, Judge Hand demonstrated he and Russell Kirk had never met before this date, and that Russell Kirk had never consulted with him on preparation of the book?

Ungodly humanism was the issue, of course.

When the defendants had their chance, they offered a mix of experts in order to establish that secular humanism was neither a religion nor a spiritual philosophy. For every point the plaintiffs made showing that the textbooks — all forty-five of them — established secular humanism, the defendants rebutted such facts with comparisons to existing recognized religions and the dissimilarities between them and what secular humanists believe. From the beginning the trial was a battle of the experts, and after two weeks and thousands of pages of testimony, with witnesses and attorneys picking books from stacks arrayed on a courtroom table and reading selected passages, the trial came to a close. It had been more than year in preparation, more than five years in development, if one wanted to go back to the early days of the Jaffree case. At stake were forty-five textbooks and whether they should be censored.

In early 1987 Judge Hand came down with his opinion, and not surprisingly, he declared the textbooks supported secular humanism which he felt was a religion. "For purposes of the First Amendment," he wrote, "secular humanism is a religious belief system, entitled to the protection of, and subject to the prohibitions of, the religion clauses." The textbooks, therefore, must be banned.

On August 11, 1987, however, the Eleventh Circuit Court of Appeals reversed, clearly and firmly. Judge Frank W. Johnson Jr. delivered the opinion: "[N]one of these books convey a message of government approval of secular humanism," he wrote. "There is simply nothing in the record to indicate that omission of certain facts regarding religion from these textbooks of itself constituted an advancement of secular humanism or an active hostility towards theistic religion."

And so the books survived.

PART THREE

WHO BANS BOOKS?

10

The Power of Words

One day, Peggy, a social worker who was also a published poet, was asked to join a meeting at the local high school with the mother of a student who had objected to one of the books in the school library.

"You could show her how a writer thinks," the principal said. "The book deals with a teenager's gay experience and the importance of going public on sexual preference."

"I don't believe in censorship," Peggy told him. She asked about the mother's religious affiliation.

"She filed this complaint as an individual," said the principal, "but I think she belongs to a conservative religious group."

"As I said, I don't believe in censorship," Peggy reiterated. "But some of these people do."

On the afternoon of the meeting, Peggy took her seat at the conference table in the board of education office.

Seated with her were two language-arts teachers, some students and the principal. Across from them were the mother who had complained about the book, her son and several friends who would remain as spectators.

The principal made an opening statement and presented the issue as fairly as he could. They were there, he said, to decide what to do with the complaint.

"I've tried to read this book and see the other side," the mother said. "But what this author writes is sinful and dangerous because others will read it and be affected. Maybe even try it themselves." She took a deep breath. "I know it's wrong. As a mother I can't sit by and watch my son and the children of others be so—so dirtied. They have to be protected."

The discussion went along for a couple of hours, growing heated at times. The mother never wavered, in spite of rational arguments about the First Amendment and free expression. "I'm sorry," she would say quietly. "I'm sorry."

Finally, a vote was taken, and Peggy joined the majority in deciding to keep the book on the shelves. Access to the book was the important thing, she felt. Parents and students could decide whether to read it or not.

But Peggy had unexpected reactions. "I went into the meeting with a stereotypical portrait of the mother," she recalled. "I was going to be dealing with an extremist, and I was prepared to have the completely opposite view." As the discussions progressed, the human side of each person emerged. "I saw someone who was experiencing anxiety and I became empathetic. I realized she was no extremist. For whatever reason, she had her point of view." It didn't change Peggy's opinion about retaining the book, but she came to see the mother not as a monster but as a concerned parent. "She had some serious feelings about the matter, and they came out of her values and beliefs."

Peggy smiled. "I still don't believe in censorship."

The mind of the bookbanner has baffled civil libertarians and scholars for centuries. How can bookbanners justify control of the written word, goes the argument, when there is no way to control what is thought or felt? It's like killing the messenger. The bookbanner answers by pointing out that the written word, itself, is devilish, capable of great harm and destruction if not controlled. Better to wipe away that devil than to trust the best instincts of mankind. Bookbanning prevents evil influences from infecting us all.

"It's not words which cause us trouble," wrote the respected librarian, Eli M. Oboler, a few years ago, "but rather the role in our lives which we permit them to have. Words control us because of our desire, our willingness, to be controlled by them." Take the word, "No!" From infancy we've come to see it as a symbol for displeasure or disagreement. It isn't merely a label we put on something without adding emotional underpinning. When we say "No!" or when we hear it, we recognize intuitively that a wall between us and the next person has been created. Depending upon the ferocity of the response, that wall might evaporate in the next instant or it might remain for some time.

Bookbanners see in words certain power that transforms the written page into a dangerous instrument. Words aren't words so much as they are weapons which can be used against the welfare of all people. Gerald Haslam, an English professor in the California State College system, has told about his difficulties in getting to read John Steinbeck's *The Grapes of Wrath*. Haslam grew up in Kern County, California, where much of the novel was set, and one day in 1952, when he was fifteen and had just realized his geographic touch with history, he went to the public library and asked for the book.

"What do you want with *that* book?" asked the librarian.

When he stammered a response, she said, "You'll need a note from your parents to check out *that* book."

So he went home and asked his mother for a note. To his astonishment she said no. (It was now thirteen years after the novel had first appeared.) "It's a filthy book, and I won't have you reading it," she told him.

But Haslam, his curiosity piqued, took a bus to Bakersfield, twenty-five miles away, and bought a paperback copy, which he devoured in a weekend. "It turned out not to be the erotic tale I had anticipated," he wrote, "but I wasn't disappointed. The great, enobling theme of Steinbeck's work—we are a human family, and together we can transcend life's challenges—reached into me. I was enthralled."

But Steinbeck's words could also bring disapproval and disgust. There were those who saw the book oozing with inaccuracies and insult. Just as Gerald Haslam did, some of the citizens of Kern County—themselves former migrants—could react to the underlying meaning of what Steinbeck wrote as well as to the labels the words projected. In their responses to Haslam these citizens (now fifteen years after the book was published) portrayed the power they sensed in the words.

"That Steinbeck guy's full of it." Here was a man who had had different experiences, and he disputed the words on

their face. Words should have offered accuracy, and if they didn't, the entire story was meritless. If it wasn't factual, it couldn't have happened.

"That Steinbeck and his nasty words! Decent folks don't talk thataway." As a former migrant worker this person saw her struggle, and herself, as upstanding and righteous. She saw unfair criticism and felt the power of this disapproval.

"That sombitch oughta mind his own business." Highlighting the sorry lifestyle of the "Okies" and the cruelties they suffered intruded on privacy and resurrected difficult memories and events. If there was personal agony, some preferred to let it lie, but Steinbeck's words prevented that: they enlivened everything. The power here was that the words served as a memory-refresher: they could kick in an entire scene or story.

Gerald Haslam sensed the power in Steinbeck's words, and now, looking back to when he was fifteen, he portrayed what he felt: "My first magical reading of the novel had convinced me that its greatest power was not social and political but mythic and spiritual. The book does not pretend to be an accurate history of the Okie migration, but it is a powerful evocation of the human spirit's resilience."

Bookbanners understand word-power and it gives them a springboard for censorship. Writers have a sense about such motivation because the mind of the bookbanner is not obscured or cloistered. When the bookbanner wants to ban books, the reasons are clear and definite.

For example, author Mark West recently talked with several children's book writers and then published his interviews. The general topic was censorship, and what was surprising was the variety of reasons the writers gave for why the censor censors. Each of the writers had been through the censorship struggle with at least one of his or her books, and there certainly was no dearth of feeling and anger.

For the late Norma Klein, whose children's books were under constant attack, it was clear where the bookbanner's motivation sprang from—fear. "One of the fears is that children will do what they read about in books." She offered the example of masturbation. Bookbanning parents, she felt, would be distraught that a child of theirs might masturbate after reading one of her books. Sardonically, she wondered if the opposite might be true, as well: would the child never think of masturbation if he or she were not exposed to the book? It's the fear of the *possibility* that's a prime mover for the bookbanner. Blame the book, and the parent has a convenient scapegoat, she argued. "These people want to believe that their children are living in a little cocoon with no contact with the outside world."

The fear she painted is that the world, through books, will discover and corrupt the bookbanner's child. It's both unreasonable and impractical because the child will be exposed to the world in many small ways that the parents can't control. What's not in books may be on the lips of friends at the school, church, camp. Norma Klein saw this fear in the bookbanner's mind as a threat to free expression precisely because it can't be answered with rational dialogue. Fear is not reasoned reaction; fear is irrational, emotional outpouring, and it's not easily contained with slogans beatifying the First Amendment. Bookbanners *fear,* they don't offer dispassionate socratic dialogue.

Betty Miles, another children's-book author, was concerned that the censorship urge grows ever wider. It used to be, she said, that what disturbed censors most was "foul language," and here, most of us could agree, there was room for give and take. But lately, she sees censors "beginning to question the whole morality of books," judging them as good or bad because of tone or general theme or overall effect. It is, at best, a disturbing trend because it is such an imprecise standard — one person's mystery story, for example, might be another's plunge into the occult. But it does offer the bookbanner a sword to slash at the dragon of corruption. By having the entire book as a model, the bookbanner does not have to quantify objections (*"foul language on one-third of the pages"* . . . *"I counted 4.2 offensive words per page"*). The book is *immoral,* the bookbanner can say; it supports abortion or sexual experimentation or homoerotic love or atheism.

For Betty Miles, bookbanners' objections spring not from fear, as Norma Klein suggested, but from anger and resentment. "Although it is seldom discussed," she said, "I think there is an element of class conflict in some censorship cases. Many of the people who want to ban books feel intimidated by everything that books seem to stand for: education, culture, a rich life."

Given such a point of view, one can feel belittled and unimportant. We certainly know through history that whole populations have revolted when resentment over exploitation has bubbled. The case is not so different for those who see book people as intellectual snobs, who sense themselves the butt of jokes, who watch while others control their political and social affairs, who endure decisions about what their children will read in school. They may not be able to make a mark on most of these challenges, but they do know they can exercise a voice in what their children will read.

And, perhaps, when they speak up, they can also acquire some respect. It is mutual respect, after all, that allows for the peaceful resolution of disputes. Let anger intrude, or resentment, and most respect is gone. With it, also, goes a rational approach to the problem.

Betty Miles saw bookbanning in social-political terms, but that was really only the effect. The mind of the bookbanner sees it emotionally: *It's time they understand! We're not going to be pushed around any more. They're teaching immorality and atheism.*

To writer Daniel Keyes it's neither fear nor class-consciousness, but power and control that lie behind the censor's act. Keyes saw the situation as the one sure thing a parent can handle. Perhaps the parent's world grows more and more chaotic as it becomes more complicated, and the parent feels powerless to control what is happening: *I used to understand the front page of the paper . . . How can people make that much money? . . . I can't get the hang of this new telephone service. . . .*

One thing bookbanning parents have power over is what their children will read. "Banning books," Keyes offered, "is an attempt to say, 'I have power over my children. I can put blindfolds on them and plug up their ears. So long as they are under my roof, I have complete control over them.' " In a sense it's the same reaction the person with anger and resentment would show at being belittled or intimidated, as Betty Miles pointed out.

In the bookbanner's mind the idea of control becomes a justifiable act because it prevents the corruption of the young. The fact that this control amounts to censorship is not so important when young minds may be at stake. In a real sense the bookbanner sees himself "saving" children, as in theological practice, and this certainly adds motivation. In fact, according to Gary Margolis, a psychologist and author, "the bookbanner could be doing the work of the book saver." He feels that the bookbanner is doing his salvation work on two levels—for the child and for the book, itself—"saving" the book by making it unavailable for children and therefore purging it of its corrupting influence.

This notion of booksaving is a fundamental tenet of the bookbanner because he works from his own ideals of unassailable morality. His personal sense of right and wrong is beyond question, so he strives to protect the morality of others. "Censorship in the name of salvation," wrote Peter Scales, "is a good way to describe the intent of suppressing or banning of books, articles, art, or any other form of communication . . ." It is not a wish to achieve their own salvation, however, because censors do believe they are already on the road. What they want is to bring the rest of us along. Only in this way can they assure the demise of corruptibility, and their own continued salvation.

Much of this theological underpinning is not apparent to those who must face the bookbanner in the trenches. An irate parent shook his fist in the face of the librarian of a rural high school a few years ago and snarled, "You better get that book off the shelves or I'll drive my pickup right through the wall of your library, and that'll clean things up!" In such a case there isn't time or inclination to wonder about who is saving whom—unless it's the librarian seeking to save her library building. The internal urge comes out more often in expressions such as:

I know why this book is bad!
I don't have to read it to know it's bad!
Aren't there better ways to say these things?

Edward B. Jenkinson, who has written extensively on censorship, lumps the external reactions of schoolbook censors (and this, for the most part, can apply to book censors everywhere) into a composite characterization. He says, "They are convinced that they know what is best for others to see and to read. They know what is wrong with a book whether they have read it or not. They tend to judge a book by a few specific passages rather than by the book as a whole."

It's a dispute on separate parallels, people talking past one another, unable to grasp the other's certainty. The problem is expectations — those supporting free expression assume there will be rational dialogue; those supporting censorship assume there is a moral equation of good versus evil. Both see their approaches as nonnegotiable, and so expectations are never fulfilled.

The two points of view contend, basically, on the true effect of The Word, not in its Biblical sense but in its ultimate consequences. According to Dr. Thomas Moore, a psychologist and published fiction writer, words have a reality that makes them much more than mere labels. "Words have power in themselves," he says. "They always mean more to the person who hears them than is intended, they are not just letters on a piece of paper." Bookbanners recognize this, probably more so than do those who support free expression, because they *fear* the effects.

"When words are given a reality," Moore goes on, "you can't use them in a purely intellectual way. They have body, so whenever you're dealing with bodies in proximity, you're dealing with sexuality." We know, from Sigmund Freud onward, how powerful the sex drive or the sexual image can be, and if it can be attached to words, they take on substantial power. "Any object, after all, can be made into a sexual thing. You can sexualize anything, even a word."

Think of fetishes. Feet, hands, fingers, open windows, angular buildings; the list is endless. Any objects can be made into a sexual fetish by providing it with sexuality. It is not hard to imagine words acquiring the same character. Words may be mere objects when they sit on the page, simply a group of letters bunched together that we've learned to interpret as meaning something. They take on power when they have what Moore calls, "affective" influence.

Take the phrase, "I love you." We speak it or hear it, and if it's said in just the right way, we're not simply communicating words, we're offering an emotional charge. The same would be true with words on the written page. They become more than labels or pieces of nomenclature to the person who reads them. Look at the former migrants Gerald Haslam contacted in connection with *The Grapes of Wrath*. One saw some words as insulting, another felt them to be intrusive, a third considered them untrue. Each related the words to his or her own experiences; it was as if the words had leapt from the page. It means, says Tom Moore, "you're not communicating an idea or something logical, you're making an 'affective' statement. It's not a rational thing." The words affect the reader—they touch the reader.

Psychologist Gary Margolis sees the threat bookbanners feel from words as cries for help. They want to ban books because of deep feelings of helplessness in the face of their emotional reactions. "If I confuse the symbolic nature of the word on the page so it is not only communication but action as well, and if I then make an equation that the word equal a list of negative things, my reaction has to be a kill the word, ban the book. I have to make the word disappear." Otherwise the sense of powerlessness and personal anxiety would continue and probably get worse.

I must ban that book! The bookbanner, in his own mind, no longer has a choice. A word becomes The Word, and it projects its own power; it is no longer a metaphor for something else. The Word becomes symbol and action in one, and it takes on gigantic form, overpowering reason and emotion and taking control.

A bookbanner facing this adversary could have only one reaction — *ban the book*! In his mind, the bookbanner senses the power of The Word, it's an image that can corrupt and destroy, especially those things the bookbanner wants to protect.

Four-letter words for example. *Such language is fit for the sewer. Children shouldn't be exposed to that sort of thing!* The bookbanner will, most likely, speak of the effect on children when he or she criticizes four-letter words in books. The urge to protect children is strong, indeed.

And on the surface that would appear appropriate. The bookbanner is acting for the welfare of his own child as well as other children. But psychologist Tom Moore warns not to take this too literally. "What's going on at a deeper level," he says, "is that the person is trying to preserve the archetypal child, the child within himself." This person, he feels, is not really interested in children generally or in his own child so much, only in his own personality. He knows he can be corrupted, and so he strives to protect the child within himself by censoring certain books. It is the effect of the books on *him* that is the key. He may say it is for the benefit of children, but in the recesses of his personality he knows it is for his own protection and welfare.

Essentially, it seems that when a person sees or hears of a book containing four-letter words, these words immediately acquire an image beyond their status as labels on the page. They become The Words, creating an emotional reaction which conjures threat and budding catastrophe. It is for the children, the bookbanner tells himself, we must protect the children. But actually his emotional reaction is triggered by the threat he perceives personally. He senses his own corruptibility.

So he fights back in the only way he can: he seeks to ban the book.

It's a situation most of us view from the edges of the arena because we don't see ourselves as bookbanners. But perhaps we haven't probed deeply enough. Some years ago John Phelan wrote, "The censorious mind will always be present in all men, good and evil, great and small. It is based on fears that we all share: the fear of combat and the fear of communion. Both threaten to annihilate our identity." To many psychologists and psychiatrists there is a bookbanner in all of us. It is a matter of repression, they say; we tend to repress those things which we fear, and all of us certainly have fears. When those fears are challenged—when, for example, the idea of four-letter words brings highly charged sexual images which we know are *wrong*—we can turn to bookbanning. All of us repress, all of us fear, say the professionals, why wouldn't we try to do away with the threat by banning it?

'I think the bookbanning part of all of us needs to be recognized," say Gary Margolis.

Recognized, as well, should be the essence of the dispute between bookbanner and civil libertarian. When one comes on with emotion and the other responds with reason, there can't be much useful dialogue. "There's no rational basis for the bookbanner," says Tom Moore, and it's obvious the more determined the civil libertarian is to be rational, the more the opposite reaction will take place in the bookbanner. If it's true that a touch of the bookbanner exists in all of us, then perhaps it's time to recognize it, to realize that there is no such thing as total opposite in this framework.

"Listen to what the bookbanner is saying beneath the literalism of the banning," Tom Moore urges. "Ask 'what are they really afraid of, what is the fear here, what is my role in that fear?' "

Understand the bookbanner, he says. Know yourself, too. The power of Words need not consume us all.

11

"Let Us Publish Your Book"

In this cavernous place where booksellers and publishers (with a sprinkling of authors and literary agents) wade through ninety-six hours of each other's company, there was a cornucopia of readers' delights. It was the annual convention of the American Booksellers Association, a gathering of bookpeople large and small, east and west, liberal and conservative, mainstream and alternative. Booths and exhibits formed avenues and cross-streets, foot traffic heeded no rules of the road, deals were made by handshake, and once-a-year friendships were enlivened or shelved by scrutiny of projected sales.

Not all of the fifty thousand books published each year were on display, of course, but one could get an idea of the limitless influence of books by noting the variety of titles offered. It is the business of publishers to publish, just as it is the business of writers to write. In this cavernous place there was powerful acknowledgment that books were to be read, to be savored, to be passed along, and above all, to be sold. Books could fill most any void.

It was surprising, then, to meet up with a senior editor and find that a book's winnowing can include subtle and not-so-subtle censorship. What is ultimately between the covers may reflect a basket of biases running up and down the editorial ladder. This editor (who requested anonymity, given grudgingly) worked for a small publisher and his booth was but a tiny corner of someone's larger space. He, like his employer, was unpretentious, but it was clear he understood his marketplace. "There's quite a bit of self-censorship going on in the publishing business," he said, adding that much of it was fueled by the fact so many publishers are now owned by conglomerates.

The bottom line controls the editorial output, he meant. "Suppose you work for one of these conglomerates, suppose you want to do a book on industry abuse. . . ."

Suppose your publishing company is owned by a chemical company. Would you publish a book on the horrors and the ineffectiveness of toxic-waste control? Or on the laxness of safety precautions and quality control in the manufacture of insect repellent? Or a work of fiction on development of a secret chemical device that could bring about corporate control of our government?

Self-censorship doesn't appear in a court docket or in a school-board meeting transcript or in a letter to the editor or on a librarian's restricted book shelf. It's an event that happens, and nobody outside the conglomerate knows.

The editor beamed now, as if to say, *but look at us, we're independent, not part of a large organization. We don't have to self-censor.* A copy of the book materialized, and the editor read from the introduction: *Random House and William*

Morrow both turned this book down, they thought it was too controversial.

The editor leaned forward. Crowds were surging in the aisles, the din was severe. He tapped the book. "What was going on here was that this was the first book criticizing the Israeli lobby in the United States. It is not an anti-Semitic book, but it was published to cast light on lobby tactics, and to encourage free debate."

A new question pops up: suppose your publishing company is owned by someone sympathetic to Israel, would this book have been published?

The editor could not be sure, but he saw himself and his employer as one sure alternative to bookbanning: "The strength of the independents is that in an industry climate where there is less and less diversity and less and less choice for the reading public, we are there to provide an alternative."

He returned to the book's introduction: *Random House and William Morrow turned this book down because they did not want to appear controversial.*

"We think these issues have been excised from the public debate, and we don't want that to happen."

By now there were others waiting to talk to this editor and the book and its introduction were placed back on a shelf. One question remained: How many copies sold?

"70,000, already," the editor answered.

Every graduating senior in America's high schools carries away one lasting memento — his or her yearbook, that compilation of sayings and doings that memorializes the range of adolescent school experiences. It is not only a record but a living testament to survival and maturation, and it acquires an element of eternal truth from the vantage of later years.

No wonder, then, that high school seniors have a particular fondness for their yearbooks. It is their final statement on themselves before adulthood, and they contribute to it with an expectation of permanence.

Imagine, then, opening the just-out 1986 yearbook of Farmington High School in Farmington, Arkansas, and discovering that one page had been clipped away. One page only, but a significant page.

The yearbook advisor, librarian Janice Boersma, said yes, she had instructed that the offensive page be removed. This yearbook would certainly not memorialize *everything* that had taken place that year at Farmington High School.

But Janice Boersma seemed an unlikely culprit, librarians being the foot soldiers in the censorship struggle, often the first to face bookbanners, to cope with complaints.

Sure enough, Janice Boersma was not the culprit, not at all. She said she had acted at the direction of the school superintendent, Myrl Massie. *He* was the one.

Yes, Myrl Massie admitted it. He wanted the offensive page removed from the yearbook. He was the censor.

And what was offensive about this page? The editorial it carried — a memorialization of what the year had been like at Farmington High School — was not so laudatory. A student, Heather Inman, had written it, saying the school was stagnant, a "prison of supposedly [sic] learning." It was this to which Myrl Massie objected.

So, out came the censor's scissors, and snip! The offending words disappeared from the yearbook. Myrl

Massie's motives were certainly plausible because he said, "It was done for the purpose of trying to prevent some real harsh feelings from the staff and teachers."

In a school environment that might make more sense than in the open marketplace, but nevertheless, one has to wonder at the price to be paid for staff and teachers' emotional peace.

And of course, one has to ask — whose yearbook was it, anyway?

What happened to the Farmington High School yearbook in 1986 is expurgation, or the changing of a text following its publication. Thomas Bowdler, a nineteenth-century British physician, and other members of his family gave their name to the practice. Their target was the work of William Shakespeare, and through the first quarter of this century, the Shakespeare studies in school came from *The Family Shakespeare*, the *opus magnum* of the Bowdlers.

But the fact is that the William Shakespeare being read in 1920 was not the William Shakespeare as originally written. Bowdlerism saw to that, and throughout the nineteenth century and into the twentieth, the custom of expurgation had a wide following. Thomas Bowdler's purpose was simple enough: to cut out whatever "cannot with propriety be read aloud in a family or is unfit to be read aloud by a gentleman to a company of ladies."

This, of course, did limit things, and by some counts *The Family Shakespeare* contained over 100 excisions in *Hamlet* and a like number in *Romeo and Juliet* and in *The Merchant of Venice*. For example, the following is often omitted from *Hamlet,* Act 3, Scene 2:

Hamlet: Lady, shall I lie in your lap?
Ophelia: No, my lord.

Hamlet: I mean, my head upon your lap?
Ophelia: Aye, my lord.
Hamlet: Do you think I mean country matters?
Ophelia: I think nothing, my lord.
Hamlet: That's a fair thought to lie between maid's legs.
Ophelia: What is, my lord?
Hamlet: Nothing.
Ophelia: You are merry, my lord.

In 1900 there were more than fifty bowdlerized editions of *The Family Shakespeare* on the market, and even today one need not search far to find a copy in active use in the schools.

Some publishers have adopted their own version of bowdlerism, relying on subjective concepts of what needs to be in and what should go out. A 1980 Harcourt Brace Jovanovich edition of *Romeo and Juliet,* for example, left out about ten percent of the text (while announcing they were omitting "trivial or ribald wordplay and especially difficult, static passages of poetry"). Yet two-thirds of what was left out had sexual connotations.

The list of books expurgated by publishers during the nineteenth and twentieth centuries read like an honor role of the literary great and near-great. (Jonathan Swift's *Gulliver's Travels,* for instance, felt the lash of expurgation almost as many times as William Shakespeare.) There's *The Diary of Anne Frank, The Autobiography of Benjamin Franklin, The Ox-Bow Incident, The Adventures of Huckleberry Finn, Fahrenheit 451,* and many more, all classics in their own way. All bowdlerized at one time or another.

And what of censorship? Is its effect any different? The censor deals with material not yet published, while the bowdlerizer manages material that has already been published. But both control the text.

Some years ago author Judy Blume offered a manuscript, *Tiger Eyes*, to her publisher, Bradbury Press. They had published several of her previous books for young readers but controversy surrounding her work had not presented undue concern.

With this new work, there was a bit of a problem. Richard Jackson, her editor, noted a brief passage dealing with masturbation, and he wondered how much controversy it would create.

Only four lines long, the passage was hardly a major portion of the book.

I'm not telling you to take the lines out, he said to her. It must be your decision. And it isn't as if this passage is inappropriate or psychologically unsound. (He told an interviewer that Judy Blume never made mistakes about what is or isn't psychologically unsound.)

BUT, he continued with her, these four lines could be the focus of one more controversy.

So she removed them from *Tiger Eyes*.

And Richard Jackson said to his interviewer, "I really did not think I was asking her to censor these lines."

Fear plays a part in all of this. Fear on the part of the publisher, that is. Bottom-line fear. It used to be that most publishers were independent, not tied to any conglomerate-corporate breathing apparatus. Decisions to publish included lofty concerns: "This book *should* be read!" . . . "It needs to be said!" . . . "The author has a great future." There were no hard-eyed accountants who insisted that editorial considerations be governed by bottom-line results. If a book had merit, it could get published.

Not any longer. Publishers are now BIG targets, fair game for libel and invasion-of-privacy hunters. Publishers have money, they have visibility and they face a litigious world. Readers see gleeful announcements of six- and seven-figure advances to authors; they read the bestseller charts and note many thousands of copies already sold. They read of blockbuster sales of movie rights or paperback rights or book club rights or foreign rights— and they conclude that this must be a rich industry.

Of course, any writer will say (and most publishers, too) that what makes the headlines is simply a reflection of the need of the marketplace for "star" quality, that these high-dollar events are not a true picture of how well-off any publisher really is. Most writers will also say (publishers, too) that for every blockbuster deal there are thousands of little deals (advances under ten thousand dollars; a single printing; sales of subsidiary rights in four figures). It's these little deals that hold the industry together, and there's not a lot of money to be made under these circumstances. But somehow the myth of publishing-gold continues to exceed the reality.

And when a plaintiff senses possible injury in the written word, there's little reluctance to sue. Especially if there is a multi-billion dollar corporate patron standing behind the publisher. It's a formula every lawyer learns by the end of the first year in law school: Find the one with the deepest pockets—the one able to pay the judgment, the one who can afford it.

It also adds a layer of censorship to the publisher's already fixed inclinations because the bottom line controls so much. "Lawsuits are expensive," say the accountants. "They reduce income, they take up a lot of time; sometimes they even force us to create a reserve against a possible loss." The subtle message rings clear: *With fewer controversial books, there would be less danger of lawsuits, and with fewer lawsuits there would be more heft to the bottom line.*

The direct corporate response is couched more informally: "Forget it, we'll be sued; we'll go to court; cost us a bundle; it's not worth it; it'll only sell a few thousand copies."

So what does the compliant editor-publisher do? Perhaps turn down a manuscript here, delete a paragraph there, rewrite a word or phrase, recast a description. In short, rework the book to make it less controversial, acceding to the accounting mentality.

Publishers, in fact, often see the threat of a lawsuit as a major obstacle. Speak with John Baker, Editor of *Publishers Weekly,* and the fear grows lifesized. "The chief thing that worries most publishers," he says, "is the threat of litigation. All publishers bear this in mind constantly." Baker has been monitoring his industry for a long time. He sees the litigation-fear having a profound effect on what is ultimately published. "In the last twenty to twenty-five years, publishers have become far more timid about what is potentially libelous. Everyone feels that if there is the slightest critical remark made in a book, someone out there can sue the author and the publisher and make a bundle. That sort of attitude has crept into things."

Publishers know some truths about litigation. They know juries tend to be biased about media people. "There's an actual resentment of the less educated toward the more educated," John Baker feels. "They see reporters and journalists as smart alecs and people who know it all."

They misspelled my name!
I hate it when they push that tv camera in your face!

*They asked that poor woman how she felt with her son dying
at her feet!
They didn't even quote me right!*

So publishers do some censoring — in the name of stay-
ing out of court.

Or they might not publish at all. Jim Valvano, former
basketball coach at North Carolina State University, no
doubt ran an effective basketball program. His record
attests to his skill. He is not above criticism, however, and
a writer named Peter Golenbock discovered there were
problems in the way the program was administered. The
book, to be called *Personal Fouls — the Broken Promises and
Shattered Dreams of Big Money Basketball at Jim Valvano's North
Carolina State,* was scheduled for publication by Simon and
Schuster.

Then, suddenly, after the book's dust jacket made the
rounds and Jim Valvano denied the accusations appearing on it, the book was withdrawn. Simon and Schuster
issued a terse statement declaring the book "did not meet
publishing standards."

Hanging over the affair was the threat of a libel suit
announced by Jim Valvano and, surprisingly enough, by
the Attorney General of North Carolina who called the
book "irresponsible and unsubstantiated."

Case closed? Not quite.

Roughly six weeks later it was revealed that a
university-wide panel (appointed prior to the withdrawal
of the book by Simon and Schuster) continued the investigation into whether there had been "academic irregu-
larities." Interviews and records-checking were not sus-
pended, even though state university officials grew
increasingly impatient for the investigation to end ("They
were asked to look at the school. They've had ample time

168 BOOKBANNING IN AMERICA

to do that," said the university's board chairman), and there had been repeated denials of any wrong doing by Jim Valvano.

But the investigators plodded forward.

The book that Simon and Schuster wouldn't publish didn't die so easily. In fact, it didn't die at all. Some six months after its seeming demise, up it popped, still called *Personal Fouls*, though this time published by someone new—Carroll & Graf, a smaller yet certainly reputable New York house. The book appeared without major changes, and it immediately skyrocketed into the public consciousness.

Was this simply a good business decision (Carroll & Graf) versus a bad business decision (Simon and Schuster)? Possibly, but then perhaps Simon and Schuster took the threat of libel more seriously than did Carroll & Graf; perhaps one publishing house had a greater aversion to risk than did the other. Speculation about Simon and Schuster's no-publish decision centered on the fact that most of the damning allegations about Jim Valvano's basketball program seemed to come from one source (who, arguably, was less than disinterested in the outcome) or from other, "unnamed" sources.

But, then, Carroll & Graf also contended with the same dragons, and they published.

Ultimately, Jim Valvano gave up his coaching post at the university. It was the university philosophy that appeared to be the culprit rather than the coach or the players. The subtlety of blame is sometimes difficult to distinguish, but a clue could be found in the resignation statement of Bruce Poulton, the university's chancellor, some eight months after the matter first blew up. (He claimed he was leaving to take the heat off the university, not because he felt he had done anything wrong.) Jim Valvano was not to blame, he should not be forced to resign. "This university over the years has made a very bad mistake in that we have admitted too many athletes as exceptions. We knew when we admitted them they were high risks. If we are honest, their academic performance to date does not come as a surprise."

This was a book that *should* have been published, reviewer after reviewer said. But, of course, Simon and Schuster didn't see it that way.

Sometimes outside pressure and the threat of litigation does push the censor button on a publisher (and there isn't a Carroll & Graf around to answer to door). In 1980 Deborah Davis wrote a biography of Katherine Graham, owner of the *Washington Post*. She called it *Katherine the Great,* and Harcourt Brace Jovanovich published it.

It met with high public approval—first printing sold out, a Literary Guild selection, riding up the best seller ladder, its reception, no doubt, spurred by the fact it was an unflattering portrayal of Katherine Graham and her late husband. It seemed, according to the author, that the *Washington Post* disseminated information helpful to the U.S. government, acting more like a propaganda organ than a major, unbiased, facts-or-nothing newspaper. Not only this but the *Post* also maintained *very* close ties with the CIA, and one had to wonder what price was paid for that.

When the effects of Deborah Davis's book began to appear, when the *Washington Post* sensed its reputation begin to tarnish, the newspaper acted like any other wounded corporate bear. It attacked. Owner Katherine Graham and executive director Ben Bradlee (of Watergate note) got in touch with publisher William Jovanovich. There was no record of who said what to whom, but the results appeared quickly.

The publisher yanked the first printing from book stores, the book was CANCELLED. There was no *Katherine the Great,* not any more (though to be fair, the book finally did see publication six years later when it was brought out by a much smaller publisher, National Press).

Some speculate that the original publisher knew what might happen if it got on the wrong side of the *Washington Post* — no more favorable reviews, no more favorable mention of Harcourt Brace Jovanovich books and authors. A big market lost, potential readers sacrificed.

Fear? Of course, and the book became banned — for six years at least.

Then, before the end of the 1980s, another similar case arose. This time the locale was Louisville, Kentucky, and the publisher was Macmillan. But there was an eerie likeness to what transpired with the *Washington Post.* David Chandler wrote a book with some unflattering asides on the Bingham family of Louisville (owners of *Louisville Courier-Journal* and *Louisville Times*). Macmillan printed the book and was about to distribute it to bookstores. There was excitement and anticipation in the publishing house. An exposé, of sorts, seemed ready to fly.

Lawyers for the Bingham family obtained an advance copy of the book. They read it, they grilled their clients and they set out to challenge the publication. The lawyers produced a legal memorandum five inches thick that called into question some of what writer David Chandler had produced. In particular the family lawyers disputed Chandler's portrayal of Mary Lily Bingham, the source of the Bingham wealth. Mary Lily Bingham, according to

Chandler, became a morphine addict and was then allowed to die of neglect. Her husband and her doctor were alleged culprits, and the sorry mess cast a distasteful net over the entire Bingham family.

Publish at your peril, the family lawyers announced.

Macmillan knew the consequences of libel, they understood the reach of a powerful newspaper family. It didn't take long before they withdrew the book from publication, and theirs was an easier task than Harcourt Brace Jovanovich's because few copies had been shipped.

Macmillan never bothered to confirm the accuracy of the challenges in the Bingham family lawyers' five-inch-thick legal memorandum, nor did it offer writer David Chandler the choice of revising his copy. A one-track decision was made: withdraw the book.

David Chandler survived the Bingham family lawyers' memorandum. Macmillan did not publish his book, but Crown Publishers finally did. The Bingham family of Louisville, Kentucky, was bared to the world.

Then there's Barney Rosset, for whom the idea of publisher-censorship simply doesn't exist. Barney Rosset, whose Grove Press introduced Americans of the 1960s to *Lady Chatterley's Lover, Memoirs of a Woman of Pleasure* (Fanny Hill), *Tropic of Cancer, Naked Lunch* and other titles. Rosset, who found himself in and out of court throughout the 1960s on charges of publishing and selling obscenity. Rosset, who survived legal challenge time and again so that erotic classics could be read by Americans openly and without shame.

Grove Press doesn't belong to Rosset anymore but he is still publishing. The erotic-book market has been pretty tame for a number of years, and he is aware that most of the foreign erotic classics have long passed through the customs shed and into the welcoming arms of American readers. But there's another side to Barney Rosset, one that still tingles with excitement and adventure.

It's Barney Rosset, the political activist. His personal file takes up pages in CIA and FBI depositories. It traces him back to his youth when he sought to enter the OSS in the early stages of World War II. He was not considered a good intelligence-service candidate because he was invariably on the side of free and open exchange of information.

In short, Barney Rosset is no bookbanner. If there is a publisher who will not bend to the inclination to bookban, it is Barney Rosset. Yet, even he, at this latter stage in life, has questioned his own resolve in the face of censorship pressure from the powerful.

In the 80's he published a book about Allard Lowenstein, the late New York congressman, who fashioned a strong reputation during the 1970s as an avid anti-Vietnam war activist. Lowenstein had many friends and supporters and was considered the archetypal anti-establishment liberal. He was assassinated in 1980.

"The pressure on us not to publish that book was tremendous," Rosset said. "Allegations were made that Allard Lowenstein was employed by the CIA — several hundred pages of extremely detailed information involving many, many people. We spent an enormous amount of time researching this book because we knew it could be a real troublemaker . . . and I think it was!" He said. "We didn't hold anything back. We let many people read the manuscript, including Allard Lowenstein's brother."

Reaction inevitably set in. "A group was formed against the book before it was ever published, and a great deal of money was spent, far more than we spent on the book itself." Friends created a foundation for the purpose of preserving the Allard Lowestein good name and to pressure Barney Rosset about the book. A major campaign developed, and Rosset was painted as the attacker of a good man's reputation.

The book was published anyway, and it ultimately cost Rosset his job (he had sold Grove Press a couple of years before, but had remained as chief executive officer). The book did not sell. "No one was interested in Allard Lowenstein except the people who liked him, and they certainly weren't going to buy our book."

He looked back now and couldn't help second-guessing himself. "That's one book I think a lot of people would have backed off from doing; maybe I would have too, if I'd known in the beginning what the hell was going to happen."

There are no absolutes with bookbanning. Barney Rosset is among the *least* likely to succumb. Yet even he, when faced with powerful adversaries, could make a case for a refusal to publish. It's fair to say that if Barney Rosset wouldn't publish a controversial book, there are few who would.

But Rosset's resolve is not shatterproof.

Publishers have their own ways of choosing what they will publish, and for most there's a personal element in the final selection. A bias in favor of good writing is standard and proper, and no one calls it bookbanning if the manuscript doesn't measure up. Yet there are some biases that don't work this way, some biases that are simply unfair—or even illegal—and represent subtle bookbanning.

John Baker, Editor-in-Chief of *Publishers Weekly,* points

to a peculiar bias that hangs over many an editorial desk. "A lot of editors in publishing are women," he says, "and there are certain authors they regard as anti-women or misogynist. They will not accept work from these authors regardless of their actual status. They simply will not take them on." It's certainly distasteful to read of a personal attack on one's gender, but don't these editors have a greater responsibility to readers than to censor because of personal distaste?

Let the marketplace decide the value of these works, say the First Amendment purists. If they spark little interest or offend to the point of dissatisfaction, they will die away.

Baker points to Kingsley Amis, the British novelist, as one who is on the receiving end of this editorial-desk bias. "He's enormously successful in England, but, believe it or not, his books are published in America very slowly, if at all, and I think that's largely because he is relentlessly misogynist. He thinks rather poorly of women, his men characters are invariably sexist, chauvinist, and I think a number of women editors have gotten together and said, 'no Amis around here'!" To be fair, Kingsley Amis does get published in America, but not, perhaps, with the fanfare one would expect for a writer of his stature.

On the other side are certain women writers who have had their difficulties because of political positions. Writer Andrea Dworkin, considered a radical feminist by many, is an example. There's little doubt her work skims the edge of stridency, and she is adamantly against all pornography, considering it classic enslavement of women. She has had considerable trouble getting her work published. Male editors simply don't like to read what she writes, and the fact she may write well or have meaningful things to say counts for little when an editor feels insulted by what he is reading. No one in the editorial office will admit it works this way, but John Baker is sure it does. "Bookbanning certainly comes into play with political things from the sex point of view."

12

The Textbook Holy Wars

She stood comfortably before the large audience, an attractive woman in middle-age, stylishly dressed. "Why do we have this urgency?" Beverly LaHay, President of Concerned Women For America, asked with quiet dignity. "Why this planning and the preparation, the prayer? Why have we joined together in this extraordinary way?

"My friends and fellow laborers, Norman Lear and his group, People For the American Way, have branded our group as the most dangerous organization in America. Can you imagine, us?"

Tall, slender with curling gray hair and metal-framed glasses, the middle-aged man spoke with confidence. He was being interviewed on a radio show that would go round the world. Robert Simonds spoke of the grassroots organizations spawned by his National Association of Christian Educators: "Primarily, their interest is in getting school-board policies that protect the children, protect them from some of the gross things that are happening to our kids within the public schools.

"Government and true Christianity, I think, are inseparable. You can't rule fairly without morality. Every law you make is a moral law or an immoral law."

It was a regular studio telecast of Pat Robertson's 700 Club on the Christian Broadcasting Network, and the genial host welcomed a thick-bodied, forty-year-old man with dark wavy hair and glasses. "We're a grassroots organization that focuses on local issues," Reverend Billy Falling, founder of the Christian Voters League, told Pat Robertson, "our school board, our school curriculum and our city councils. We have successfully eliminated *Playboy* from cable television channels. We've gotten transcendental mediation out of our high schools."

"Tremendous!" Pat Robertson said.

Reverend Billy Falling pointed to the battle between the wicked and the righteous. "It's very naive to think there's a peaceful co-existence existing today, and the bottom line is it's either us or them."

Two generations ago there were few battle lines in the sedate world of local school affairs. Except for shrill red-baiting and finger-pointing by communists, most paid modest attention to who taught what, when and how. It was the way things were done. Schools were bastions of authority. Parents understood this. They rarely questioned it, and breathed easier when they didn't have to make a nightly journey through textbook pages with their student son or daughter.

Then, a generation ago, things changed. Along with

the Vietnam War the young began to question adult authority, and suddenly reasons — good reasons — needed to be found for almost anything that had been an accepted fact. *Why?* became an aggressive challenge instead of an intellectual invitation, and one area that attracted great interest was how some people or groups were portrayed. The civil rights movement played an important role because for the first time racial and religious minorities had more than simple moral persuasion on their side — now they had the law and the people. Many depictions taken for granted through the years were suddenly challenged; no longer could we safely assume facts and circumstances our parents and grandparents assumed. These depictions were *wrong;* they were demeaning, and they had to be changed.

A logical place to look was in school textbooks because this was where so many of the unflattering stereotypes or wrong-headed notions had appeared. Groups blossomed where, in the past, a single individual might have surfaced, and the pressures mounted accordingly. This is not to say there were no book protests in the earlier decades, only that now they became more organized and more focused. Edward B. Jenkinson, an authority on these matters, wrote that "nearly all of the schoolbook protests before the early 1970s were free of violence. Individuals and organizations became emotional about schoolbooks, and frequently heated words seared school board meetings and scorched the offices of publishers. But schoolbooks were not burned and people were not hurt."

But things became different. People were *used* to protesting, and they knew that in numbers there was power. It didn't seem like a war at first because it wasn't the sort of thing that caused people to die — like Vietnam — or to suffer second-class-citizen status — like a racial or religious minority. These were simple words on the written page, embarrassing to some perhaps, but hardly dangerous.

Yet it was war, nevertheless.

An early shot was fired in 1973. A religious fervor hadn't appeared, but militancy was clearly there. In Drake, North Dakota, the school board was offended by several books, including Kurt Vonnegut's *Slaughterhouse-Five*. School boards had been offended by a book like this before, and the usual step was to restrict it to a certain shelf in the school library or — in the extreme case — ban it altogether. This school board, however, took things one step further: They threw every copy of *Slaughterhouse-Five* into the school furnace.

Nationwide, the public outcry was great enough to save the other books the school board had targeted, but, suddenly, school textbooks had become vulnerable to literary auto-da-fé just as had popular classics such as *Memoirs of a Woman of Pleasure, Lady Chatterley's Lover, Ulysses* and *Tropic of Cancer*.

The war had begun.

The first battle occurred the next year, 1974, and now a religious fervor developed. The place was Kanawha County, West Virginia, a rural location in coal country. As in North Dakota, the school board was where things started. The County had ordered 325 language-arts textbooks for English classes, and a first-term school-board member got a glimpse of their content and was not pleased. She was the wife of a self-ordained minister, and immediately she and her husband began a campaign to keep the books out of the schools. Their objections were largely religious; they were seeing their beliefs demeaned and held up to ridicule.

Many on the school board, however, did not agree, and in quick order the situation went public.

As with any war, it was more difficult to call a halt than to signal a beginning. People soon chose sides, and matters grew ugly:

— coal miners went on strike in support of the school board member and her objections to the books;
— twenty-seven local ministers denounced the books from their pulpits; ten ministers supported the school board;
— snipers fired at school buses;
— teachers were threatened repeatedly;
— an elementary school was firebombed;
— three cars were dynamited; school buses were vandalized;
— shotguns blasted out windows in the board of education building.

In the middle of the turmoil arrived Mel and Norma Gabler, at that time the most prominent school-textbook critics in the country. They spent six days in a rush of speaking assignments in and around Kanawha County, trying to deflect approval from these language-arts textbooks, and their efforts were applauded by supporters across the country.

But, ultimately, they didn't succeed. Nine months later this battle finally ended and the books were kept on the shelves. The drum roll, however, would leave a hearty echo because the religious equation would rise again and again.

In many ways Mel and Norma Gabler, from Longview, Texas, were the agenda-setters for today's textbook holy wars. Through the 1970s they were the ones who established what would—or could—pass muster in the nation's textbooks. In a good year they would travel more than 200 days to meetings and speaking engagements across the country, spreading their "faith ministry" in the name of textbook purity. Theirs was a creed that refused to acknowledge the debasing of "traditional" American values. In their case "traditional" meant religiously-based and God-involved. They operated with a small staff, usually fewer than ten persons. They called their organization *Educational Research Analysts.*

The crux of their work was done in their home state of Texas. It was here the major battles were fought—and won—year after year. At stake was the $60 million that Texas spent each year for textbooks. And until the early 1980s the Gablers had solid credibility with Texas school authorities that they knew best what should go into the textbooks and what should stay out. Each year they would read Texas school texts *line by line,* noting which passages were objectionable and which texts should be eliminated. The state of Texas acknowledged their judgments without much question. In one year, for example, the Gablers provided 659 pages of objections to twenty-eight state textbooks in literature and American history. "God saw fit to direct the State Textbook Committee to remove eighteen of these objectionable textbooks in the first stage," they wrote to their followers. "*Many* others should have been eliminated."

The Gablers' views were resolutely held. "Too many textbooks leave students to make up their minds about things," they believed. Schools were riddled with "crime, violence, immorality and illiteracy." The seeds of decadence were being taught. They had the answers: more control, more emphasis on those traditional American values.

And they had influence far beyond the borders of Texas. This was because of the nature of textbook publishing. Economically, it is impossible for publishers to issue fifty editions of the same textbook in order to satisfy the particular demands of each state. What might work in North Carolina might not be acceptable in Texas; what might pass muster in New York might be vetoed in California. So textbook publishers, being business people, try to minimize their costs by catering to the common denominator, and in this case that happened to be best represented in Texas.

For a number of years it was accepted that if a textbook was approved in Texas, it would survive in every other state. Here is where the Gablers' power reigned. It wasn't only the $60 million yearly textbook budget in Texas, *it was the multi-billion dollar textbook budget across America*. If Mel and Norma Gabler said no, few textbook publishers would issue a separate edition for California or New Jersey or Michigan. "Traditional" American values, no matter where they surfaced, had a peculiar Texas twang.

By the early 1980s the textbook wars had a coast-to-coast reach (though the Gablers' influence had receded when the Texas attorney general questioned their right to censor in the face of the First Amendment and its protection of free expression). The battles now intensified across the country as school boards and school commissions were challenged in state after state. In the White House, Ronald Reagan offered ideological support, and the legions that had cheered a return to conservative politics now saw a way to put an idelible stamp on what would be taught in the schools. What started out as politics soon graduated to zealotry, and now the textbook holy wars erupted larger than ever.

"It's either us or them," Reverend Billy Falling told Pat Robertson on the 700 Club broadcast. The textbooks are right — or they are wrong; support us — or support them.

The militancy was more political then religious for awhile, but it was militancy, nevertheless. Conservative, anti-feminist Phyllis Schlafly and her Eagle Forum were in the fray at an early date, and matters now moved to the big stage. Schlafly had become nationally known because of her unrelenting opposition to — and ultimate success in defeating — the Equal Rights Amendment, yet it was obvious she was more than a one-issue stalwart. The quality of school textbooks concerned her and her organization — so much so, in fact that the Eagle Forum formed the *Stop Textbook Censorship Committee,* and Schlafly could declare that liberals were the most ruthless textbook censors of all. "The list is endless of the topics and the books which the liberals have censored out of the school curriculum, out of school and public libraries and the media," she wrote. There was creationism, prayer and all references to God, to be sure, and words, pictures and concepts that could influence young women to be homemakers instead of careerists, as well as the dangers and disadvantages of sexual promiscuity. All of these censored out.

The purpose of the committee, however, was anything but anti-censorship: those books which don't carry what we support — KEEP THEM OUT!. The committee wanted nothing but "balanced treatment" of what students would read. Balanced, however, meant tilted in their favor because the approved content would have to reflect narrow, conservative, ideological points of view. A newsletter from the committee urged parents to "Read textbooks, and encourage your child to bring home all worksheets, workbooks and any questionnaires that might be filled out." An instruction sheet the committee handed out, "How to Examine a Textbook," admonished parents to see if the textbooks reversed traditional roles: does Father bake a pie, does Mother drive a truck? The *Stop Textbook Censorship Committee* had no doubt where the evidence lay:

> "The emphasis on patriotism and the fact that the United States of America is good and great has been censored out. The positive portrayal of the free enterprise system has disappeared. *And in their zeal to 'separate church and state,' the moral values embodied in the Ten Commandments have fallen victim to the censors."*

It was no longer Mel and Norma Gabler and their handful of believers in the backwash of Longview, Texas. Now the might of all those women who had followed Phyllis Schlafly through the ERA fight, who had cheered her victories, who had gladly joined her Eagle Forum, were ready to follow her into the next battle. The legions — 50,000 strong — of the *Stop Textbook Censorship Committee* were on the march.

But that was nothing compared to what was building in the mind and heart of Beverly LaHay, the pleasant mother of four in San Diego who had worked alongside her minister-husband while he had developed a prominent ministry, who ran family-life seminars and had written several books. One evening in 1977, she was watching Betty Friedan, on national television, telling interviewer Barbara Walters that she wouldn't rest until humanism ruled the United States. Turning to her husband, Beverly

LaHay announced in a shocked voice that *she* wouldn't rest until the humanism challenge was defeated. She organized a prayer rally to call attention to what Friedan had announced, expecting a modest handful of believers. But before the rally was over more than twelve hundred people had shown up, and a major force in the textbook holy wars had been born.

Beveryly LaHay is no Phyllis Schlafly; she is not as confrontational nor as politically intense. She is, though, president of Concerned Women for America, the largest women's organization in the country. They claim to have five hundred thousand members — ten times what Phyllis Schlafly can muster, all dedicated to one simple purpose: "To preserve, protect, and promote traditional and Judeo-Christian values through education, legal defense, legislative programs, humanitarian aid."

Concerned Women make up a vast army that can be recruited into the textbook holy wars, and that, among other things, is exactly what has been happening. Beverly LaHay, the wife of Reverend Tim LaHay, is a major spokesperson for the religious right, but she is no longer dependent upon her husband's reputation for the development of *her* legions. She has become a public personality on her own, and from the early days Concerned Women for America has shown keen interest in what goes between the covers of school textbooks. "The sad fact," she has written, "is the educational system in most American schools has already removed any reference to God or teaching of Judeo-Christian values that is the most important information a child can learn."

Beverly LaHay spins her message in genteel fashion; she is not a guerrilla fighter in the textbook holy wars. For her public appearances (and there are many of them,

often replayed in the pages of the glossy monthly magazine her organization puts out), Beverly LaHay is femi-
ninity itself: well-groomed with make-up and nail polish,
dressed in chic though understated manner, dignified yet
friendly. She offers herself and her organization as the
compassionate alternative to points of view that embrace
feminism, abortion and sex-education in the schools. It is
this latter item particularly that is embodied in the textbook holy wars. Recently in discussing teen sex and
pregnancy, she wrote, "This has reminded me once again
of the battle CWA has before it — to protect the youth of
America and to educate people on the destruction that is
taking place right in our public school systems."

One answer that Beverly LaHay and Concerned
Women for America found was to urge that certain books
be banned from schools. But this was no public-relations
effort. LaHay and her organization decided to sink their
teeth into the morass of school-textbook quicksand. They
found their battlefield in Hawkins County, Tennessee.

Seven families in this rural area had objected to a
reading series adopted by the county school board. The
series was well regarded by many educators because it
had been offered by Holt, Rinehart and Winston, a major
New York publisher. But the parents were unmoved by
that. Look here they said, there are passages about witch-
craft, astrology, pacifism, feminism, evolution. Where's
anything about *our* religion, about what we believe?
There's no mention of God or the mainstream church.
The entire reading series ignores these important things.

Enter Beverly LaHay and Concerned Women for
America. We'll help you bring your case, they offered.
These books need to be changed or kept out of the system

altogether. It is wrong that schools use books which gloss over traditional American values.

The matter went to court, and testimony showed that these books did, indeed, pay scant attention to mainstream religious history and practice (the Protestant Reformation was barely mentioned, for example). What also came out was that these plaintiffs objected to the textbooks' failure to discuss "creationism," or as one parent put it while clutching a text which labelled chimpanzees man's "closest relative": "We did not descend from a common ancestor." Evolution was not the scientific truth they followed, and evolution was what this reading series promoted.

Out! demanded the parents.

We're behind you, said Beverly LaHay and Concerned Women For America.

The trial judge in Hawkins County, Tennessee, was sympathetic. Yes, he said, the way these textbooks read, Christian parents' free exercise of religion is heavily burdened. They and their children are exposed to offensive religious beliefs, and this interferes with their own religious exercise; it puts the state in the position of favoring one belief over another.

Pay these plaintiffs $50,000.

We'll keep the books in the schools, though, the judge added. But you parents will be allowed to educate your children at home — you won't have to expose them to this offensive reading series.

A major battle had now been fought and won. Beverly LaHay could show her delight by announcing that Tennessee would no longer run schools "in a way which systematically forces Christians . . . out." Major news organizations blinked. The textbook holy wars were suddenly *hot*. One called the trial "Scopes II"; another headlined its story "A Bombshell Court Ruling in Tennessee."

For the losers there was some consolation: at least the books hadn't been banned from the schools—yet. But it was obvious another challenge could accomplish this. With a more sympathetic judge and more resolute parents, the principle might be broadened, and direct censorship might result.

Ten months later the Court of Appeals reversed. There was no violation of the Constitution; exposure to offensive religious beliefs is not the same as requiring them to be accepted. No damages, no home-schooling, no censorship.

Beverly LaHay and Concerned Women For America had not won, but they had served notice: we are no longer toothless and weaponless, we have our legions, and they can lead us to victory. School textbooks are the battlefield, and the war is far from over.

On the tenth-anniversary celebration of Concerned Women For America in 1989 Beverly LaHay could take pride in her hundreds of thousands of supporters. At a huge day-long celebration in Washington D.C., ladylike, dignified, she couldn't resist, one more time, naming her antagonists. Looking into the television camera, she said, "We're facing the American Civil Liberties Union . . . and we are standing against the Godless views of those like Norman Lear and the People For the American Way."

Mighty applause greeted her.

Meanwhile, a continent away, in Costa Mesa, California, another textbook warrior has been waging *his* fight. Robert Simonds is a former pastor, high school teacher and principal, and in 1983 founded the National Association of Christian Educators. His concern is simply that "the children of our nation receive the very best education possible in both academics and in moral and spiritual values." Through his Center for Excellence in Education he has dispatched advice and guidance to textbook objectors in school districts throughout the country. These are the foot soldiers of his army, local citizens who have joined the cause at the local level and formed Citizens for Excellence in Education chapters. A recent count put the number of them above fifteen hundred — an average of thirty chapters *per state.*

And for them, as for Robert Simonds, it is WAR! "There is a great war being waged in America," Simonds wrote, "but not on the battlefield of conventional weapons. This battle is for the heart and the mind and the very soul of every man, woman, and especially child in America . . ."

Simonds is clear on who is fighting whom: "The combatants are 'secular humanism' and 'Chistianity.' " It is the God-believers versus the Godless, Good versus Evil, nothing less.

It is at the schools and local government that Simonds and *his* legions have directed their guns. There can be no neutrality here. Unless God is part of the teaching mix, there is only humanism, and every good Christian *knows* where that can lead. "For Christians neutrality does not exist."

Since 1983 Simonds has been developing his program, and his believers have pamphlets and booklets and newsletters that promote the cause. There's "How to Elect Christians to Public Office" which provides a questionnaire to put to school-board candidates. Sample question:

Do you believe that textbooks with pornographic or foul-language materials should be removed? An election agenda is set out, describing the duties of the committee members, development of training seminars and finally "getting the vote out . . . involving the media . . . promotional strategies . . . coalitions . . . PARLAYING VICTORIES."

There are other booklets: "How to Start A Parent Group"; "How to Deal With School Boards"; "Tips on Writing Good Press Releases." Simonds is thorough. He knows that a winning strategy is only as good as the abilities of the believers to carry it out.

But as with any war, matters are not so easily dictated. In Gwinnett County, Georgia, Jo Ann Britt had become the director of the local chapter of Citizens for Excellence in Education. She and two friends had demanded a right to read several English texts the school board was considering for the high school. There was *Migrant People* by John Steinbeck which had a line, referring to the desert, "She'll cut the living Jesus out of you." Jo Ann Britt was agitated. "That offends me," she announced, "I'm a Christian. Jesus is a precious name to me. It's not to be used like that."

There were three other books she objected to, as well, and before the school board met to pass on the textbooks she had prepared critiques, line-by-line. She wanted the school board to ban the books because they offended her and the other members of Gwinnett County's Citizens for Excellence in Education.

"I'm a Christian . . ."

This is WAR.

But the school board voted to accept the books in spite of her critiques. She may have lost this skirmish but the broader war was far from finished because Jo Ann Britt announced that her Citizens for Excellence in Education now realized there were other books in the overall 52,000-pupil system that needed challenge. Ten to twenty books in fact, and the county school board would be hearing from them shortly.

"I know this will probably be a long, drawn-out process," she told a reporter, "but we're prepared to take this as far as we have to go."

Robert Simonds would applaud her tenacity because in war the only victory that really counts is the last one. And the final battle certainly has yet to be fought.

Then, again, it may never be fought. The textbook holy wars are capable of endless controversy because the issues are so irreconcilable. So long as one side remains adamant about the presence of God in a child's learning experience, and the other sees such messages as subtle and not-so-subtle religious propagandizing (and, therefore, a violation of the Constitution) the wars will probably go on. It's apparent that in the past fifteen years religious conservatives have become adept at promoting their cause. They see themselves discriminated against in school texts, and they have learned how to fight to be heard. On the other side there has been a willingness to brush off the challenges, at least until Ronald Reagan was elected, because they seemed so convoluted. Who, after all, would want to ban a book because they *disagreed* with it? The First Amendment covers everybody . . . doesn't it?

It all depends, apparently, on whose First Amendment is being applied.

13

The Burning of Salman Rushdie

It was still dark in Berkeley, California, when Andy Ross was awakened by the telephone.

It was not a voice he knew well. The caller was a janitor who worked in a building near his bookstore.

Andy Ross heard frightening words—*flames . . . your store . . . fire . . . alarm. . . .* A bookstore fire was a major dread because the stock was paper and the burning could become a roaring conflagration in moments.

Andy Ross rushed out of his house. What could have happened? Cody's Books—his bookstore—had an enviable reputation—clean, well-managed, up-to-date; some called it the finest general bookstore in the west.

What had happened?

When he arrived, he saw the fire department had things in hand. The fire had been contained before a great deal of damage had been done, and Andy Ross knew he could reopen later that morning. A spot check showed about a thousand dollars damage.

But what had happened?

A firebomb, he was told. Someone had thrown it in a back window. A deliberate act.

He thought he understood. Fourteen days earlier, the Ayatollah Khomeni of Iran had called for the murder of British writer Salman Rushdie because of blasphemy in his treatment of the Islamic religion in his new book, *The Satanic Verses*. Andy Ross and his bookstore had been selling this book right along and, in fact, had sold out. There had been no warning of reprisal during these fourteen days, even though a large Muslim population lived nearby.

He got a cleaning crew for the bookstore, but four hours later a different kind of shock awaited him. In the poetry section one of the crew came upon an unfamiliar cylindrical object, rolling about. It looked harmless enough until someone examined it closely.

An unexploded pipe-bomb.

A call brought Berkeley's bomb squad who defused and exploded the device harmlessly outside the bookstore. Andy Ross witnessed the detonation. He heard windows rattle, he saw the building shake.

He knew, then, the searing truth: people could have been killed. "It's a feeling that words can't describe," he told an interviewer, "except to say that it's something that for as long as I live I will never forget."

It is the bookbanner's ultimate weapon—the burning of books. It evaporates the offensive words, it disintegrates them. Salman Rushdie and his *Satanic Verses* were but the latest victims. This auto-da-fé, however, required a double sacrifice — the books *and* the author, just as the Inquisition demanded of heretics and non-believers hundreds of years ago. Even the Nazis, who burned books by the thousands and executed Jews by the millions, didn't resort to this medieval remedy (along with the horrendous solutions they did devise). But the Iranians saw their Islamic God blasphemed, their religion mocked; they saw a devilish threat.

The Satanic Verses, itself, is a tale of good and evil filled with metaphoric allusions to some of the most revered aspects of the Islamic religion. As it plays out, the story seems to call into question certain essential Islamic tenets. For instance, a major character, Mahound, resembles the Prophet Mohammed but his actions and thoughts are distinctly unprophet-like — so much so, in fact, that his imperfect human side appears on the verge of winning out. The motif and setting are in the present and the future, and Rushdie explores Islamic myths and Koran pronouncements against this backdrop, instead of allowing his tale to unfold in the past. To Islamic fundamentalists this represents effrontery and disrespect, a dismissal of centuries-old reverence for tradition and certainty.

In our secular world we have difficulty understanding why a book could create such havoc. It is, after all, only a book, it's not an armed invasion. We're puzzled by the extremity of the Islamic reaction because in our society there are attacks on religion all the time. No American clergyman would *dare* order the execution of a writer because of something he wrote which happened to criticize the religion. No American government official, in fact, would order the execution of a writer because of something he wrote. In our self-concern for democracy and free expression we congratulate ourselves on the civilized manner with which we deal with dissent or criticism. We have a First Amendment (the Iranians don't), and that guarantees us that the Ayatollah's medieval remedy can't happen here.

Perhaps.

Certainly the variety of religions in the United States means that none—even if they considered it—could get away with issuing a death threat and have it backed up by government force. We have no state religion, nor are our religious leaders free to punish a reviler with death. There are, however, other situations where the circumstances could change.

Suppose we came across a book that:

—joked about the Holocaust
—made fun of the assassination of Martin Luther King
—portrayed Abraham Lincoln as whoremaster and thief

True believers could feel all those things the Muslims felt—insult, embarrassment, fury, vengeance. They could feel justified to do whatever it took to wipe away the stain of ridicule; they would believe their purpose was beyond reproach because it was pursued to achieve sanctity and glory.

The Iranians called Salman Rushdie's book "blasphemy," and this justified the extreme reaction. "Even if Salman Rushdie repents and becomes the most pious man of all time," the Ayatollah Khomeni said, "it is incumbent upon every Moslem to employ everything he has, his life and wealth, to send him to hell." Blasphemy is a form of apostasy under Islamic law, and that makes it a capital crime. Khomeni was so adamant in his condemnation of Salman Rushdie that he put a price on his head for any bounty hunter: "If a non-Moslem becomes aware of his whereabouts and has the ability to execute him faster than a Moslem, it is incumbent upon Moslems to pay a reward or a fee for this action."

In our sometimes-smug world of First Amendment protections we might scoff at this naked display of power and vengeance. None of that murder stuff for us, though our religious heritage could offer a counter-argument. We may be secular all the way, yet in the Old Testament Book of Leviticus it's written: "Whoever blasphemes the name of the Lord shall be put to death. And the whole community shall stone him." That command clings to many of our religions, and we might find it hard to deny its role in our culture as we so willingly criticize Islam.

There's no ignoring that blasphemy is as much a part of our religious and cultural heritage as it is in Islam. In the days when church and state were barely separate, blasphemy was a direct challenge to the established order because it offered disrespect to the combined authority of God and the government. Right up to the seventeenth century it was not uncommon for blasphemers to be executed for their strong criticisms and to have their books burned alongside them. Most of this took place on the Continent rather than in England, but that doesn't mean there wasn't cheering from across the channel.

The authority of the church and how it fit with the state was never more in evidence than in 1676 when Lord Hale announced in court that "Christianity being parcel of the laws of England, therefore to reproach the Christian religion is to speak in subversion of the law." If a writer blasphemed the church, he was also violating secular law.

This close tie between religion and government was carried to America by the Puritans who saw blasphemy in perhaps starker terms than did the English. Blasphemy was a direct challenge to established order in Colonial America, and to make it vividly understood, three colonies — Maryland, Plymouth and Massachusetts Bay — not only declared it to be a crime *but established the death penalty for violations.*

Usually, however, things didn't go that far. Typical was the tale of William Pynchon whom history notes for two things: he was founder of Springfield, Massachusetts, and he suffered a book burning — the first ever in Colonial America. It was 1650 and William Pynchon had written a religious pamphlet (most of the writings in those days were religious) which he called *The Meritorious Price of Our Redemption.* It dealt with the doctrine of atonement which he wanted to clear "from some common errors."

William Pynchon arranged to have his pamphlet published in London where there were many more printers than in Colonial Massachusetts. But several months later when copies began to show up in Massachusetts, the reaction was quick and stern. The Puritan authorities confiscated what they could and asked the General Court to ban the pamphlet. The court responded willingly, and on October 19, 1650, it condemned the pamphlet because it held "many errors and heresies."

The Meritorious Price of Our Redemption was burned in the Boston marketplace the next day, the sentence carried out by the public executioner.

It was the first book burning in America.

Even after the First Amendment came along, the notion that blasphemy might be protected as free expression was barely recognized. Pity a poor New Yorker by the name of Ruggles who found this out a generation *after* the First Amendment made its appearance. One day, most likely in a fit of temper, he announced: *Jesus Christ was a bastard, and his mother must be a whore.* Whereupon he was arrested and found himself before a glowering magistrate.

I have my opinion, Ruggles argued. I can say what's on my mind.

The court did not agree. "Liberty of conscience hereby secured shall not be so construed as to excuse acts of licentiousness or justify practices inconsistent with the peace or safety of this state."

Convicted!

Though the court didn't say it, what upset everyone was that Ruggles challenged the sanctity of oaths. Allowing him to get away with blasphemy would make it easier for anyone to challenge the omniscience of God, and this, in turn, would make the penalty for violating oaths a farce. Reverence for the Almighty allowed ultimate questions to be decided by a single authority.

Convicted!

The blasphemy laws have never really died out, even though they became less and less used as the decades wore on. With our wide variety of religions there could never be one that spoke for the government, as in England. And as the First Amendment's separation of church and state became more significant and more widely honored, the idea of Lord Hale that the laws of Christianity and the laws of the land were one simply didn't hold up. But few have been willing to wipe the blasphemy laws away entirely. Through the generations there have been enough pious prosecutors, judges and jurors to insure they survive, barely breathing perhaps, but breathing, nevertheless.

In 1953 in Massachusetts a stir was caused during

Christmas week when a comic book titled *Panic* included a depiction of Santa Clause flying aloft with a cupid and a ballet dancer pulling his sleigh instead of a reindeer. A placard on the sleigh read, "Just Divorced," and Santa looked as if he was enjoying himself. The Massachusetts Attorney General didn't find it amusing, though, saying, "In my opinion it desecrates Christmas."

Newstand owners wondered what to do.

Sell it and I'll prosecute, the Attorney General told them.

The comic book disappeared from the newstands.

Today it's true there are fifteen states which still have blasphemy laws on their books, but the "crime" of blasphemy is rarely prosecuted. That doesn't mean, however, that blasphemy can't offend just as easily as it did when Ruggles shouted his vitriol about Jesus Christ and Mother Mary. It may not be important enough to incite the *legal* process, but there are those who can pick up a book and feel an acute sense of ridicule and insult.

Look no further than a school district in Los Angeles County, California, in 1989. Realize it is *today, right now,* and that a parent has a child in the tenth grade in one of those schools. English-class assignments are given out, and this student receives a copy of *The Catcher in the Rye,* J.D. Salinger's classic coming-of-age novel, used across the country, in school after school.

The parent finds it "filthy" and insists it has "absolutely no literary value." Then, the most telling objection of all: it's *blasphemous!*

It took a major review by teachers and school officials to retain the book. It was not an easy win over the bookbanning parent, and the notion that blasphemy might be a relic of another time was clearly put to rest. Blasphemy offends—now!

The blasphemy challenge, which comes in different words and phrases, means essentially a "written reproach maliciously cast upon God, His name, attributes or religion," according to historian Paul Blanshard. Cast an eye on the challenge in public schools recently: in Alabama it's "attack on religion" in John Steinbeck's *Of Mice and Men;* in Colorado it's "incorrect depiction of hell, and offending religious beliefs" in Mary Calhoun's *The Big Sky;* in Maine it's "a distorting picture of the Catholic faith" in Doris Bett's *Still Life With Fruit;* in Michigan it's "sacrilegious language" in Jack Schaefer's *Winning* and *Shane;* in Oregon it's the "offensive nature it had toward religion" in James Baldwin's *If Beale Street Could Talk;* in Wisconsin it's "making a mockery of Christianity" in Stephen King's *Children of the Corn.*

Blasphemy charges, all.

For hundreds of years books that blasphemed suffered the ultimate penalty—they were burned, like William Pynchon's pamphlet in 1650. Burning as a remedy offers a double theological effect: it cleanses and it eradicates. Cleansing purifies the soul by allowing the flames to destroy any remnant of evil; eradication purifies the atmosphere by wiping the book off the face of the earth. Bookburning came out of pagan practice, long before it was adopted by Christianity. There was Protagoras, an ancient Greek philosopher, whom many considered the first avowed Agnostic. In his book on the gods, he began by announcing he couldn't be sure the gods really existed.

The Greeks didn't appreciate his uncertainty. They knew the gods were there, why couldn't he?

Protagoras had no answer, so his books were rounded up and publicly burned. A thousand years later he would have burned with them. But Christianity and the auto-da-fé were still a long way off.

Bookburning in our time isn't limited to Christian vengeance; the religion of Islam pursues it, too. Not long after the Ayatollah's death-order about Salman Rushdie, a dispatch came over the AP wire from Iran. Professing to speak with full authority, a leading Iranian official declared that the international crisis could be resolved if *The Satanic Verses* — all copies — were burned. Otherwise "it will remain forever a source of rebellion and it would be impossible that peace would come between real Muslims and the supporters of this book."

It is time, said this Iranian official, "to issue a strict order to seize all copies in the entire world and burn them."

It probably came as no shock to Salman Rushdie that Iran would urge his book be burned, since he had already been singled out for murder. And, realistically, there was no possibility that *all* copies of the book could be rounded up and burned. The Iranian rhetoric appeared more designed to inflame than to resolve, and Salman Rushdie could comfort himself with knowing that his chief tormentors were book burners in the grand Christian mold.

And it's not far-fetched to say that book burning has a lively history in America; it crackles right along today.

Look to Morgantown, West Virginia, on a Sunday evening in early September. The time is *now,* in the receding years of the twentieth century. In the parking lot of the Riverside Apostolic Church, forty believers gather along with their minister, D.M. Hudson, and they come with staunch revulsion against rock music and anything that promotes it.

The believers throw books, tapes, albums on a pile, as Reverend Hudson watches and waits. The pile grows higher, and there is growing excitement. Then, the minister lights the pile and stands back to watch, while the believers crowd around and stare into the first wisps of smoke that soon become the flicker of tiny flames.

"We see these as a threat to personal consecration, trying to draw a closing way from the Lord and to carnal things," intones Reverend Hudson, "I'm not looking for ridicule here, I'm trying to make a point."

Yes, indeed. Among the books that burn this night under the West Virginia sky are: *The Hobbit,* by J.R.R. Tolkien, some Harlequin Romance novels, and volumes on astrological projections and Eastern religions. For forty believers and D.M. Hudson this is more than the cleansing of the soul, it represents a *statement: We disapprove.*

The question, of course, is: In this land of free expression does disapproval include the right to decide for those who might have read the books if they hadn't been burned? Reverend Hudson could argue that this burning was symbolic; it couldn't possibly destroy all copies of the books. An expression of disapproval, that was the intention. But in the process someone else's right to free expression was also affected, removing the choice others might wish to make.

Salman Rushdie would certainly understand. The way Islam read his book is *not* the way he wrote it. "The thing that is most disturbing," he said, "is that they are talking about a book that doesn't exist. The book that is worth killing people for and burning flags for is not the book that I wrote."

But if all copies had been burned, many would not have had the chance to decide for themselves. Whose right to free expression, then, does it become?

For the book burners, the decision is clear. They have the strongest right, and they have the fewest doubts. Book burnings in America are replete with evidence of this. Observe the Reverend James Davenport in New London, Connecticut in 1743. He was part of a cult called "New Lights," and he was a spellbinding speaker. One day his rhetoric rose above its usual level, and he exhorted his people — *Destroy your idols!*, pinpointing frivolous attire and "subversive" religious books. His people marched to the town wharf and tossed their clothing and book after book into a huge bonfire — the works of Increase Mather, John Beveridge, J. Favel, Benjamin Coleman, Joseph Sewall and Jonathon Parsons. Some books lay smoldering for hours, until rescued by onlookers once the book burners had sated their zeal.

As for clothing, it burned alongside the books, and history doesn't record whether the faithful pulled off what they were wearing or stood around and watched in more appropriate attire.

Book burnings have hardly diminished in the twentieth century:

- in 1922, 500 copies of James Joyce's *Ulysses*, printed in London, were burned by the U.S. Post Office;
- in 1935 and 1936, a massive burning of books declared "obscene" by the courts occurred at New York Police Headquarters. Among the victims: 130 volumes of *John Krugge*, 184 copies of *Ladies of the Parlor*;
- in 1939, three copies of *The Grapes of Wrath* burned in St. Louis by official order;
- in 1964 in Philadelphia, a major book burning joined in by the Police Commissioner and the Superintendent of Public Instruction;

— in 1985 in Colorado Springs, Colorado, two book-stores set afire by arsonists;

— in 1987 in Seminole, Oklahoma, sixty people helped burn books, records, tapes, clothing, cosmetics ("we were burning things of the devil, not things of God");

— in 1988 in Alliance, Nebraska, more than $10,000 worth of books, tapes, records, posters were burned at the end of an evangelical crusade because they held a "satanic message."

In Salman Rushdie's case the book-burning scenario in America is less direct but no less permanent. No one can say *The Satanic Verses* was victimized here as it was in Islamic countries, but in a real sense Rushdie and his book suffered some of the major effects of book burning in America. Consider, first, that blasphemy is not dead in the minds and hearts of the pious American; consider, next, that book burning is, for some, as ingrained in the American culture as Thanksgiving. Put them together, and it's not surprising that certain Americans could react harshly to *The Satanic Verses*.

By the time of the Ayatollah Khomeni's death threat, the book had already been banned in some Islamic countries, and several book burnings had occurred world wide. There had been a cutback in Salman Rushdie's publicity tour in the United States because vague rumblings had made his publisher, Viking-Penguin, apprehensive for his safety. "Neither we nor the author of this novel published the book with intent to offend," the publisher declared.

You can never be forgiven! the Ayatollah thundered.

The burning of Salman Rushdie in America was already in progress. Shortly before the Ayatollah's threat, an inkling arrived in the form of a decision from Revenue Canada, the Canadian government's customs service, to halt importation of the book until they could decide whether it was "hate literature" and thus barred from the country. For five days an unknown clerk in Canadian customs held the power to decide what Canadians could read. In the meantime, Coles, the largest bookstore chain in Canada, decided to remove the book from its shelves.

He was "embarrassed," Brian Mulrooney, the Canadian Prime Minister said, obviously relieved when Revenue Canada released the book into the country. We may have to change the law, he added, while most eyes now turned to the United States.

Waldenbooks, America's largest book chain, acted first. 5000 copies of the book were in inventory, but they would no longer be on public display. Waldenbooks would sell *The Satanic Verses* to anyone who asked for it, but it would not be promoted because forty anonymous threats had been received. "Our people are not Foreign Service officers," argued Harry Hoffman, the president. "The problems of international terrorism are not best solved by a bookstore chain."

B. Dalton and Barnes and Noble, a large chain and discount and college bookstore conglomerate, joined in. They removed all copies of *The Satanic Verses* from their shelves. "The safety of our employees and patrons must take precedence," insisted Leonard Riggio, the chief executive officer.

Help from Washington was sought. Certainly the government would be the staunchest defender of this vicious

Iranian attack on First Amendment principles. Yes, indeed, said President George Bush, this is a deplorable situation. "However offensive that book may be, inciting murder and offering rewards for its perpetration are deeply offensive to the norms of civilized behavior." A little later he added, "My view is that we are an open society. None of us like everything that's written, but certainly people should have protection of the law if they decide to go ahead and sell a book of this nature."

A book of this nature . . . it sounded almost as if President Bush found the book offensive. At no time did the president come out with a ringing endorsement of the principle of the First Amendment and free expression. At no time did he excoriate the Ayatollah for violating that basic precept of civilized man—the right to think and speak without fear of reprisal. It was muted endorsement, at best.

A book of this nature.

The burning of Salman Rushdie continued. Now it was the turn of the Catholic church. John Cardinal O'Connor of New York, through a spokesman, announced he encouraged "everyone not to dignify the publication of this work." He saw it as blasphemy to Islam, but he never actually ordered the book banned. Instead "he left it to [Catholics'] own mature judgment how to deal with the situation."

But he couldn't help adding a bit of advocacy. He was "confident they would do the right thing."

A book of this nature.

In the end, bookstores across America received eighty-seven threatening phone calls, ninety-one threatening letters about *The Satanic Verses*. In addition to Andy Ross's bookstore in Berkeley, another in California was firebombed, and a printing plant in New York with ties to the book was severely damaged. The author and his reputation have been charred by negative—or less than enthusiastic—public and private reaction to a naked international attack on free expression. There have been no bonfires of *The Satanic Verses* yet, but the author will remain hostage to his words for the rest of his life, victimized not by a malicious spirit of his own, but by the all-too-human need of others to burn away the seeds of challenge, doubt and criticism.

14

Careening Through the Looking Glass

With apologies to Lewis Carroll, suppose the White King and the White Queen had tea.

"My goodness, you are frowning," the Queen said, fluffing a dainty nappy across her lap.

"Would you read a book that confuses light with bright, glimmer with dimmer, shower with glower?" The King wondered. "Would you read a book that begins nowhere, leads nowhere, ends nowhere?"

The Queen beckoned for his tea cup.

"Hmmm . . . nowhere is exciting, it's so . . . unknown." She poured.

"Confusion, I hate confusion!" The King drank his tea in one gulp.

The Queen patted his arm. "I like little words, they're so . . . cuddly, especially the ones with i's and o's."

"Confusing words make confusing books." The King reached for a cherry tart. "I counted 2.4 confusing words on each page. And that's without the index!"

"I thought nowhere was more popular," the Queen said, shaking her head. "Are you sure you didn't skip?"

"My mind is made up," the King said, his voice solid as oak. "I shall outlaw confusing books. No more books to nowhere."

The Queen pursed her lips. "What is confusing to some can be art to others."

"All right, then, only 1.3 confusing words per page."

"That won't get anyone to nowhere."

"Books can't go to nowhere. It's the law, now."

The Queen grew sad. "Such a shame," she said, "nowhere is very nice in spring. . ."

What's confusing to some, of course, doesn't have to be confusing to others. Most of us would agree that literary value has little to do with a book's confusion level, yet once we're confused with the text, how many of us read on? It isn't hard to imagine thoughts like . . . *I wouldn't recommend this book to anyone . . . garbage, pure garbage! . . . I paid good money for this?*

It should be banned!

Mark Twain would understand. In 1885, the public library in Concord, Massachusetts, banned *Huckleberry Finn,* finding it coarse, crude and inelegant. "Trash suitable only for the slums" was the view. Instead of hanging his head in shame, Twain actually rejoiced because he could see that his condemnation in this tight-minded

Puritan stronghold would add allure to the book else-where. His disposition grew positively radiant when Louisa May Alcott, that proper author of proper novels such as *Little Women,* couldn't resist a public comment. "If Mr. Clemens cannot think of something better to tell our pure-minded lads and lasses," she wrote, "he had best stop writing for them."

Ah, Mark Twain must have thought, such a gift! Slyly, he didn't tell the truth about *Huckleberry Finn*: the book was not selling, few people wanted to buy it; this new story from the pen of the great Twain caught readers between yawns.

A spark from the Concord Public Library changed all. Two weeks after the banning Twain wrote a letter to his nephew Charles Webster, who happened to be a publisher:

"Dear Charley:

The Committee of the Public Library of Concord Mass., have given us a rattling tip-off puff which will go into every paper in the country. They have ex-pelled Huck from their library . . ."

Many authors would have been incensed — how *dare* they! — But the great Twain understood that immutable law of political success: the more a thing was mentioned, the more important it became.

Until it became essential. He added a final line to his nephew:

"That will sell 25,000 copies for us sure."

Actually his prediction was modest. Within two months of the banning, *The Adventures of Huckleberry Finn* sold more than 50,000 copies.

It's often true that what bookbanners hope to accomplish ends far from the goal they seek. In the reflection of the looking glass they see clear purpose with undiluted pride. They hold themselves with honor and duty, yet they understand only the dimensions of their own self-image, never imagining that another image awaits beyond the reflection. What they see of themselves does not carry eternal verities, though they tend to believe that it does. But the looking glass renders a skewered reality and, at times, a nonsensical apparition.

Purpose and pride are the twin sovereigns of the bookbanner's heart, and the erasable line that separates the discriminating from the undiscriminating can turn purpose and pride into arrogance. When this happens, bookbanning becomes farce.

Take a woman by the name of Mary Boyce Temple. In the 1920s she lived in Knoxville, Tennessee, and she was head of the United Daughters of the Confederacy, a well-heeled, tradition-minded organization. It seemed that a Somerset Maugham short story, *Rain,* had been made into a play and it was to be performed in Knoxville. The story took place in Pago-Pago and involved the conflicts between a missionary couple and a prostitute. The missionaries attempted to "save" the prostitute even though she resisted, and they made her life so miserable she eventually succumbed — until the male missionary was driven to have sex with her. She resumed her prostitute ways, the male missionary killed himself and the dream of religious renewal was shattered.

There was not one word of obscenity or blasphemy in the story, not one scene of graphic sex. There was only subtle suggestion, but this appeared to be enough for Mary Boyce Temple whose United Daughters of the Confederacy wished to prevent the play from opening.

First came clear purpose: "We do not fear the effect which such a play would have on us," Mary Boyce Temple insisted. "We of the D.A.R. and the United Daughters of the Confederacy have had the advantages of education and travel and have been prepared for such things. Such a play would not injure us; it would only disgust us." But there are others, she said, who would be unduly influenced, those who hadn't had her advantages, her experiences. "It is for their benefit and protection that we seek to prevent the showing of such plays in Knoxville."

Now came pride. "Such a play would not injure me," she went on, "but I have seen the world. Nobody knows the world better than I. No woman has had greater educational advantages, has been more in social life or has travelled more than I."

Nobody knows . . . No woman has . . . her purpose and pride have become arrogance because she could not imagine those whose tastes were different. *I am the judge!* she announced.

And why did she feel justified? "It is the duty of us to protect those who have not had our advantages."

It was in the excess of her response that we make fun of her today. By wrapping herself in a cloak of arrogance she nullified her own credibility. It was her self-importance that had to be established, not the fragile sensibilities of the less advantaged she purported to protect.

There are more than two million words in the English language. It is one of the richest languages in the world. We have two, three, four words for the same thing and we can use the same word to mean different things. We can shade our meaning in the subtlest way (where do we sleep? A bed . . . a pad . . . a sack . . . a cradle . . . what can "bed" mean? A place to sleep . . . a dirt pile that holds flower seeds . . . a roadway underlayment . . . the bottom of the ocean . . .) While we bask in the word-glow of our language, we should also be aware that the very strength of our language provides its most vulnerable side.

To the bookbanner.

A simple word with several meanings might offend with one of those meanings. A simple meaning illuminated by different words might offend with one, or more, of those words.

Dictionaries ride the point here. They are, after all, compilations of words and meanings; they don't try to dazzle with style or conjure word-pictures in the reader's mind. Dictionaries are like the nail barrel in the country store; reach in, make your selection, apply what you get, insert it, install it, inspect it. Does it fit? Fine. If not, go back for another.

Dictionaries are not insidious works of art dedicated to preserving offensive, obscene, blasphemous language. They compile and offer, they do not create. But there are bookbanners who think, even so, they should be sanitized.

A man by the name of Max Rafferty was California's Superintendent of Public Instruction in 1963. He picked up a book that had been resting unobtrusively in school libraries, and he saw some things he didn't like. "A little bit of censorship" is what he decided, and he suggested that *A Dictionary of American Slang* (published by T.Y. Crowell) had to go. It was like ringing an alarm bell. Rafferty's supporters flocked to his side, combed through the book, and from about 8000 entries they found 150 "dirty" passages which they then listed and published.

Slang is the colloquial underpinning of our language;

without it our communications become forced and formal. Slang by its nature comes from the rougher side of life, but like the upwardly mobile yuppie, it will acquire the trappings of gentility as it becomes more acknowledged. Today's slang could easily be tomorrow's sublimity.

But this possibility did not move Max Rafferty and his supporters. They continued their campaign against *A Dictionary of American Slang,* and in a handful of communities they claimed success. The book was, indeed, banned.

And in one place it was burned! As if the offensive slang could have been eradicated by a conflagration of righteousness. But even if the words on the written page vanished, the spoken slang will of course remain.

To be used again, and again, and again.

In the 1970s the Dictionary Wars heated up. Texas was a prime battlefield, and the bookbanners focused, not on slang, but on prime, A–1, top-of-the-drawer word-meat. They went after the established dictionaries: *Webster's Seventh Edition, Random House, Doubleday* and the *American Heritage Dictionary.* It was a battle over words, individual words, not style nor graphic description nor blasphemous connotations.

Such as:

— "bed" defined as a verb;
— "knocker" given a slang definition;
— "balls," "nuts," depicted with slang meaning.

There were a few more, but not many. Especially not many when measured against the ninety-nine percent of words that passed muster. The chances are that any of us could have found objectionable words in a recognized dictionary. Our language, rich as it is, offers a marvelous spectrum of word choices, and some are bound to insult or anger or embarrass.

But we don't have to read them. We don't have to dwell on them; we don't have to make them part of our reading experience. It's not the same as a piece of fiction where the offensive words or passages may be integral portions of the text, where we could lose the flavor of the storyline if we skipped or jumped or passed over them.

Pity the poor dictionary, then. It was the victim of its own thoroughness. A reference book whose referencing was challenged not because it cut corners but because it tried to do the opposite. It did its job too well.

The dictionary wars continued. In 1987 in Alaska, that old veteran, the *American Heritage Dictionary,* was banned by the Anchorage School Board. The vote was close, but the banning happened, and the words that offended were pretty much the same as those Texas had pinpointed a decade earlier.

Sometimes a word can bring offense even if it doesn't carry a slang meaning. The effect of a word of blasphemy, obscenity, clear treason can be explosive, incendiary.

We all know them, we've read them, we've probably used some of them. One single word: can it — or should it — destroy a piece of creativity? *But why can't we use a substitute,* some ask? Another word, another phrase. Surely our rich language can come up with an adequate replacement.

The artist, the creative person will answer simply, "Words are not like bars of soap on a supermarket shelf. They perform the organic equivalent of a mating dance. They must fit, they must carry a certain flavor!"

Myra Cohn Livingston, a poet, told of the life and death of a five-line limerick she composed for a textbook. She entitled the verse "Fourth of July," and in it she related the lighting of fireworks which are, after all, consistent with the patriotic theme.

But there was one word in the limerick which caught the editor's eye. The limerick must go, the editor decided; not a thing could be used.

Matches was the word.

The editor said, "we can't have anything about children playing with matches."

But what do you light fireworks with?

Sorry . . .

A single word. The five-line limerick was not used. And the Fourth of July was celebrated with one less poem.

We remember the myths of our childhood, the nursery rhymes by which we could glean the inklings of moral rule. There were good people and bad people, and sometimes bad things happened to good people and good things . . . well, the litany is familiar. Virtue and honesty and helpfulness would be rewarded, greed and dishonesty and cruelty would be punished. These were the learning tools of our childhood, and we came to rely upon them as guides and truths.

Imagine, then, an attack on these myths and nursery rhymes, as if they were recent products of a wordly society rather than the sedate moral gridiron most of us took them to be. Imagine this headline:

"Jack and the Beanstalk Declared Subversive!"

The old, old story of the young boy who planted the magic beans and climbed the stalk into the sky where he met the mean old giant whom he consistently thwarted and outthought. Countless generations have been fascinated by this story.

Not so one particular modern parent. He thought the giant should have won, and in fact he made a complaint to the school where his child was a student.

"That story should be removed," he said.

The school officials were dumbfounded. Why, they asked?

"It teaches disrespect for persons in authority," came the answer.

There was puzzled silence.

"The giant," the parent pointed out. "He's the one in authority. He gets no respect."

Are our myths and nursery rhymes so easily categorized? They have been around much longer than we have. They must possess some universal truths or they wouldn't be part of our learning process.

Bookbanners see a threat in even the most innocent tales. In Texas, for example, it was *Little Red Riding Hood* that had to be defended. A teacher, in fact, initiated the complaint, calling the book "violent" (the antics of the wolf, of course, give this some substance). But this was not all. What appalled the teacher as much was a picture of the grandmother drinking wine!

The tale did not survive this challenge. The book was placed on the "restricted" shelf, available only to those who requested it by title and author.

It's a skewed looking-glass that presents reflections to us in some of these incidents. Reality and moral purpose become bound in a strange search for truth, but the effect is often plain silliness. Some years ago in Los Angeles that magnificent figment of the creative genius of Edgar Rice Burroughs — *Tarzan* — was summarily removed from the elementary-school libraries. In a wholesale banning, books by the cartload were wheeled away.

And the reason? Tarzan and Jane (his nubile, fresh-faced mate) did not have the blessings of marriage on their union. They cohabited, but they were not wed, and to some stiff-necked people, this was not good role-making for young children.

So Tarzan and Jane were whisked to the densest part of the banned-book jungle, and a large coterie of school children were left to wonder at the strangeness of it all.

Then there was the test that our well-remembered friend from long ago, Robin Hood, had to endure in Indiana a few years back. It was the time of Joseph McCarthy, political suspicion poisoning the air. For Mrs. Thomas J. White, a Republican on the Indiana State Textbook Commission, the culprit was clear. Robin Hood had to go! The story had to be removed from Indiana textbooks!

It's a tale from long ago, she was told, more myth than reality. Hardly a threat today.

She was undeterred. "There is a Communist directive in education now to stress the story of Robin Hood," she insisted. "He robbed the rich and gave to the poor. That's the Communist line."

The truth was, like so many other bookbanners, Mrs. Thomas J. White saw the story of Robin Hood through a most narrow prism, unable to recognize that what she was objecting to was precisely why the tale had attracted so much interest through the years—the story of the underdog striking for equality. If Mrs. Thomas J. White had had her wits about her—which she apparently did not—she could have seen that such striving for equality is an essential ingredient of this country's ethic.

No one, it seems, is immune from a case of the sillies when it comes to bookbanning. Elected officials, for example. They seek reasonable solutions to sometimes vexing problems, and they seek consensus. Debate, discussion and dissection might be an appropriate shorthand for the way they solve problems.

Imagine, then, a law in Oregon which attempted to control what would be written about figures now dead for two hundred years or more. There is no ancestor worship in America, but we have our Founding Fathers, and it is from them we find the solace of legitimacy. We *are* a Republic, and we have emerged and continue to prosper because of these brave people.

St. Thomas . . . Jefferson?

St. George . . . Washington?

School textbooks were forbidden where they spoke "slightingly of the founders of the republic or of those who preserved the union . . ." To belittle or undervalue these men and/or what they did would be a crime, and it would be punished.

Did this not prevent an honest appraisal, a true and factual rendering of history? Perhaps we are better off for knowing that George Washington's plantation had slave quarters, that Thomas Jefferson, himself, fathered an illegitimate child by a black woman. To speak "slightingly" of them is to see them as human, and to understand their motivations and their statements. They come alive this way, and so they strike us with special resonance; we feel close to them, and we identify with them, and their so-called "historical" secrets.

But legislators sometimes have their eyes on a more distant goal, never imagining that means have a way of not justifying ends. Take that thorny period in the 1950s, the "McCarthy era." No doubt the menace of Communism was perceived as real enough, and to some, the most effective form of combat was the loyalty oath. Get a person to sign an oath of fealty to the United States, and no one could then be corrupted by the material they produced.

Behind the loyalty-oath supporters marched the book-banners. If you don't sign a loyalty oath, we will remove your books from the shelves — an easy rationale. You are what you sign — or don't sign! But drumming up patriotism through loyalty oaths had its drawbacks, and in a couple of instances the bookbanners bit off more than they could chew:

- in Texas, publishers submitting books for adoption in the schools had to state whether the authors, illustrators and editors could qualify under the Texas "nonsubversive" oath. More than 600 titles needed this stamp of approval.
- in Alabama, publishers and authors had to state that neither they nor anyone cited in a book advocated Communism or was a member of "the party." Literal interpretation of this provision meant the political pedigrees of twenty-eight *million* authors had to be checked in order to vet the 150 thousand textbooks in the school system.

Needless to say, these two laws did not stay in effect for long, but they point out the bookbanner's long reach: censorship is clearly an effective tool to preserve certain values.

Bookbanning silliness isn't confined to a single aberrant period in this century. It continues right along. One day in 1982, the George C. Marshall Research Library at Virginia Military Institute in Lexington, Virginia, received a visit from members of the secret-secret National

Security Agency. They asked to see the documents James Bamford had used in writing an already-published book, *The Puzzle Palace* — an unauthorized look at the National Security Agency.

The documents were unclassified, so no one at the library saw a problem. But then, the NSA people announced that, by virtue of a recent presidential order, they had the power to reclassify material. And they intended to reclassify the material that Bamford had used for his book.

The college librarians objected: some of this material has been declassified for more than twenty years! It's been sitting on our shelves open to anybody.

Not any longer, they were told. Consider it all reclassified and no longer available to the general public. This is serious business.

No amount of argument prevailed. The NSA did not want its old laundry — dirty or no — to be aired. There's no subtlety in the message: perhaps James Bamford got away with it, but the next author won't.

RECLASSIFIED!

Author James Bamford was able to get the last word, though: *The Puzzle Place,* he wrote, "is the only book in history to have been totally unclassified as it was being written, yet top secret by the time it was published."

Now suppose the White King and the White Queen met again for tea. This time it is the Queen who is wearing the frown:

> "I have canceled my trip to nowhere," she said, irritably. "It's on the banned list."
>
> "Only somewhere is banned. Nowhere is . . . nowhere." The King answered.

"But nowhere has such nice beaches." The Queen sipped her tea delicately.

"Getting to nowhere is confusing, and you know how people write books on that sort of thing."

"Are all nowhere books confusing?"

"I have already banned confusing books. Perhaps I shall ban confusing places mentioned in confusing books." The King stroked his ample chin.

15

Censors in the Spy Pit

Joseph Burkholder Smith lives quietly on a suburban street near the beach in northern Florida. In his late sixties, Joe Smith is recently widowed, and his life is filled with the nuances of aging: a memory that isn't as snappy as it once was, a tennis game that seems to glue him behind the service line, a writing career that grows more difficult to grapple with and subdue.

It is the last—the writing career—that offers a book-banning footnote in the life of Joe Smith. Some years ago, shortly after he retired, this pleasant-faced, soft-spoken man began to write a book about his former employer. It was neither diatribe nor paean, simply a realistic portrayal of the work he had done and what his former employer had made of it.

His progress was steady, and he began to pile up the pages. Then, one day, his ex-employer informed him, informally, that his manuscript had to be "approved" before it could be published.

But how do you know I'm writing it? Joe Smith asked, more surprised than disturbed.

His former employer was the Central Intelligence Agency, and on a lovely spring morning in the thin air of Mexico City, where he lived at the time, he found out how long its reach could be. He had just returned from New York where he had signed a book contract with G.P. Putnam, Sons, after showing only an outline and a sample chapter. He was eager to work on his book, but a phone call from one of his friends at the CIA station in Mexico City dislodged him.

"How about a cup of coffee?" his friend — we'll call him Nate — suggested.

They met in a quiet café. "We understand you're doing a book," Nate said softly. "We hear you've got a contract."

Joe Smith felt surprise, but no concern. "I'm writing a book," he admitted.

"You're supposed to show it to the agency," Nate said. "Remember, you signed an agreement to do that when you joined."

That had been in 1951, Joe Smith recalled. He hadn't given the agreement a thought since that date. "I only know in general terms what the book will be about," he said.

"We'd like to see it, anyway," Nate responded.

I *did* agree, Joe Smith realized. "When I make some progress, I'll send it in," he said.

About a year later, the book was finished, but Joe Smith had heard nothing further from the CIA, nor had he sent in any material. He did, however, tell his Putnam editor about the conversation with Nate. "Let's not send this thing to them until we have to," advised his editor.

"I want to live up to my agreement," Joe Smith insisted, but he wondered about the depth of CIA interest. During the year while he was writing the book, he and Nate had continued to meet for coffee every six weeks or so, swapping tales and discussing "tradecraft."

But the book never came up — not once.

Finally, Joe Smith asked, "What's Headquarters say about my book?"

Nate responded with a shrug. "I haven't heard a word."

By this time the publication process was well underway, and Joe Smith was caught up in final editing. Putnam had put together pre-publication promotion and set the first printing at ten thousand copies, an unusually large number for a first book. By June of 1976, Joe Smith had the galleys of his book, now titled *Portrait of a Cold Warrior*. He tried to show how and why perfectly intelligent and decent people could become ardent cold-warriors and think they were doing the right thing, even if zeal and narrow purpose could exact a high human cost from time to time. The book was not an apology, it was an attempted explanation.

In August, 1976, Joe Smith saw an ad for his book in *Publishers Weekly*. Publication date was only weeks away. Then, he received a phone call from an old friend in the CIA legal department. "Joe, we better see this manuscript."

Joe Smith tried to explain that the book had already been printed and was sitting in warehouses, waiting to be distributed.

"We need the manuscript, Joe."

So his editor sent it, and in a couple of weeks the CIA came back with several changes they wished to see — not big changes, but extensive enough to require the reprinting of the book.

"You better get an attorney," the CIA advised Joe Smith, and he did so. He also informed his Putnam editor of the changes the CIA wanted, and this created a crisis immediately. Who will pay for the changes? Do they *have* to be made?

Within a few weeks there was a meeting in New York. Joe Smith's editor and the president of Putnam faced representatives of the CIA and the United States Department of Justice. Surprisingly, neither Joe Smith nor his attorney had been invited. But Joe Smith and his book were the single topic discussed.

The Putnam people, concerned about the cost of making the changes at this stage, argued that the CIA had had ample time to review the manuscript before this, having known more than a year earlier that it was being written. The CIA argued that Joe Smith had signed an agreement, and that it was his duty to turn the manuscript over to them, regardless of financial consequences now.

The meeting broke up inconclusively, and Joe Smith recalled what happened then: "My attorney telephoned the CIA, and they specifically said they weren't sure what they would do about me. They reserved their decision."

In a few weeks the book came out as planned, *without* changes.

"They never did get back to me about anything," Joe Smith said.

Such a laissez-faire approach to the pre-publication obligations of former employees would not occur again, as far as the CIA was concerned. Joe Smith represented a watershed in the sense that thereafter, the CIA would look with hard eyes on anyone wanting to publish, when sitting in the files was a document signed upon joining up. The document, a "secrecy agreement," reads, in part:

"I hereby agree to submit for review by the Central Intelligence Agency all information or materials including works of fiction which contain any mention of intelligence data or activities, or contain data which may be based upon information classified pursuant to Executive Order, which I contemplate disclosing publicly or which I have actually prepared for public disclosure . . ."

This agreement or one similar to it was what CIA people had been signing since the birth of the agency in 1947. It was totally embracing: "*all* information or materials" . . . "*any* mention" . . . "data which *may* be based" . . . "contemplate disclosing . . . actually prepared for public disclosure" . . . And it covered fiction as well as non-fiction.

It was broad enough so that its scope began to worry some people in Congress, especially after Frank Snepp became ensnared in its uncompromising tendrils. Within three months of the Supreme Court decision to force a return of book royalties from Snepp because he didn't let the CIA see his manuscript *before* publication, a subcommittee of the House of Representatives Select Intelligence Committee met in room H-405 of the Capitol. They had a question to consider: If the CIA had this secrecy agreement, how many other government agencies in the spy business had it, too? It was an issue that, until the Frank Snepp case, few members of Congress would have bothered with.

Representative Les Aspin of Wisconsin gaveled the hearing to order at 9:45 in the morning. A parade of witnesses offered testimony on what various agencies did, and it was obvious the CIA was not the only one with a secrecy agreement or a review requirement.

By late morning, the prepared statements were concluded, and Congressman Aspin fixed his gaze upon George Zacharias of the Defense Intelligence Agency, the Department of Defense's spymaster arm. "First of all," the Congressman asked, "who signs the agreement? Everybody who comes to work?"

"Every individual who comes to work," Zacharias answered.

"Military and civilian?"

"Yes."

"Subject to a pre-publication review?"

"Yes."

Congressman Aspin then asked when the agreement was signed, and he was told the employee signed one at the beginning of employment and another when leaving employment.

"And the provisions of the contract are to last during employment and beyond?"

"Yes," responded Zacharias.

"So an employee is forever bound by the provisions of the contract. There is no time until the end of the contract?"

"That is right."

In a few moments, Congressman Aspin turned to Daniel Schwartz, of the National Security Agency, the government's top cryptographic organization, whose speciality was super-secret codes.

"What we have," said Daniel Schwartz, "is an indoctrination oath which reminds all entering employees and assignees to the agency of the criminal laws related to the various statutes relating to the release of classified information."

"And the provisions of the secrecy oath or the oath of classified information are to apply, no matter whether the employee is current, former or whatever?" Congressman Aspin asked.

"The provisions of the criminal law apply wherever that person is, in NSA or anywhere else," Daniel Schwartz responded. It was obvious NSA considered its oath the equivalent of a secrecy agreement.

Congressman Aspin turned to Lloyd Dean of the FBI. "Does everybody who works at the FBI have to sign a paper?"

"That is correct, the employee agreement," Dean said.

"And it does commit them to a pre-publication review?"

"Yes," Dean answered, "by the director. . . ."

In the spy business, it was pretty clear that secrecy agreements and a "clearance" process were part of the administrative procedure structure. The CIA agreement was not alone in its requirements for pre-publication review, and in a sense this was reassuring, because it meant that those in the spy business could speak with one voice. It wasn't only one agency, or one director, burdening the First Amendment, it was the entire spy community. They all saw their work as demanding an exception to the guarantee of free expression. Congressman Aspin was sympathetic, saying "I an not arguing with the case that you are making, Mr. Dean, or the case Mr.

Schwartz is making. I can see the point you are raising in those kinds of cases, and even in Mr. Zacharias's case . . ." Pre-publication review *should* be in place when people work for these agencies. The only question was how broad the review should be. Congressman Aspin allowed the issue to dangle: "What I am saying is, there are some tough judgment calls here."

Particularly when it came to the CIA. Even when Joe Smith's book-idea was little more than a speck in the mind of its author, another former CIA employee was jousting with the agency. Victor Marchetti, along with co-author John D. Marks, had published *The CIA and the Cult of Intelligence* in 1974, but not without delay and difficulty. Herbert Hetu, Director of CIA's Public Affairs Office in 1980, described the circumstances.

"In 1973 we learned that Victor Marchetti was preparing a book. We asked him to submit it to the Agency for security review. He did. A task force was formed in the Agency to review Mr. Marchetti's book. We took exception to some of the things he had in there on the grounds of security, and he took exception, and it went into litigation."

It went into *extended* litigation, with at least two separate appellate cases following from struggles at the District Court level. The outcome? The CIA won some, Marchetti won some, but it was a protracted, expensive fight, leaving bitterness and dissatisfaction. Alfred A. Knopf published Marchetti's book and inserted a publisher's note that said the CIA had ordered 339 passages in the book deleted. But, following litigation, the number of passages deleted had been reduced to — one hundred and sixty-eight!

That's almost one passage every other page. Swirling

through this arduous confrontation were innuendo and subtle speculation. This book was not complimentary about the CIA; perhaps the criticism, implied as well as direct, motivated CIA to fight more diligently than it might have; perhaps it smarted under fault-finding public scrutiny.

And the unsaid challenge: would the CIA fight as hard over deletions in a book that didn't spear it with criticism?

Within a couple of years, the chance presented itself: *Portrait of a Cold Warrior,* by Joe Smith. It didn't criticize; it didn't embarrass; and it didn't carry any CIA changes, even though the CIA did suggest some. There was no litigation, as there had been with Victor Marchetti's book. The book survived intact, and Joe Smith became a book-banning footnote because he and his publisher had stared the CIA censors down.

But somewhere a persistent thought nagged. . . what if Joe Smith's book were critical of the CIA? Would the fight have been won so easily?

It wasn't long after Joe Smith's book appeared that the CIA decided to institutionalize its review apparatus. Stansfield Turner became CIA director under President Jimmy Carter; the Vietnam war had been over for a couple of years, and former CIA people were beginning to write and divulge uncomplimentary profiles of the agency and its work. Something permanent and official was needed, and so a Publications Review Board was created inside the CIA, expressly to deal with what current and former CIA employees might write.

But the review board was only the end of the cycle; to understand its scope one must trace it back. It all began with that secrecy agreement the employee signed when entering CIA: "I hereby agree to submit for review. . . all information or materials. . . ." The employee gave up the right to free expression for the security and adventure of a career with the CIA. It may not have been an even bargain, but that was probably not uppermost in the employee's mind when he began work. The secrecy agreement only developed life when, years, later, the employee — now an ex-employee — decided to write a book and discovered he had an unwanted editor and partner.

"I shouldn't have signed it!"

"You did the patriotic thing."

"You'll ruin my book!"

"We're protecting classified information."

The Publications Review Board is composed of six people, one from each CIA directorate (Administration, Operations, Science and Technology, Intelligence, Public Affairs and DCI Staff). It meet regularly. "All types of manuscripts are reviewed, both fiction and nonfiction, in all forms" according to Eileen Roach Smith, in 1989 the chairperson of the Publications Review Board. She listed what comes in: "books, articles, short stories, essays, book reviews, letters to the editor, speeches, lectures and testimony — in short, any writing concerning intelligence or other subjects covered by the author's secrecy agreement."

If there is no classified information in the manuscript, it is freed from restriction. If clearly unclassified, the board secretary "will recommend that the chairman *authorize* its publication on behalf of the board." Authorize. Allow. Agree to. Ordain, Decree. These aren't words of advice or suggestion. These are words of power. *Authorize* — to legitimize.

If the manuscript contains classified information, there is a clear procedure. Again, Eileen Roach Smith: "When the board requires deletions from the manuscript, the legal adviser notifies the author of the required changes." Power words abound: *"requires* deletions. . . *required* changes . . ."* Seemingly, no potential to negotiate, no bow to relativity. Everything is absolute.

"In very rare instances," Eileen Roach Smith added, "the manuscript is so replete with classified information that, in the board's view, revision cannot salvage it. *In such cases, the author is denied permission to publish it altogether."* The final decision on whether and what to publish rests not with author, not with publisher, *but with the Publications Review Board!*

"In the board's view. . ." is nothing more than the power to bookban, and it really doesn't matter that Eileen Roach Smith attempts to minimize its effect by allowing that it happens only "in very rare cases." According to students of the First Amendment, the power to censor once is the power to censor again and again, and the burden to avoid such a result is put squarely on the author. Convince us there isn't classified information in your book, the Publications Review Board says; show us how you came by this information from public sources; point us to where the government has authorized disclosure of the information.

Prove it!

Eileen Roach Smith, again: " The author is invited to present any argument or evidence he may have for believing that the information is unclassified." And when the Publications Review Board takes a look at what the author provides. . . .

"The board will either affirm or modify its decision accordingly."

How active has this board been? From a modest few

manuscripts checked in 1979, it examined more than 18,000 pages in 1988, roughly 300 separate pieces of work. Some were obviously critical of the agency, yet the questions of a decade before, on differing treatment depending on how critical the manuscript was, seem muted now. Eileen Roach Smith can say in 1989, "Under no circumstances does the agency delete material solely because it is embarrassing to or critical of the agency." And she is echoed by Anne Fisher, her legal adviser: "We must be legally indifferent to anyone's opinion, pro or con the agency; we can't care whether it's supportive or not."

Merely saying it, of course, doesn't make it so, but at least now there seems more awareness of possible bias in the review process. And yet this very awareness establishes the inherent censorship-potential of the Publications Review Board. It must proclaim its freedom from one type of bias in order to project its credibility, yet by its very nature it remains biased in another way because it has set ideas on what shall be written about the agency. Even assuming its review can remain objective (and there are those who think *all* censorship ultimately becomes subjective), the bias is built-in: Protect the agency, protect the information! At the least, there will be shadings, in self-defense, when humans follow human urges.

But that's what happens when the censorship bottle is opened. The genie will concoct a mess of mischief, and the results are often not quite what one expects.

Ralph McGeehee, for example, finished, in 1980, a book manuscript critical of the CIA which he called *Deadly Deceits — (My 25 Years in the CIA)*, and dutifully, he showed it for review. A few weeks later he was presented with a list of 397 deletions. He was shocked because much of what was on the list was publicly known. So he had a meeting with the CIA to clear things up. The first thing said to him was, "It's too bad you didn't work for the Israeli intelligence service. They know how to deal with people like you. They'd take you out and shoot you!" That set the tone, and McGeehee spent the next two and a half years wading through the censorship morass, a victim of severe hair-splitting.

For example, on finding *New York Times* articles that described an incident he wanted to write about, he called "Bob," the assigned CIA censor.

"Do the articles name specific American officials?" Bob asked, adding that a reference to an unnamed CIA official didn't count.

"Ambassador William Kintner made a statement," McGeehee said.

"Is the statement in quotes? If it isn't," Bob said, "it doesn't constitute official disclosure. Reporters could write anything."

No official disclosure, no use. CENSORED!

McGeehee's book finally appeared in 1983, but, even so, he had to endure a final thrust. Much of what the CIA objected to in the manuscript, McGeehee claimed, can be found in the *New York Times Pentagon Papers* of some years before. It was material which had gone through litigation and been the subject of a landmark U.S. Supreme Court case. What's in the documents was part of the public record, McGeehee claimed.

No so, said the CIA. These documents have never been "officially" released. The Supreme Court has ruled *only* that the government could not enjoin publication. The executive branch has never officially agreed to disclose what's in these documents.

And, the CIA added, since we're part of the executive branch. . . .

Then, two years after McGeehee's book was published,

Stansfield Turner, the CIA director who gave teeth to the Publications Review Board, came out with *his* book. Called *Secrecy and Democracy: The CIA in Transition,* it was a lengthy examination of world affairs from his own perspective as America's chief spymaster. However, he wrote the book after he and his patron, Jimmy Carter, had left office, and he found himself facing down a less-than-supportive CIA, now responsible to Ronald Reagan. In fact, a large portion of the book's Introduction was devoted to complaints about the time and the effort he had gone through in order to get CIA clearance. "Since every chapter was processed three or four times, the delays were very costly to me. . . more than one hundred deletions were made by the CIA. These ranged from borderline issues to the ridiculous. I appealed many of the questionable deletions to the higher levels of the CIA and obtained only three minor concessions."

He was clearly vexed. Ten to fifteen per cent of the time he took to write the book was devoted to fencing with the CIA, and he saw himself as a victim. "It was all most unreasonable and unnerving," he wrote, blaming his administrative successors. "There are two problems: timeliness and arbitrariness."

But, in truth, there is delicious irony here. From the pen of the man who admitted he had urged Attorney General Griffin Bell to prosecute Frank Snepp in 1978 because Snepp had published his book, *Decent Interval,* without allowing the CIA to see it first, we read of grumbling, even gnashing of teeth, because, having followed what he preached, Turner sees that the course is not so steady, that the censorship genie, once out of the bottle, is elusive and troublesome. He provides a vivid example of his travails:

"I had given in on most of the deletions demanded by the CIA but two requests were particularly egregious and unnecessary. Anthony Lapham [CIA General Counsel] on my behalf, sent the CIA a letter stating that unless they either (1) provided me with a convincing reason for their position, or (2) obtained a court injunction against my publishing the information, I would proceed to do so. The CIA. . . chose to do neither. Instead, they replied that I should do whatever I deemed to be 'appropriate,' but that the CIA reserved the right to take whatever action it deemed appropriate. . ."

Left to pursue his own course, Stansfield Turner decided to delete the material, but his attitude was unreconciled. "This was the most irresponsible position they could have taken."

One has little sympathy with a man who helped design the track and now complains about the trains that are using it. The only certainty is that once a restriction is placed upon free expression, it will be enforced in ways no one can truly predict. The limits to free expression carry a subjectivity that varies and varies; one man's limitation will be another's unburdening, making it impossible to forecast what will develop.

Except that a cost will be paid.

Three years later, Stansfield Turner appeared on Capitol Hill before the House Committee on Government Operations. His views had not changed, and he called his experience with manuscript clearance "painful and costly," claiming that he had suffered "gross abuse" of his constitutional rights. His writing schedule had often been interrupted as he would wait, sometimes for two weeks,

for approval of a chapter, and many more weeks following each appeal of a Publications Review Board ruling.
The CIA, he charged, had "no concept that time is money
to an author," and he acknowledged that in all probability
he received better treatment than most.

Stansfield Turner seems not to appreciate the irony.
Congressman Jack Brooks of Texas asked him, "How
important are pre-publication contracts to our national
security?"

"They are useful but not critical," Turner replied.
"Other than in the CIA and the NSA we have got along
well for a long time without them."

16

At the Barricades

The beige stone headquarters of U.S. Customs in Washington D.C. is not a building that welcomes the casual visitor. There is the hard-eyed guard, another lurking nearby: "Whom do you wish to see?"

"Is he/she expecting you?"

Followed by: "Sign the log—name, address, purpose of visit, time in."

All within five feet of the front door. A waist-high wooden railing bars a straight path. To the side is an electronic frame. "Through there. Walk slowly."

One guard monitors a screen, the other stands beyond the electronic frame. Another machine has already examined briefcase and tape recorder. The first guard repeats the name of the person to be seen, picks up the phone, gives visitor's name and location and receives a response.

"Be here in ten minutes," the guard says, handing back

briefcase and tape recorder. "Wait over there," indicating a wooden bench.

The guard reaches under a console and produces a badge. "Wear this in plain view," he says. "Always." The badge reads: *Visitor.*

"What room number?"

The guard shakes his head. "Everyone's escorted in this building. No one walks these halls alone."

It isn't easy to get inside the U.S. Customs Building in Washington D.C. Drugs and drug violence are among the reasons; imagine the coup if a revenge-seeking druggie could plant a bomb, carry out assassination, destroy the large cache of super-secret files!

The function of policeman is not foreign to members of the U.S. Customs Service. They know how to enforce the law, and they are confident about doing it.

Customs mans the barricades. Customs is responsible for controlling what comes across the borders, and through the decades this responsibility has been shouldered gravely, sometimes zealously. Customs is serious about protecting us.

Even if the threat happens to be a book.

Not drugs, not weapons, not laundered money; simply a book. Here's what current customs regulations say: "Customs officers have the legal authority to scan documents and correspondence to determine whether the documents or correspondence are obscene, treasonous, seditious (i.e., inciting or producing imminent lawless action). . . ."

Then, if scanning raises the custom officer's antennae, he may read more thoroughly, and if *that* produces "reasonable suspicion" the work is obscene, treasonous or seditious, the customs officer can "detain" it (the word, no doubt, less offensive to civil libertarians than *impound* or *confiscate*) until a legal proceeding decides whether he is right.

A book can be prevented from coming into this country because a customs officer has a *reasonable suspicion* about it. No probable cause, no search warrant, no finding that this customs officer appreciates literature well enough to decide its literary value. "The customs service is the most powerful organ of government," according to Michael Fleming, a customs officer with the Los Angeles office. "We don't require search warrants at point of entry to the United States, and our search standard is 'suspicion.' "

The Supreme Court has made it clear that this is perfectly proper. "We've been challenged many times," Michael Fleming says resolutely, "but our authority has been upheld again and again." No warrant needed, no probable cause required, no well-read customs officer expected.

The customs service as censor and bookbanner: there has been quite a history. It began innocuously enough, in 1842, with the passage of the Tariff Act allowing customs to seize "obscene" works that might be coming into the country. No one actually knew what "obscene" meant, but the general feeling was, "I know it if I see it." The problem was no one really policed the policers, so in each port of entry — New York, Boston, Baltimore, New Orleans — different works and different words offended different censors. Obscenity in New York might not have been obscenity in Boston, because each collector of customs had what amounted to an independent fiefdom. Sure, the Tariff Act called for judicial review whenever customs seized books, but, until the early twentieth century, most of these reviews were formalities. The customs bureau, itself, did little to harmonize the different local offices; only the most general regulations were circulated; there was no attempt to bring out a uniform decision on "obscenity"; no one put together a list of prohibited titles for all the offices to follow.

Customs officers were left to decide these things on their own, and it should be no surprise that bias and prejudice became rampant. Authors and publishers and importers whose books were seized had recourse to the courts, but they saw the courts rubber stamping the decisions of customs officers so this was no option at all.

The situation prevailed through the first third of the twentieth century. In 1917, the Espionage Act added "treasonous and seditious" to the types of books the customs service could seize. In 1926, the customs service even got its own specialized court — the Customs Court — to deal with appeals from the seizures of customs officers'. Heady times, to be sure.

A book by Marie Stopes, *Enduring Passion,* was fairly well known during the 1920s, especially in Europe where it had been written and published. An importer tried to bring it into the United States, claiming it had substantial educational value (it provided sex education to the inexperienced and offered aid to frigid spouses). No sir, said the customs service. It was obscene. But the book was written by a well-known doctor, said the importer; the book is scientific, useful, needed.

The customs service was not moved. If you, the importer, were a doctor, things might be different. Look at the contents: "Excessive Virility," "Undersexed Husbands," "The Frigid Wife." Is this what Americans should be reading? It allured the reader, it excited his morbid curiosity about sex, it had no redeeming virtue. The author, in fact, should know better than to write this kind of book.

So the book stayed out of America.

By the late 1920s, the customs service was like a strict father reproving wayward children for harboring impure urges. Book after book was stopped at the border, local customs officials employed vivid prose to beat back the advance of sexual permissiveness:

- "obscene in every sense of that term" — *Droll Stories* by Honoré de Balzac;
- "thoroughly rotten and putrid" — *The Wild Party* by J.M. March;
- "impure suggestion clothed in pleasing attire allures and corrupts" — *Aphrodite*; *The Songs of Bilitis*, poems by Pierre Louys.

Other classics were not spared: *The Decameron, Candide,* the works of Rabelais — all banned. Current, accepted works such as *Lady Chatterley's Lover, Ulysses, Jurgen* — all banned. The customs people got together with the post office people and they drew up a list: 700 books to keep out of the hands of people living in America, 700 books that could not be mailed here, 700 books that could not be imported here.

America's first *Index Librorum Prohibitorum!*

Then, in 1930, after a decade of confrontational litigation, a weary public began to question the judgments of the customs service. Where they right? How did they know? What was wrong with sex and erotica?

Why are we being suppressed?

The questions were answered by a new tariff act which

clipped the customs service wings. The secretary of the Treasury, to whom the customs service answers, could allow literary classics and books of recognized value across the border, even if a customs officer at the barricades thought they were obscene. No longer could one customs officer's views on obscenity decide the fate of an imported book. The power shifted, and it shifted even more a couple of years later when Judge Woolsey in New York decided the famous *Ulysses* case against the customs service, calling Joyce's book a modern classic.

The floodgates swung open, and the 700 items on the customs-post office *Index* dissolved to just a handful. Books which for decades had been smuggled into the country in brown wrappers or in the false bottoms of suitcases now flew by the border searches, openly and carefree. Bookbanning at the border was no longer a major development.

Now, more than half a century later, who could be blamed for assuming the customs service had found other, more pressing concerns to focus upon? Bookbanning, after all, doesn't carry the same danger, the same menace to Americans as do drugs or secreted weaponry or assassination teams or plans for imminent political upheaval. Such an assumption would be reasonable, even automatic. But matters haven't quite worked out so easily.

While the obscenity issue does seem to be fairly resolved (the Marvin Miller case in 1973 settled what was or was not obscene), that little add-on by the 1917 Espionage Act — "treasonous and seditious" — gave new breath to whatever weakened instincts for bookbanning there might have been in the beige stone building on Independence Avenue.

The customs service today remains in the business of

bookbanning, and while it doesn't pursue its role with the zeal it showed a half century ago, it takes its responsibilities seriously, and it has never given up its power to seize (read: "detain" or censor) any book it considers to violate the laws of the United States.

Customs has an ally now it didn't have years ago—the Immigration and Naturalization Service of the Department of Justice. As Michael Fleming of the customs service says. "They deal with people, we deal with what people carry." If a foreigner seeks a visa, the immigration and naturalization service jumps in. They grant, deny, take away or otherwise control who comes through the barricades, and under what conditions.

The McCarran Act (true cold-war-vintage legislation) is the authority, and under it foreigners can be kept away or deported because of their political and ideological beliefs. Banned, in other words, if:

- "engaged in activities which would be prejudicial to the public interest";
- "members of the Communist Party";
- "advocat[ing] the economic, international and government doctrines of world communism."

The immigration and naturalization service enforced this law just as zealously as the customs service enforced its right to seize offensive books. Since the early 1960s they have banned a number of people, including writers and journalists.

For Example:

- *Gabriel Garcia Marquez*—he could come here only if his traveling companion was an FBI agent;

—*Carlos Fuentes*—in 1964 his visa was valid only for five days, and he was restricted to Manhattan Island;

—*Dario Fo,* a prominent Italian playwright—was not allowed to come here in 1980, or in 1983, because he "never had a good word to say about the United States."

There were others—Nobel Prize winner from Poland, Czeslaw Milosz; English novelists and short story writers Graham Green and Iris Murdock; French writers Michel Foucault and Regis Debray; Italian novelist Alberto Moravia. All were banned from the United States. In 1990, finally, some relief appeared: people with radical views, especially radical political views, would no longer be kept away. But, of course, history had already been written.

When the immigration and naturalization service banned a writer, it was clearly buttressing the customs service's banning of books. If one proceeded with zeal, the other would also. Banning the writer kept the symbol away, but banning the book blanketed sweet reason.

In the mid-1930s and after a series of embarrassing defeats in the courtroom over what was or was not obscene, the customs service reached for an outside viewpoint that would guide it in the face of a continuing traffic in books and photos carrying the depiction of erotica to its ever-expanding limits. They hired a man named Huntington Cairns to be their official conscience, and he came to occupy a unique place, not only with the customs service but with *any* government agency. His job was to advise on book seizures. Is it obscene? Is it a classic? Is it of literary merit?

He was an author and social scientist, a man with

varied tastes, well read and sophisticated. He was also a lawyer, and quickly established himself within the customs service. His decisions became acceptable even for the customs inspectors at the barricades. Of D.H. Lawrence's *Lady Chatterley's Lover,* he said, it is a "work of literary standing in the sense that it is constantly discussed in the best literary journals. . . [It is] a serious work put forward by an eccentric but indubitable genius."

Judgments like these marked the 1930s and 1940s, and for many years the customs service — and their conscience kept away from controversy. Whenever there was doubt about erotic portrayal in a book, Huntington Cairns's opinion was sought — and followed. In the words of one well-known authority, ". . . Washington and to a large extent Mr. Cairns, fixed the minimum standards of fitness of foreign works."

But Huntington Cairns has been dead a long time, and while the subject of obscenity now seems relegated to a back shelf, there remains the political side of the bookbanning equation, since "treasonous and seditious" books can also be banned. There is still *this* monster to slay.

It started simply enough. On January 16, 1985, a journalist named Edward Haase walked off a plane in Miami and proceeded to the customs desk. He did not hide the fact he was returning from Nicaragua after a stay of several months, or that he had made several trips to that country through the years. On his declaration card he mentioned he was carrying reading material. Yes, he affirmed to the customs inspector, it was reading material acquired in Nicaragua.

Nicaragua! (The court subsequently found there was no "official" policy requiring undue suspicion about travelers from Nicaragua.)

But the customs inspector didn't let him pass. Over there, he directed Edward Haase, take your bags over there. He indicated a second customs inspection station, and a new customs inspector.

The inspector, named Oliveros, was much more thorough than his predecessor. He was also a student-trainee, though Edward Haase didn't know this. Oliveros dug through the bags and he found some of the reading material that Edward Haase had declared. It was not light fiction, nor was it inoffensive nonfiction.

It was political—books and magazines, mainly. Then, as he examined other items in Edward Haase's bags, he came across a picture frame.

In a moment, Oliveros removed the backing on the frame, and discovered a single sheet of paper carrying a list of names and addresses. It was enough for him to call his supervisor, because Oliveros suspected he was staring at "seditious" materials. He knew what his authority allowed; he could seize "any book, pamphlet, paper, writing" that contains "any matter advocating or urging treason or insurrection against the United States or forcible resistance to any law of the United States."

Olivero's supervisor examined what Edward Haase was carrying, and he picked up the phone and called the FBI. A problem, he told them. You'd better get over here. While he waited for them to come, he photocopied the list Oliveros had found behind the picture frame.

Shortly, an FBI agent by the name of José Miranda appeared. Now it was customs *and* FBI facing down Edward Haase. José Miranda looked over the photocopied list, and then he announced he would make his own search of Edward Haase's bags.

Miranda pulled out Haase's personal address book; his diary; two articles he had written; five sheets of paper with the names and addresses of organizations involved with Nicaraguan and Central American affairs; other papers concerning the "National Network in Solidarity with the People of Nicaragua"; and a few more books and magazines. The cache had now expanded mightily.

But Edward Haase needed to make a connecting flight, and he had to buy a ticket first. Go ahead, he was told, get your ticket and then come back. We'll decide what to do with these items while you're gone.

In fact, José Miranda and the customs people knew what they would do, for while Edward Haase was gone, they photocopied as much of the books, magazines and papers as they thought they needed. When Edward Haase returned, they gave him back his originals.

We have copies, they said.

But that violates my constitutional rights, my right to privacy, Edward Haase asserted. You can't keep copies of *my* books and papers without my permission.

This a seizure, they told him. We want to determine the legality of what you are carrying—and reading.

One month later Edward Haase sued, demanding return of all the photocopies and asking damages because his civil rights had been violated. But neither the customs service nor the FBI flinched. That little add-on from the 1917 Espionage Act, giving the customs service the right to seize books and other materials because they were "seditious and treasonous" was their ally. What Edward Haase brought into the United States was "seditious," they claimed.

But sedition is a tricky word, one man's sedition being another's patriotism, so a rather fine line must be observed. In an August, 1986, internal memorandum to the field, an assistant customs commissioner flayed the sedition devil:

[You] will recognize seditious matter in such forms as printed and graphic exhortations to the reader, encouraging or promoting *imminent* acts of armed or other violence against constituted government and military authorities and institutions. . ."

But there were limits:

[You] must distinguish matter that merely advocates lawless action, which is admissible, from prohibited matter that is directed to inciting or producing imminent lawless action and is likely to incite or produce such action. . ."

A customs inspector at the barricades was expected to distinguish between "advocating" and "inciting"—at least superficially—after a cursory reading.

It was one thing to yell "Fire!" falsely, in a crowded room. It was another thing to make the same exhortation in the pages of a book.

Pity the customs inspector who must make those hair-thin distinctions in an instant. Is it any wonder the copier becomes the customs inspector's best friend? Copy now, buy time to analyze, apologize later if it comes to that.

But above all. . . copy!

Of course, copying is, in and of itself, an intrusion on a person's right to privacy, but all the customs inspector needs is "reasonable suspicion"—not clear proof, not absolute certainty—to seize the materials and hold them for a later determination.

When Edward Haase left Miami International Airport in January, 1985, he had his original books and papers, but the government had copies which they intended to keep and place under seal in the registry of the district court so they would not be further disseminated.

It was that "reasonable suspicion" which held the copies of Edward Haase's books and papers hostage at the barricades. *And the government wanted to retain copies of materials it seizes!*

But then, in early 1988, customs overstepped. Perhaps the Edward Haase matter gave them confidence, but whatever the reason, the customs service continued to copy the books and papers of a number of travelers returning from Nicaragua (among them a nurse and health educator, the operator of a political bookstore and two university professors whose area of academic interest was Nicaragua). Something different happened, though. In some of these cases the seized materials were *not* seditious.

Give us back the copies, the travelers demanded.

Customs complied. *But* before doing so they created a "record of non-violation" consisting of reports, notes and tallies describing and commenting on the materials which were to be returned.

The travelers found out about the "record of non-violation." We want this, too, they insisted. It belongs with our books and papers.

Sorry, customs said. We have a right to make this record. We've returned everything we examined.

You have a record on us, the travelers maintained, and we have not violated the law. That is unconstitutional!

It's *our* record, not yours, customs insisted.

You wouldn't have a record if you hadn't seized our books and papers, the travelers answered back.

On and on went the dispute, until it fell into the lap of a federal district court in California. A wise judge by the name of J. Spencer Letts listened to both sides carefully.

Yes, he said, customs does have the right to make border searches, and it doesn't have to follow the constitutional requirement about probable cause. "Reasonable suspicion" is okay.

But, — and here the customs service must have blinked a bit — I don't think anyone has the right to keep a record of someone else's lawful conduct. If I haven't violated the law, why should you keep a record of it?

Judge J. Spencer Letts put his thoughts into more appropriate legal language:

The mere existence and retention of the Records of Non-Violation, therefore, threaten Plaintiffs with future seizures and can have no effect but to impermissibly "chill" Plaintiffs' conduct in the future as to their constitutionally protected expressions.

And so one small battle in the bookbanning war was won, but the overall right of the customs service to seize and destroy books at the borders remains largely intact. The barricades are sturdy, and those that guard them are resolute. In these last few years of the twentieth century, the ogre has become seditious and treasonable literature, and nothing seems more certain than that seemingly reasonable minds will disagree on the reach and scope of these designations. In this war, however, the censors have an advantage: they man the barricades and they control the traffic. It is a tight world they manage, and they manage it very well.

Just ask Edward Haase.

17

"Politics, Mr. President, Politics"

"The American impulse," writer John Garvey insisted, "is to turn morality into law." Good is legal, bad is illegal. It's no secret that morality can derive absolutes from seemingly innocuous conduct and that such morality is easily translatable into a broad rule for society. If *we* think something is bad, shouldn't it be bad for others, too? What offends me *should* offend you.

Incidents revealing this sort of thing have risen throughout our history. Loyalty oaths, for example. During the 1950s these became an established way to distinguish the true American from the imposter, the patriot from the traitor. "Are you now or have you ever been a member of . . . ?" was the often-asked question, and the response determined the individual's loyalty level.

"Are you prepared to defend the Constitution of the United States and the government under which it operates, now and in the future . . . ?" was another type of

253

loyalty oath often put to those who entered federal
service. Loyalty was a big issue in the 1950s; it was the
era of Joe McCarthy, the early stages of the Cold War
and the urge to purge unclean Americans from positions
of influence and power. Facing the loyalty oath quickly
attracted ardent supporters and detractors. "A job? You'll
need to sign this little document first."

I am not now nor have I ever been a member . . .

Loyalty was tested by where one traveled, whom one
traveled with and why one traveled. The private work-
place was contaminated by measuring one's loyalty level,
and if the gauge didn't register well, sometimes, it was—
"Sorry, we can't afford embarrassment."

Thousands felt the sting in the 1950s, and the reasons
were just as John Garvey predicted: loyalty became more
than symbol, it became law. A good American was a loyal
American, so we'll make it a crime to be anything else.

Good was legal, bad was illegal.

My sense of loyalty may be different from yours.

*No one who believes the way you do can talk of loyalty to
America!*

Ludicrous results came from this urge to legislate the
morality of patriotism. In Alabama a state statute was
passed which required each book in state libraries to have
a certification that author, publisher and every major
character in any non-fiction work have a loyalty oath on
file attesting to their status as good Americans. When
someone began paging through the books in the Alabama
library system, it was soon apparent that to make this law
effective more than twenty-seven *million* loyalty oaths
would have to be checked, so the law was quietly forgot-
ten. Of course, the politics inherent in passing this legisla-

tion undoubtedly was quite vivid, invoking terrible consequences for generations unborn should the peoples' representatives not perform their duty. Who, after all, wanted to vote against a system that would protect the citizens of Alabama from seditious writers and publishers and booksellers?

To vote against the loyalty oath was to vote against the interests of America. Politicians understood this very well.

In this context books became an easy target for politicians bent on creating law out of morality. In the world of politics a book is both an easy victim and a solid protagonist. What it is and what it can be are viewed without difficulty.

"This book should be banned!" shouts the politician, and he has merely to raise the book over his head, show it and offer a casual insight or two about its contents. The crowd has no doubt he's correct because they can see, they can read for themselves. It's much safer than calling someone a thief and relying on a witness.

Books are easy targets for politicians. The 1986 Meese Commission on Pornography showed us why. It started with eleven board members and a staff of nine. It was a public commission using taxpayer dollars and investigating a presumed public menace—pornography in books, magazines and films. It should have come forth with few preconceived notions about the subject, it should have sought answers to presumed vexing questions, it should have striven for something akin to truth.

But it never came close. Somehow, here, politics became too important to take a back seat; we had a Republican administration within an ideological straitjacket: pornography was bad, it was immoral, it should be illegal at all levels and wiped from the consciousness of all Americans.

Six of the eleven commission board members were on record as favoring some type of regulation of erotic literature. On record *before* the commission heard a single witness, saw a single exhibit or caucused for its first meeting. It was hardly an unbiased group, but it did sense a mission. In those sunlit days of the Reagan second term it knew where the power of moral purpose lay, and it knew such power would begin to wane as the term ran out. Now! We have the power to make a difference now!

If politics is the exercise of power, nowhere is it more unvarnished than when it is suited up with moral purpose. "The conclusion is unmistakable," said the commission, "that with respect to the criminal laws relating to obscenity, there is a striking underenforcement, and that this underenforcement consists of undercomplaining, underinvestigation, underprosecution and undersentencing."

A call to power—"Let's go get 'em!"

The issue of morality arose as the commission sought to examine, and ultimately control pornography—"Sexual explicitness." Some pornography, insisted the commission, even if it's legal, is "still considered by many people to be harmful, offensive, or in some other way, objectionable." A call to morality followed—"What's legal may not be moral."

And so the Meese Commission examined and analyzed and scratched its head for the better part of a year (mindful, of course, that it had had a predecessor, a 1970 commission which studied these same issues and concluded there was no link between pornography and anti-social behavior) and finally produced a massive two-volume compilation of its work. Politically, it was in step with the Reagan administration because it had little good to say about anything erotic or pornographic that might appear in a book or magazine.

Yes, it believed, there *was* a connection between what people read and what they would do. Yes, pornography would excite and incite the rapist, the child molester, the deviate sexual practitioner. Yes, violent pornography would prod some to violence against women. The evidence? Some testimony from a few social scientists and law-enforcement personnel, but not at all a strong, fact-filled, substantiative case. At best, information the commission had gathered was ambivalent on the question, and for several members it was simply not persuasive enough. "Some of us . . . except for material plainly describing sexual activity with minors or targeted to minors would urge that materials consisting entirely of the printed word simply not be prosecuted, regardless of content." There was no clarification of how many "some" is, but obviously it was more than one and fewer than the majority.

But the commission didn't let go so easily. "Others of us, however, while sharing this special concern for the written word, would not adopt such a rigid rule, and would retain both in theory and in practice the ability to prosecute obscene material regardless of the form in which the obscenity is conveyed." Once again no light on the extent of the vague, collective "others of us," but as with "some" it meant more than one and possibly fewer than a majority.

"Others of us" felt all obscene materials should be prosecuted. "Some" of us felt there should have been no prosecutions.

Hardly a resounding affirmation in either direction. But politics being what they are, the commission understood where its power could lead. It could recommend, it could persuade, it could even bully if it wished.

One day, in February, 1986, an innocuous-looking letter arrived at corporate headquarters of Southland Corporation in Dallas, Texas, a major business enterprise which included, among other holdings, 7–Eleven, the largest chain of convenience stores in the United States. A multi-billion dollar operation, run for many years by the quiet, seemingly imperturbable Thompson family of Dallas, the company was not likely to fold under pressure.

The letter was from the Meese Commission, signed by Alan Sears, Executive Director, a former federal prosecutor from Kentucky. The commission, according to the letter, had "received testimony alleging that your company is involved in the sale or distribution of pornography." The Thompson family was unpleasantly surprised because they had never considered themselves purveyors of material characterized this way.

Alan Sears asked them to explain why their company might have been targeted in the testimony. Then, in an ominous turn, added, "Failure to respond will necessarily be accepted as an indication of no objection." The burden was on them to show they were not pornographers.

Most lawyers would say that the hardest thing to prove is a negative: *I am not . . . I never was . . . I can't be. . . .* But Alan Sears was telling the Thompson family to prove that their business did not sell or distribute pornography, and that they'd better do it fast, too! *Failure to respond . . .*

Sears had attached a copy of a page of commission testimony, so the Thompson family knew he was serious:

> "The general public usually associates pornography with sleazy porno book stores and theatres. However, many of the major players in the game of pornography are well-known household names. Few people realize that 7–Eleven convenience stores are the leading retailers of porn magazines in America."

Who provided this testimony? Alan Sears didn't tell the Thompson family. *Failure to respond . . .*

A few weeks later *Playboy* and *Penthouse* were removed from 7–Eleven stores. No one was willing to admit a direct causal connection with the letter from Alan Sears, but the suspicion certainly lingered.

And it hardly abated when a couple of other facts came out. The same letter from Alan Sears was sent to a number of major corporations around the United States, and the person whose testimony accompanied the letter to the Thompson family was Reverend Donald Wildmon, based in Tupelo, Mississippi, the executive director of a far-right, religiously-oriented organization called the National Federation of Decency. There was no reason to question Wildmon's sincerity as he propounded his convictions, but one had to ask — why?

Why an accusatory letter from a taxpayer's commission seeking answers — not prosecutions?

Why overt credence to the legal conclusions of an extremist?

It had to be politics. The politics of pornography, the branding of political opponents to show that those who supported pornography were bad; those who fought it, and who were able to ban it, were good.

Little was offered to distinguish the fact that not all pornography was illegal; that some of it, most of it, in fact, was not obscene under the Supreme Court definition spelled out in the *Miller* case in 1973 (where, among other things, the work had to appeal to the prurient interest of the average person and had to be utterly without redeeming virtue). And if the book or magazine was not obscene, then it didn't violate the law, regardless of how pornographic it might be. But pornography was a big, bad word to the Meese Commission, and for maximum effect it had to have designation stronger than "offensive" — it had to have one with teeth!

Morality into law, a bookbanner's equation. Pornography should be illegal! But not all of it is, and the result of trying to make it so is to bring bookbanning into the political circle, the only alternative to leaving the law where it is. Attorney Maxwell Lillienstein, counsel to the American Bookseller's Association, says: The issue is "whether or not a governmental agency, by placing its seal of disapproval on certain kinds of constitutionally protected books and magazines, can cause booksellers to engage in what is perhaps the most insidious form of censorship (i.e., self-censorship), whereby thousands of mainstream booksellers may eliminate from their stock matter protected by the First Amendment."

Why would booksellers do this? To duck the label as a "distributor of pornography," to avoid being stigmatized and perhaps worse. Of course, what Lillienstein describes works right down the line — when booksellers decide they won't sell a book, they don't buy it from the publisher, and when the publisher sees he can't sell it to the book-sellers, he won't accept the manuscript from the writer.

And when the writer sees he can't sell his words, he'll drop the book idea.

Self-censorship from top to bottom offers the same result as overt bookbanning, and it affects our First Amendment rights just as vividly. Politics creates the opportunity; morality suffused with power fills the vac-uum; and what is recommended as legal or illegal is no different from what is considered good or bad.

Morality that becomes law — the politics of bookbanning.

Many politician's attitudes toward books and art and creativity are a curious mixture of suspicion and support. *I don't understand these people, but I know they have a right to express themselves this way.* . . . Such tolerance is commend-able but it isn't unlimited. Every politician has an offend-me gauge; nothing can offend quite so readily as the written word, or an artist's rendering. The politician's antennae are forever cued to a rise in his or her offend-me gauge because it presents an opportunity to be decisive and *on the right side!*

Books do present a challenge to the politician, and no doubt the written word is capable of tripping the offend-me gauge. Benjamin Disraeli, the celebrated ironist and nineteenth-century British Prime Minister whose la-bors on behalf of Queen Victoria allowed the Empire to circle the globe, could offer, (while believing not a word of it):

"Books are fatal" they are the curse of the human race. Nine-tenths of existing books are nonsense, and the clever books are the refutation of that non-sense. The greatest misfortune that ever befell man was the invention of printing."

Most modern politicians won't go this far, of course, but lurking in the minds of some is the suspicion these people—writers and artists—are up to something . . . *I don't understand these people* . . . and such a politician watches and waits. He sees or reads something that starts the motor on his offend-me gauge, he wonders if he's missing something, he asks himself, *but is this art?* Soon he hears others asking the same question, and now he knows he's not alone . . . *it can't be art!* His offend-me gauge jumps to the red, and he speaks out. . . .

Ban it! Remove it! Burn it! The politician becomes a censor, his suspicion turning to certainty.

A drama such as this was played out in the Congress of the United States in the late 1980's. At issue wasn't a book but several photographs that were part of an exhibition funded by the National Endowment for the Arts. The medium of expression, however, was not so important—the photographs could have been books. It was the approach of the politician to a work of art that provided a window so we could spot that tiny pebble of suspicion, always there, always solid.

Two photographers, Robert Mapplethorpe and Andres Serrano, offered their photographs, and the National Endowment for the Arts turned them into a traveling exhibit. Mapplethorpe's collection was a fulsome display of homoerotic art while Serrano offered one photograph which showed a crucifix hanging upside down in the artists urine. He called it "Piss Christ."

Word reached Congress that the National Endowment for the Arts had granted $45,000 for the exhibit. As it happened, the annual budget for the NEA was currently under debate. For the politician who found his morality swimming with his sense of what should be legal or illegal, it was an opportunity not to be missed.

First off the mark was Congressman Dana Rohrabacher from California. Florid-faced, jaw set, he strode to the rostrum in the well of the House. He proposed to do away with the National Endowment for the Arts entirely. "Those who gave artist Andres Serrano 15,000 taxpayers dollars to fund his work of art entitled 'Piss Christ' did more than offend most of the Nation. They set off a national debate on the value of Government funding of the arts. Is a picture of Jesus Christ hanging from the cross submerged in a jar of urine worthy of Government funding? The answer is no. . . ."

Rohrabacher went on to describe the photographs of Robert Mapplethorpe with equal distaste, addressing his colleagues with the admonition, "Your votes will decide if this is worthy of subsidization." The answer, he claimed, is to get the government out of the arts, otherwise, abuses such as those described were bound to happen. He mentioned—with less than enthusiasm—a magazine for homosexuals, *Gay Sunshine Press,* which the NEA funded for several years. "I don't care if it's heterosexual literature," he said, "Our taxpayers shouldn't be subsidizing these kinds of questionable projects."

Congressman Rohrabacher continued, "We should leave this money in the hands of the people at the local level . . . I can guarantee the Members that if this money was in the hands of the people, the taxpayers, they would not be sponsoring this other type of pornographic art . . ."

"Artists say that the Government has no right to interfere with or censor the work of artists," the congressman thundered. But "The taxpayers shouldn't have to pay for whatever outrage or trash an artist dreams up."

The moral equation was clear . . . trash art (books included) is "bad" art and the government won't pay for it. If the Congress agreed with Dana Rohrabacher, a law would be passed to make it so, and morality and law would become one.

"Artists can do whatever they want with their own time and with their own dime."

The debate flowed back and forth for a while, but as a vote neared on Dana Rohrabacher's bill to disband the NEA, Congressman Pat Williams of Montana rose, and suddenly the issue of politics and censorship and morality and law was clear. "We are here today politicizing the National Endowment for the Arts," he said. "That is perilously close to censorship. We are exerting political pressure on them. We can couch it in good language. We can couch it in the grandeur of the Congress of the United States, operating in this Chamber, but it is censorship."

The way it works, said the congressman, is quite simple: we slow the flow of money to artists, we "hobble" their creative freedom. It is the freedom of artists in the United States that is at stake.

Slow the flow and politicize the artist. Morality into law.

"Indirectly, but in a very real sense," asserted Congressman Williams, "the Congress of the United States is herein today practicing censorship."

Censorship, bookbanning, the offend-me gauge, all bouncing with Congress's control of funds for artists. Because Congress is a political body, it follows that most matters taken up will find their way into the political ledger, and it's not surprising that a seemingly non-partisan issue, such as freedom for artists, will somehow surface with a political face. But because politics is often a case of narrow choices, what might satisfy one craving can bring a new and different ogre.

As happened here. Congressman Rohrabacher's bill was defeated, not least because the price for artist-funding control convinced many it was thinly disguised censor-ship. Yet there were enough on the floor of the House of Representatives who remained offended by the photogra-phy of Robert Mapplethorpe and Andres Serrano that they wished to send a message of sorts. In a classic exer-cise of the narrow choices politics can develop, the House of Representatives voted to reduce the NEA budget for the next year by the amount of the grant for the offensive exhibit, $45,000.

It was still censorship, and if this were a book instead of photography, it would have been bookbanning because the Congress hadn't *refused* to act, it had simply widened its control. There was still a moral judgment here, and Congress, by reducing the NEA budget, had allowed such morality to become law.

A couple of months later it was the U.S. Senate's turn, and following the same script, Jesse Helms of North Carolina introduced a bill which would prohibit the NEA from funding obscene or indecent materials (which would, presumably include books), as well as anything which would denigrate any religion or person because of race, creed, sex, handicap, age or national origin. His bill, he said, should "ensure that the American taxpayers' money will never be used again to pay for pornography or attacks on religion."

Once, again morality into law. For Jesse Helms and his supporters the shapes of good and bad were clear and certain; the law can only make them more definite.

But doesn't this restrict artists and writers, doesn't this interfere with their right to produce what they wish? Their freedom to create?

Isn't it censorship and bookbanning?

No, no, Senator Helms was quick to respond. "Censorship is not involved, I say it over and over again."

But others in the Senate chamber were not so convinced. "Almost any work of art could be declared ineligible for funding," insisted one of Jesse Helms's colleagues, and another said with some vehemence, "We will be restricting the atmosphere in which the creative process occurs."

Not censorship, not censorship, Jesse Helms repeated. We're not preventing publication or distribution — only the use of taxpayers' money. His reasoning echoed that of Dana Rohrabacher in the House: "Any artist can produce anything he wants to, but nobody has a preemptive right to raid the pocketbook of the American taxpayer."

The bill that Jesse Helms pushed relied on the moral equation that what is good should be lawful, what is bad should be unlawful. The politics, just as in the House of Representatives, dictates that narrow choice as to whether or not any restrictions should be placed on the use of public money for artists. To reconcile the moral equation and the politics one must assume some limit on what can be published or produced, regardless of what that limit is or who is enforcing it.

Senator Herb Kohl from Wisconsin answered Jesse Helms with dramatic reference. "I fear that we take a step toward the Iranian model of literary criticism," he said. We may not pronounce a death sentence against the author, as was done with Salman Rushdie and *The Satanic Verses,* but prohibiting NEA funding for the book would occur if the Helms bill passed. "We would not banish an author like Alexander Solzhenitsyn, but we would banish him from being eligible for federal funding," because there may be some who would object to what he writes.

What we're doing, Senator Kohl insisted, is taking a meat-axe to something that needs some fine-tuning. It is demeaning to the arts, and it ignores the Constitution. It needn't be done this way.

Yet, he said, we *do* take the Helms bill seriously. "And you know why?" he asked.

He glanced toward the rostrum. "Politics, Mr. President, politics."

Two months later another bill was introduced, this time outlawing the use of taxpayer money for any "obscene" work of art. The wording in the legislation followed the Supreme Court definition of obscenity. For the first time, Congress could place a limit on the *content* of a work of art, if taxpayer money was involved.

Politics being what it is, this bill was approved by the House and passed by the Senate, 91–6. The President signed it readily.

18

The Newest Bookbanners

When he wrote *The Adventures of Huckleberry Finn* in 1885, Mark Twain knew he would be tweaking Victorian morality. His characters and situations repelled a conventional work ethic and wisdom gained through formal education. His heroes were not high born, yet they tantalized with their sense of adventure and their underdog role in a life harsher than most readers could know.

Many were attractive rogues and criminals, often speaking with fractured syntax and in street vernacular; others — particularly the runaway slave, Jim — spoke in crude misstatement but offered insights and judgments both accurate and humorous. Mark Twain knew his characters would offend, because he understood the conventional morality that would judge his book.

But, of course, he had made a career of poking fun at that morality, so he never really hesitated to write the book. And when the Concord, Massachusetts, Public

268

Library banned his book shortly after its publication, he was not surprised.

That was more than one hundred years ago, and conventional morality has certainly changed; so much so, in fact, that what the blue-nosed set in Concord found objectionable in 1885 would cause nary a stir today. The troika of bookbanning categories — political, religious, sexual — that has blanketed the field for so long would find no home for *The Adventures of Huckleberry Finn*.

But the book continues to be banned. In fact, since the late 1950s it has been condemned in a number of states and by a number of organizations. The reason is not one Mark Twain could have imagined.

To some, *The Adventures of Huckleberry Finn* is racist.

The first inklings came in New York City. In 1957, the National Association for the Advancement of Colored People brought pressure on a local high school to remove the book from its shelves. To those who sought answers from past bannings of the book, this challenge was unforeseen. For almost three-quarters of a century (and in this time the book had reached that zenith of literary longevity — the "classic") no one had muttered an objection like this.

Black author Ralph Ellison helped to explain: "Jim's friendship with Huck comes across as that of a boy for another boy rather than as the friendship of an adult for a junior; thus there is implicit in it not only a violation of the manners sanctioned for relations between Negroes and whites, there is a violation of our conception of adult maleness. . . ."

In short, *The Adventures of Huckleberry Finn* demeaned the stature of a black man, portrayed as something less than he actually was. This was racism because only the black man was singled out for this treatment and because the effect was to force the reader to lose respect for the character, not because of what he said or did, but because of his skin color.

This was a new approach to bookbanning. Usually, challenges to books galvanized from the Right where established ideas and doctrines had girded to fight off change-provoking threats. From the sputterings of the Colonial government in John Peter Zenger's 1734 case to the shouts of obscenity in Boston in the 1920s to the accusations of secular humanism in 1987 Alabama, the bookbanner had seemed to materialize from the conservative side of a controversy.

Now all of a sudden the bookbanner came from a different direction. The NAACP, and other groups which had joined them, were not mired in stereotypical value judgments. They desired change; in fact they were beginning to *insist* on change. They did not have an established political base to protect, nor were they concerned with the religious or sexual aspects of the book. They saw it in altogether different terms: as a slur upon their sense of being, and in this regard no conservative bookbanner could find quite so emphatic a likeness. Banning a book because it offends one's sensibilities is strong enough; but banning a book because it slurs one's very nature is something else again.

And so the people who thrive on categorizing things began to sift through this new bookbanning sortee. In the meantime *The Adventures of Huckleberry Finn* continued to be attacked, every year or two bringing a fresh challenge because of its perceived racist cast. And sometimes the attacks succeeded: in 1984, for example, the book was removed from a public high school reading list in Waukegan, Illinois, because a black alderman found the language offensive. By this time it was clear bookbanning was no longer the purview of the conservative right; those who sought equality and freedom from discrimination also felt the urge to bookban.

And from the categorizers came the word: a new bookbanning category was born.

Social issues, they called it.

And now there were four.

This one is less definable than the others, mainly because its victims pass across the behavioral and cultural spectrum. Its broader reach makes it more encompassing. Look at the trials of Raymond English who worked with an educational research organization some years ago as a writer for social science textbooks. As a political science professor he had publicly bemoaned the political ignorance of college freshmen, and he thought the problem lay in what these freshmen had been exposed to earlier in their academic lives. They had been reared on pap; they had not been forced to take a stand; they had absorbed light-hitting accounts which avoided controversy and offense. He wanted to change all that.

He and several others began work on a world history text, and for awhile things seemed to go well. They had their problems with religious depiction, at first, because of objections to differing accounts of the Reformation (the Catholics and Lutherans saw it one way, the Baptists another) but it seemed to work itself out. A little later there was a problem with political portrayals because the conservative right objected to certain economic designations (such as calling the U.S. a "mixed economy" and mentioning farm supports with some favor). But these objections, too, were worked out.

Then, in the 1970s Raymond English came face to face with a different, less malleable set of objections. Work on the history textbooks had continued, and suddenly there were new confrontations. First it was the Filipinos who objected to the account of the annexation of the Philippines at the end of the nineteenth century.

This must be rewritten, they demanded. You must show that the sugar interests in the United States controlled President McKinley and insisted he take over the islands in order to thwart the growing independence movement. It was not the product of imperialistic rivalries, as you suggest, they said.

No sooner did Raymond English and the other writers catch their breath, than it was the Zionists who came after them. You must change the text concerning the ethnic make-up of Palestine before 1947, they said. It was not predominantly Arab as you write (even though reliable statistics would have had it so). Better you remove any reference to population levels before 1947.

Then, before long, came still another complaint — this time from a state committee on ethnic and sex discrimination. You are wrong in your account of the rise of feminism, they declared. It did not begin in the 1860s and 70s with certain economic and technological advances (such as ready-made clothes and bulk canned food). It was not the fact that industrialization had made it easier for them to work outside the home. Instead, it was women's "character and self-assertion" that brought about their emancipation.

Finally, Raymond English and his group heard from a Japanese-American critic who objected to the portrayal of the Japanese-American in the history textbook. English had written that on a proportionate basis, there were more Japanese-Americans than any other ethnic group in executive and professional positions. Take this out! demanded the critic. It must come out!

But why? asked Raymond English.

"It reinforces the myth of success," came the answer. For this Japanese-American, at least, it was more important to remain modest and self-effacing, and he was willing to do it, even if it meant twisting the words in the text.

In these examples of "social issues" there are no political, religious or sexual overtones, but there certainly are sensibilities that appear offended. This is clearly a product of the last third of the twentieth century. People who find offense in the books they read grasp a ready outlet in bookbanning. Better to ban the book, they say, than to propagate the poison.

But, of course, the same argument was used in the 1920s in Boston and New York when obscenity was the dragon, and in the 1950s when communism was the monster and loyalty oaths were in flower, and throughout recorded history when orthodox religion faced the heretics. It is not enough to feel offense and simply turn away; one must act to save others. Here is where bookbanners on the left have joined bookbanners on the right in lockstep. Bookbanning becomes the only acceptable remedy.

Not too long ago in Toronto, Canada, William Golding's *Lord of the Flies* faced the fire. In the past this book had been challenged because of its political overtones and its cruel descriptions, but when it offended, it was for the familiar reasons prompting bookbanning.

Now, suddenly, a committee of the Toronto School Board ruled (after complaints by parents and members of the black community) that the book was "racist," that it must be removed without delay from all the schools. The reason? A reference to "niggers" and its general demeaning of black people. Interestingly, it was a Nobel Prize-winning author who was banned, not some obscure writer. The consequence has to follow: no one is safe from assuming that what didn't offend in one generation might continue not to offend in another generation. Certainly the Nobel Prize doesn't offer much protection.

Significantly, the bookbanning grew out of social issues. "Get rid of it!" shouted one committee member, and soon it was clear where the collective judgment lay.

When it came time to defend the book, no one spoke up.

And so William Golding's book (just as was William Faulkner's in Kentucky in 1986) was banned. While the reasons were different, the results were still the same.

At about this time, a similar case was being taken up in Amherst, Massachusetts. An eighth grade textbook. *History of the American Nation,* came under scrutiny. Three mothers found much to criticize in the way the book treated minorities — particularly blacks and Indians. These mothers did what most activists do — they organized a committee, they petitioned, they made statements, all in support of their view that the book had to go.

They even had their own expert, Professor Meyer Weinberg of the University of Massachusetts, who examined the book and offered a long list of objections, from the manner in which slavery was treated (without indignation or solid criticism) to the fact the word "racism" never appeared. The book is "distorted," the mothers' committee declared, "It's biased, filled with omissions. . . ."

Forty-one different objections, Professor Weinberg offered, forty-one different areas where the book didn't measure up. And the state of Massachusetts was listening, because they launched an inquiry, though in the end the book was retained.

But it was a close call.

Since the middle 1960s various groups and philosophies have grown more assertive as they have seen others acquire respectability, even deference, in the literary marketplace. It isn't only African Americans, or American Indians or Jews who have spoken out about their portrayals in books and films; it is the elderly who now complain about age-discrimination; the homosexuals who complain about anti-gay writing; the poor who complain about the "welfare" stereotype. The category may be new, but that doesn't change the remedy. Parents who are offended by sexually explicit materials in the schools seek the same thing as do gay men who see themselves victims of "gay-bashing."

Ban that book!

Initial reactions might seem most appropriate, at first. If a book treats us unfairly, if it denigrates us or demeans us because of our race, color, nationality, sex, age or sexual preference, there would seem little reason it should occupy shelf space. It is deeply offensive, and it serves no purpose other than to perpetuate long-held prejudices. Out it must go.

But . . . is there any more justification for censoring books than for censoring what offends us in the sexual or religious or political areas? The social-issues category may have developed a new area of potential harm and injury, but censorship, even though it might solve an immediate problem, may not be the answer.

No better arena for judging this exists than with feminism. As with other victims of discrimination, women have long pointed to certain books and authors as having treated them unfairly, unequally and with conscious disdain. It was only in 1964, with passage of the Civil Rights Act, that "sex" discrimination was declared illegal. It was a breakthrough on the federal level that enabled women to assert their right to equal treatment and equal opportunity, and it spurred an already burgeoning feminist movement. It blossomed just as the barriers to literary censorship seemed to come tumbling down, with decisions involving *Lady Chatterley's Lover, Memoirs of a Woman of Pleasure,* and *Tropic of Cancer* finally opening the door. We should be able to write whatever we want, and we should be able to *do* whatever we want. No discrimination, no censorship.

The problem was that these two freedoms seemed to go together, but actually, they didn't. There came a time when they headed right at one another, becoming adversaries.

The culprit was pornography, or more particularly, *sexually explicit material which subordinates women.* Feminists saw themselves as victims of this type of writing, and some could imagine no more appropriate solution than to have pornography banned.

Pornography *demeans us, it insults us, it puts us in an inferior position.* To certain feminists it violated women's civil rights because it perpetuated sex discrimination.

And *that* was a violation of the law.

Leading the fight were the radical feminists, and heading the charge were writer Andrea Dworkin and lawyer Catherine MacKinnon. Dworkin, a novelist, political pamphleteer and harshly critical essayist, believed that pornography created "bigotry and hostility and aggression toward all women," and that it only served to confirm the fact that "[t]he hurting of women is . . . basic to the sexual pleasure of men." For her the idea of using the obscenity laws to ban pornography could never work because the "community standards" yardstick also includes ubiquitous sentiments approving violence against women. Instead, pornography had to be recognized as a pernicious form of sex discrimination . . . and then it could be controlled by the civil rights laws.

And the only effective remedy she saw was for the civil rights laws to ban pornography altogether, as they did racism.

Dworkin and MacKinnon drafted a model ordinance and proposed it to city councils in Minneapolis and Indianapolis and Bellingham, Washington. The legislation would have allowed a woman who believed herself victimized by pornography to sue bookstore owners for civil damages, and, of course, to have the offending books removed from the shelves. It was not a complicated ordinance:

". . . Pornography is the sexually explicit subordination of women, graphically depicted whether in pictures or words . . . "

It then listed nine separate situations where this might happen, including when:

". . . women are presented as dehumanized sexual objects, things or commodities . . ."

The ordinance specifically stated that even if a woman had given her consent to this depiction it was no defense. It was irrelevant because consent under these circumstances is a sham. The male had total control and power.

These were hard-hitting proposals, but Dworkin and

MacKinnon almost succeeded. In Minneapolis the legislation passed twice, only to be vetoed by the Mayor; in Indianapolis, it was passed and signed, only to be challenged and overturned in court; in Bellingham, Washington, it had added support from writers Susan Brownmiller and Gloria Steinem, but a court proceeding brought everything to a halt.

A troubling question surfaced early: did Dworkin and MacKinnon speak for the feminist movement when they urged banning of pornographic material? The answer came quickly, and it was a resounding NO! Feminists, generally, had little use for books and stories which extolled violence, and they were quick to criticize material which tended to dehumanize women and to turn them into sex objects.

But ban such books and stories? For many feminists the cure was worse than the disease. As one feminist newsletter stated: "These [banning] laws can be used to attack and limit feminist self-expression, including women's writing about sexuality, abortion, birth control and medical self-help. Once these laws are on the books, feminists have minimal control over their interpretation and enforcement by the courts."

To these anti-bookbanning feminists the question of what really constituted "pornography" was unsettling because of its vagueness. If "sexually explicit" was used as a standard, then there were bound to be those who saw this as simple erotica and not pornography; if "sexual submission or subordination" was used, then some would see submission or subordination where others didn't, and some might even see the woman in control. Uncertainty like this could have only one result: bookbanning was not the answer.

But the voices of censorship in the feminist movement are not stilled, and there remains a wellspring of feeling that pornography is best done away with completely, that its degradation of women has canceled its right to protection under the First Amendment's guarantees of free expression. As a social issue in the realm of bookbanning, it will not go away. But for the moment, anyway, feminists who seek to continue the bookbanning battle will have to contend with the forceful logic of Federal Judge Sarah Barker who overturned the Indianapolis ordinance, after it had been passed and signed into law:

"To deny free speech in order to engineer social change in the name of accomplishing a greater good for one sector of our society erodes the freedoms of all and, as such, threatens tyranny and injustice for those subjected to the rule of such laws."

In this final third of the twentieth century we've experienced a widening of sensibilities when it comes to offensive literature, and we've seen that the traditional triumvirate of categories of censorship — political, religious and sexual — is too limited for what is being and has been written, read and judged. Now we get a glimmer of what it must be like to feel discrimination, now we sense the anger it generates and the pervasiveness with which it might be found. We've watched — or participated — as minorities and women have achieved some successes in their long fights against discrimination and denigration, and we've seen them point to specific books and authors as culprits and antagonists in the arduous struggle.

Treat us equally, they say; don't think of us in the old way. We demand the opportunity.

Has it worked? Since the mid-1960s, there has been a blossoming of minority and feminist writing; it has moved forward alongside, though not in concert with, the bookbanning demands. Where a book doesn't degrade, the tendency can be to uplift, yet the evidence of current success in minority and feminist writing is not so easily found. In fact, it may be a long time coming.

We need look no further than a 1989 survey of 500 public, Roman Catholic and private nonsectarian high schools, asking: *What books do you read in your school? What's required, what's not?* The answers showed two things: only one of the ten most-read authors was a woman, and not one of these authors was a member of a minority. Shakespeare was by far the most popular author, with Nathaniel Hawthorne's *The Scarlet Letter,* F. Scott Fitzgerald's *The Great Gatsby* and William Golding's *Lord of the Flies* read in more than half the schools. In addition, and ironically, Mark Twain's *The Adventures of Huckleberry Finn* (carrying its latest designation as "racist") was also high on the list. In terms of late-twentieth-century social issues, the conclusion is inescapable that book and author choices haven't been heard by those who prescribe the reading menu in our schools, and if the schools aren't listening, what does that mean for the culture as a whole? If women and minorities are not given equal time during the formative years, their complaints may well be treated less seriously later on.

Which, or course, would mean that their books would continue to be overlooked.

The fact is that the results of this survey (which was funded by the Center for the Learning and Teaching of Literature at the State University of New York) are almost identical with an earlier survey done twenty-five years before, and another done more than eighty years ago! "In all the settings which we examined," the study states, "the lists of most frequently required books and authors were dominated by white males, with little change in overall balance from similar lists twenty-five or eighty years ago."

If we look at the past quarter of a century and at the concerted efforts in the schools to urge the reading of writing by women and minority authors, the survey results are disquieting because they indicate that there is a strong institutional bias in favor of the status quo. Under these circumstances, it's not hard to have sympathy with those who see themselves at a cultural dead end.

Ban that book! might be their frustrated response.

The wise person, however, would remember that bookbanning only perpetuates the negative message, making it more pervasive, more solidly entrenched.

Educate yourself! the wise person urges. *Learn from our differences . . .*

And then respect us!

19

We Writers

Some years ago a mystery-suspense writer complained that his book was being challenged by a conservative religious group.

"It's a parody, for God's sake. Where's their sense of humor?"

The book concerned the shenanigans of fundamentalist Christians who attempt to compete in the wordly arena of real-estate development. They get involved in murder, drug smuggling and assorted lesser crimes, finding justification easier and easier. No one survives the story without a tarnished halo.

"They're calling it blasphemous," the writer said. "My book that took me over a year to write!" He shook his head. "Don't they realize the work I've put in?"

I could have reminded him—as others have reminded me—that controversy like this is what most publishers and writers welcome. Calling attention to a book, negatively or positively, is the surest road to greater royalties, but then I'm sure he knew that. What bothered him was that the people who wanted to ban his book never thought to consider *his* sensibilities. This was a serious writer who had written a serious book, and it deserved a more respectable fate.

What this writer felt was the same anguish a host feels when an elaborate dinner party degenerates into food-throwing: insult. What the writer offered had been dismissed; it had been kicked into an ash heap.

Bookbanning insults writers. It pays no homage to what the writer has had to endure in order to produce his book. In a society where what we do often portrays who we are, a writer whose book is banned has a certain blemish, no matter how many supporters there might be. He or she is "controversial." While some may thrive on this notoriety, many would gladly give it up if their book would be circulated.

That is the burden the writer must carry, because the insult of bookbanning is forever. The only choice for the writer is to denounce the banning publicly, and have it rescinded (if possible) or take steps to prevent its happening again. No such moves can — or will — fully atone for the insult. The writer must carry it like a part of his or her anatomy, a blemish that won't come out. It has to affect future work . . . should I leave this paragraph out? Maybe I'd better not do the book this way!

Writers have had to endure substantial agony at the hands of bookbanners, insults that became challenges to their essential notions of propriety. If a writer has to justify what he wrote, the insult is in the lack of faith in the writer's purpose. Here's James T. Farrell, author of *The Studs Lonigan Trilogy,* on the witness stand in Philadelphia in 1948. Were his books obscene? The prosecutor tried to paint them so:

> Q: . . . With this beating of the girl, and her screams, the kicking her here and punching her there; that is described in great detail in your book on Page 347 of the *Young Manhood of Studs Lonigan.* Would you say this sadism is more in the author or in the character?
>
> A: Why, of course, it isn't in me. Why do you think it is?
>
> Q: You wrote this part out at great length, covering page after page, about everything that is done to each one of these girls . . . You have the girl trying to jump out of a window because she has been raped, and you finish it with this other one.
>
> A: . . . Now, the mere directness of the presentation should cause you not to have the kind of thoughts implied in the questions asked me, but it should cause you to be revolted and repulsed, you should be shocked by it; those things shock me.

Insults like these are what every writer contends with because bookbanners have little concern for the effort and the careful planning that produces a book. They see only the effect, and they can't imagine true purpose in how the words are arrayed on the page. The prosecutor shot back at James T. Farrell the cynical rejoinder so many book-banners use:

> "They did not shock you, Mr. Farrell, so much but that you can put them on paper and get a good royalty out of it, did they?"

Once in a while writers do fight back, and because the creative mind is — well — creative, some ludicrous things can happen. In the early 1940s Henry Miller was living frugally in France, wondering if he would ever be published in the United States. For ten years his work sold in Europe, but not a word of it appeared here. The taboo, he claimed, was in a handful of words which people used in daily speech, but which never appeared in an English-language book. So he wrote an open letter to the *New Republic* where he emphasized the fullness of dedication to his art and that only in matters of daily living would he consider making a compromise.

Henry Miller needed money, so he made an offer: "I do not pretend to be a painter . . . " he wrote. "But I like to paint, and I like to think that whatever an artist does by way of avocation is interesting and perhaps revelatory." Miller proposed to sell some paintings he had done, though he was at a loss to estimate their value. "I offer them with the understanding that the buyer may name his own price . . . Anyone wishing to encourage the watercolor mania would do well to send me paper, brushes and tubes, of which I am always in need."

Miller wasn't finished with his begging. "I would also be grateful for old clothes," he wrote, giving his sizes. "Love corduroys," he added.

Henry Miller had a devilish humor, and there was the possibility that he postured in order to needle the censors. But later writings have shown that Miller did indeed suffer through a bare existence in Paris, so the question isn't really whether he was telling the truth but to what level a writer can be shoved because his books have been banned. Miller's creative spirit was insulted by the censors because they had no respect for his efforts to produce something. His labor was valueless to them, and this, in turn, meant his human dignity was worthless.

From the writer's point of view it is an insult stemming from ignorance, but it is an insult, nevertheless. The writer — in this case Henry Miller — cannot achieve appropriate satisfaction through his art, and so he must beg for old clothes. His immediate wants may be satisfied, but the insult never fades. There can be no satisfaction.

Motive is often a key. Jean Auel received a letter from a librarian in a small Texas town relating a controversy concerning *The Valley of the Horses,* one of her books. Some thought it obscene, and had consulted the local district attorney. The librarian wanted a word from the author: "Would you mind writing a letter [to the library board of directors] stating the research that has been involved in writing the book, and your intention when you wrote the book . . . ?"

Here again an insult. Jean Auel was asked to disprove a negative *show us why your book is not obscene!* The presumption is just the opposite: obscene until proven otherwise. It is a turnaround on our ages-old concept of innocence until shown to be guilty. The librarian demonstrated bad judgment, but the real culprits were those who wanted to censor Jean Auel.

Writers know that bookbanners treat the reasons why something was written as coloration for the words themselves. It is not an unreliable formula, and most writers would say that their words do reflect their motive — at least to some degree. But what if the writer sets out to produce something beautiful, and somehow his words end up by offending? Should the writer be judged by his motive or by his words or both?

In 1959, in Montreal, police seized copies of D.H. Lawrence's *Lady Chatterley's Lover* on the grounds of obscenity. (At this time it was also barred from the United States.) There was no question the book depicted sexual conduct in graphic manner, but the defense contended that this did not make it obscene. The prosecutor, however, felt the author's motive was crucial, and if he could establish obscene purpose, he was sure the book would be kept out of Canada. On the witness stand under cross-examination was M. Hugh MacLennan, a well-known Canadian writer.

"In your own books," asked the prosecutor, "have you given a description of the sex act such as those we find in *Lady Chatterley's Lover?*"

"At no time have I used such language," answered MacLennan. "No."

"Would you?"

Here, MacLennan did fall into the trap. "If necessary for the subject about which I was writing," he responded.

Motive and language working together. But a little later MacLennan extracted himself and showed why the formula isn't reliable.

Q: Would you give such a book to children 15, 16, 17 years of age?

A: If they wanted to read it, yes.

Q:You would?

A: Yes. I wouldn't impose it on them, but if they asked me for it, I'd say Yes, certainly.

Q: What would be, in your opinion the goal Lawrence wished to attain when he wrote the book?

A: He said this very well himself. His goal, his

objective, I think, was this—there is no doubt about it—he repeated it often: to show people that the sex act is proper and natural instead of dirty and sinful. That's the aim he had in mind.

What D.H. Lawrence wanted to do was to write a beautiful book, not a tawdry, lubricious sex manual. Yet the *way* he wrote it was enough for the Canadian prosecutor to challenge his motive. Bookbanners see nothing wrong in this, but the consequence has to be to restrict creativity. Most serious writers feel that the effect their book generates is the true measure of success; not everyone will feel the same way about a book, nor should they. As long as it moves people—pushes them positively or negatively—the writer has achieved something, and the question of why he or she wrote the book is immaterial. But once motive is tied to language, limits will apply, and these limits fit neatly with how the bookbanner views the world of books.

It took three years before *Lady Chatterley's Lover* could be published in Canada. The trial court found it obscene, and it was only through appeal to the Canadian Supreme Court that the book prevailed. But it was not a resounding victory. The court split in the book's favor 5 to 4.

The effects of bookbanning on writers is sometimes subtle, sometimes vivid. But always it is sad, because writers sense the manipulation and have little recourse, except after the fact in a public forum such as a courtroom or hearing or publication. In the privacy of their writing space, writers face the dragon of censorship much more directly because they are alone, and they have pieces of a manuscript before them. Decisions must be made, and the work must go on, yet how safe will it be to write this, portray that, describe her, dramatize that, characterize him . . . ? Susan Sontag, in a speech following the vilification of Salman Rushdie by the Ayatollah Khomeni, said that the real evil from such censorship is the story not written, the paragraph omitted, the sentence changed in order to pacify the bookbanners. In the privacy of their own world, writers might be excused in justifying some censorship—when their necks could be on the line.

Or for other reasons. In the late 1980s Mark West interviewed a number of children's-book authors and asked them about their clashes with bookbanners. Here's what some of them said:

Judy Blume: in her book *Tiger Eyes* she describes her protagonist masturbating. "There was just one line in the book, but my publishers said it would make the book controversial and limit the book's audience. I took it out but I wish I hadn't."

Harry Mazer: ". . . I write today with an awareness and, yes, a caution that wasn't there when I began writing. I've become 'inventive' in my use of language, finding other ways of saying what may be challenged."

Daniel Keyes: "You are at your writing desk, and you are about to use a certain word—when suddenly your fingers start to tremble. And you ask yourself, 'Do I really need to use that word?' This is where the young writer is more likely to be frightened into compromise than the well-established writer, but even the established writers are feeling the pressure."

While writers understand that caution may nullify bookbanning challenges, they also understand that the final product may be less than they had hoped for. As they seek to offend, what comes out may be pablum or inoffensive garnish instead of wild pepper or garlic spice. For the honest writer it is one more insult: he or she cannot develop what creative instincts tell them they must develop.

It's enough to be consumed with fury—which is precisely what Canadian poet Crad Kilodney felt in 1984 when Perrin Beatty, Canada's Minister of National Revenue, decided to censor certain books, periodicals and films that were to be imported into Canada. "Now is the time to put to death Revenue Minister Perrin Beatty," Kilodney publicly declared. Several major magazines published his horrific wish-list:

"Sink an axe into the back of Revenue Minister Perrin Beatty.

"Cut off the arms and legs of Revenue Minister Perrin Beatty.

"Shoot Perrin Beatty in the head as soon as you can

"Take jack handle, sledgehammer, or mace and smash in the face of Canada's minister of revenue and customs . . .

"Put cyanide crystals in the cigar of Perrin Beatty . . .

"Connect dynamite to the ignition switch of an automobile owned by the minister of revenue and customs . . .

"Train Doberman pinschers to tear him to pieces.

"Put his head in a vice and crush it.

"Lock him in a freezer . . .

"Hang, guillotine or draw and quarter Revenue Minister Perrin Beatty . . .

"Accuse him, in Iran, of adultery, drug smuggling or blasphemy . . ."

All together, there were thirty-nine creative — and torture-filled — deaths that Crad Kilodney had laid out for Revenue Minister Perrin Beatty. "Do your part *today — this very hour —*" he urged, "so that our children, grandchildren and dogs may live in a saner, healthier and happier world."

In the end, however, it is the insult of bookbanning that singles out writers especially. It goes to the root of our self-image. *How dare you*! we want to shout. It's our language too, and what we do with it is our business. You don't have to read us, but don't tell us what we shall and shall not write. Learn the lessons of history that bookbanning in America does not work, that the more it is attempted, the more it is denounced.

Understand us. We are not your enemies.

Afterword

Fortunately, we writers are not alone in the bookbanning battle, and when the fury dissolves, most of us will acknowledge that. When a book is challenged, the bookstore owner, the librarian and the publisher suffer too. Threats to the written word make allies of us, even where the ages-old battle of art versus commerce rages among us. When it comes to bookbanning, survival is at stake for us all.

People in the book trade understand this vividly, as an open letter to American readers spelled out in April, 1990, when it appeared in twenty-eight daily newspapers. Signed by Ed Morrow, president of the American Booksellers Association, and Harry Hoffman, president of Walden Book Co., Inc., the letter stated in part:

> *We believe attempts to censor ideas to which we have access —*
> *whether in books, magazines, plays, works of art, television,*

movies or song—are not simply isolated instances of harass-
ment by diverse special-interest groups. Rather they are part of
a growing pattern of increasing intolerance which is changing
the fabric of America . . .

Censorship cannot eliminate evil. It can only kill freedom.
We believe Americans have the right to buy, stores have the
right to sell, authors have the right to write and publishers
have the right to publish Constitutionally-protected material.
Period.

More than seventy-five thousand Americans clipped a
vote of approval at the end of the letter and returned it,
showing their support. It was a remarkable display of
common interest, and most encouraging. However, none
of us—writers, publishers librarians, booksellers—are
lulled by this one-time outpouring. We know bookbanning in America is a hardy virus and that if it is not
confronted consistently it will continue to spread.

Source Notes

These notes are meant to highlight some of the more dramatic quotes and references in the text, but they are not all-inclusive. In fact, they represent only a minor portion of all the published material I used. They seem, however, most appropriately placed here and in this manner. A more extensive bibliography can be found further on.

Chapter One, *pages 3 to 43*

"This was the American Dream . . ." was the opening of an essay, "On Privacy," that appeared in *Harper's Magazine*, July, 1955.

"I got a job in the power plant . . . ," on page 6, appeared in the introduction to Faulker's *Sanctuary* (New York: Modern Library, 1932) at p. vii.

"These are people that I have known . . . ," on page 12, was Faulkner's response to a question about where he got the idea for *As I Lay Dying*. It was recorded in *Faulkner at West Point,* Joseph L. Fant, and Robert Ashley, editors (New York: Random House, 1964), at pages 96–97.

On pages 17–20, the comments by Jerald Ellington and Delora English are from page 1 of the *Mayfield Messenger,* September 5, 1986; the comments by Jeff Howard and Bob Spaulding are from the *Paducah Sun* of September 5, 1986; Suzanne Post was also quoted in the *Paducah Sun* on the same date.

Faulkner's words on page 20, "If there is a villain . . . ," are from class conferences at the University of Virginia, 1957–1958, *Faulkner In the University,* Frederick L. Gwynn and Joseph L. Blotner, editors (Charlottesville, Virginia: University of Virginia Press, 1959), page 112.

Suzanne Post's comments on pages 27–28 are quoted in the *Mayfield Messenger* of September 10, 1986, on page 1.

The text of the Graves County [Kentucky] Baptist Association letter on page 27–28 can be found in the *Record of Board Proceedings* of the Graves County High School for September 11, 1986.

The comments of Suzanne Post and Billy Watkins on pages 30–32 appeared in the *Paducah Sun,* September 11, 1986.

I'm indebted to Dan Sharp for his recollection of what was said at the school board's closed session, appearing on page 29.

Billy Watkins' words at pages 30–31 are a part of the *Record of Board Proceedings* of the Graves County High School for September 11, 1986.

"God didn't merely believe in man . . ." on page 31 is from an address Faulkner gave to the graduating class at Pine Manor Junior College, Wellesley, Massachusetts, on June 8, 1953. It can be found in *Essays, Speeches and Public Letters by William Faulkner*, ed. James B. Meriwether (New York: Random House, 1965) at page 136.

Andrew Goodman's remarks on page 34 are from the *Mayfield Messenger*, September 12, 1986, page 12.

The comments by Terry Sims and Ronnie Stinson, as well as those by Jeff Howard and Dan Sharp, on pages 34–35 are quoted from the *Paducah Sun*, September 12, 1986.

"I took this family . . ." on page 39 is from *Faulkner in the University*, page 87.

On pages 40–42, Billy Watkins' words, "Since there is a board-approved policy . . ." are part of the *Record of Board Proceedings* of the Graves County High School, September 18, 1986; Robert Spaulding's comments and Jeff Howard's comments are included here, too.

"What threatens us today . . ." was part of a speech Faulkner gave to the graduating class of University High School, Oxford, Mississippi, May 28, 1951. It can be found in *Essays, Speeches and Public Letters by William Faulkner*, pages 122–123.

Chapter Two, *pages 46 to 57*

A narrative summary of this story appears in *John Peter Zenger and the Freedom of the Press*, published by the University of the State of New York, The State Education Department, the New York State Library, Albany, New York, 1985.

The full text of page one of Zenger's newspaper referred to on page 48 can be found in "The Case of John Peter Zenger" by Lincoln Barnett, *American Heritage Magazine*, December, 1971, at page 34; further quotes from the second and third issues of the newspaper appearing on page 49 can be found in the article at page 37.

Throughout this chapter there will be quotes from the trial proceedings, and these can be found in *A Brief Narrative of the Case and Trial of John Peter Zenger,* by James Alexander, ed. Stanley Nider Katz (Cambridge, MA: Belknap Press of Harvard University, 1963).

The quotes on page 49 from the January 28th and April 8th, 1734 issues of the *New York Weekly Journal* can be found in *American Heritage* at page 39.

"All the high things . . ." and succeeding portions of Andrew Hamilton's final argument on pages 53–55 appear in *A Brief Narrative of the Case,* pages 79–100.

The comment by Justice Brennan at page 57, "Although the sedition act . . . ," appeared in *U.S. v. Sullivan,* 376 U.S. 254 (1964) at page 276.

The John Peter Zenger Award described on page 57 was mentioned in a release from the Playboy Foundation, July 10, 1988, announcing the judges for the 1988 Hugh M. Heffner First Amendment Awards.

Chapter Three, *pages 59 to 69*

The text of Peter Holmes' indictment on pages 59–60 is set out immediately before the opinion in *Commonwealth of Massachusetts v. Holmes,* 17 Mass. 335 (1821) at page 335.

A description of life in the Fleet on pages 60–61 can be found in William Epstein's *John Cleland: Images of a Life* (New York: Columbia University Press, 1974) pages 162–163.

"Madam . . . Hating, as I mortally do . . ." on page 62 is the opening text of *The Memoirs of Fanny Hill* (New York: New American Library, 1964), page 15.

The "G Fenton" in the advertisement on page 63 was the *nom de publishing* of Fenton Griffiths.

For an item-by-item comparison of the indictments in the Sharpless case and the Holmes case mentioned on page 64, see *Literature, Obscenity and the Law* by Felice Flannery Lewis (Carbondale: Southern Illinois University Press, Illinois 1976) at page 5.

The words of Judge Isaac Parker on pages 65–66 are from *Commonwealth of Massachusetts v. Holmes,* 17 Mass. 335 (1821) at page 336.

". . . utterly without redeeming value . . ." on page 67 is quoted from the U.S. Supreme Court opinion, *Memoirs v. Massachusetts,* 383 U.S. 413 (1966) at page 418.

Chapter Four, *pages 69 to 83*

"Resolved that the doctrine . . ." appearing on page 70, and all succeeding quotes through page 81 from the floor of the House of Representatives are in the *Congressional Globe,* 1st Session, 36th Congress, December 5, 6, 1859, pages 4–22.

"It is a greater sacrifice of moral . . ." on page 72 appears in Hinton Rowan Helper's *The Land of Gold Versus Fiction* (Baltimore, 1855).

"Of you, the introducers . . ." and other quotes from Helper's book on pages 73–74 can be found in *The Impending Crisis in the South — How to Meet It* (New York: Collier Books, 1963) at pages 113, 114, 124, 130, 159–160.

The development of the compendium idea on page 76 can be found in *Hinton Rowan Helper: Abolitionist–Racist* by Hugh C. Bailey (Tuscaloosa, AL: University of Alabama Press, 1965), pages 43–44.

"Nothing has made . . ." on page 82 are the words of Senator William Bigler written to Robert Tyler, December 16, 1859, *History of the United States From the Compromise of 1850*, Vol. II, by James F. Rhodes (New York: Mac-Millan and Co., 1910), page 427.

"For weeks and months . . ." on page 82 is quoted from the *New York Daily Herald*, November 26, 1859.

Chapter Five, *pages 83 to 95*

"We want this book suppressed . . ." on page 84 appeared in the *Boston Herald*, April 17, 1929, page 1; a general description of the revels in Ford Hall, as well as all quotes from that evening, can be found in the *Herald*, April 17, pages 1–2; April 18, pages 1 and 3; April 19, page 3.

For background on the events described on pages 84–95, see *Purity in Print: the Vice-Society Movement and Book Censorship in America*, by Paul S. Boyer (New York: Scribner's, 1968), pages 167–206.

"Was [your book] founded . . ." on page 93 and other testimony on pages 93–94 can be found in the *Boston Herald*, April 17, 1929, at page 4.

The Dunster House Bookshop case mentioned on pages 94–95 is fully described in *Purity in Print* at pages 196–199.

Chapter Six, *pages 96 to 106*

A thorough analysis of *Ulysses*, as well as its impact on literature in general, can be found in *Ulysses on the Liffey*, by Richard Ellman (New York: Oxford University Press, 1972).

The story of James Joyce and the *Little Review* on pages 97–98 is in *James Joyce*, by Richard Ellman (New York: Oxford University Press, 1959), pages 517–519.

John Sumner and his battles against books set out in

this chapter are fully discussed in *Purity in Print,* pages 48–143.

The life of Anthony Comstock and the history of the New York Society for the Suppression of Vice, on pages 98–100, can be found in *Comstockery in America: Patterns of Censorship and Control,* by Robert W. Haney (New York: Da Capo Press, 1974).

"The golden oak furnishings . . ." on page 101 is in *Purity in Print,* page 138.

The full text of James Joyce's letter to Bennett Cerf on page 103 can be found in the American edition of *Ulysses,* published by Random House, New York, in 1934, pages xv–xvii.

Nora Joyce's modelling for Molly Bloom, mentioned on page 103, is discussed in Brenda Maddox's biography *Nora: the Real Life of Molly Bloom* (Boston: Houghton Mifflin, 1988).

Quotes from the trial on pages 104–105 are in *Censorship: The Search for the Obscene* by Morris Ernst and Alan U. Schwartz (New York: MacMillan and Co., 1964) pages 94–96.

The U.S. District Court opinion quoted on page 105 is reported in *U.S. v. One Book Called Ulysses,* 5 Fed. Supp. 182 (S.D. U.Y. 1933).

Senator Reed Smoot's quote on page 106 can be found in *Books and Battles: American Literature 1920–1930* by Irene and Allen Cleaton (Boston: Houghton Mifflin, 1937) at page 62.

The current *Ulysses* debate on page 106 is described in the *Burlington (Vt.) Free Press,* May 7, 1989, at page 5D.

Chapter Seven, *pages 107 to 118*
The interview quotes on pages 108, 109, 110, 111, and

112 appear in *Hearings before the Subcommittee on Oversight of the Permanent Select Committee on Intelligence,* Ninety-Sixth Congress, 2nd session, March 6, 1980, at pages 25–26.

The full text of the Morrison letter appearing on page 109 can be found in *Hearings before the Oversight Committee* at page 23.

"There clearly has . . . ," Stansfield Turner's testimony on page 114, appears in the trial court opinion *U.S. v. Frank W. Snepp,* 456 Fed. Supp. 176 (E.D. Alexandria, Va., 1978), at pages 179–180.

The U.S. Supreme Court opinion referred to on page 115 is *Snepp v. U.S.,* 444 U.S. 507 (1980).

"Do you know specifically . . . ," the testimony of Les Aspin and Herbert Hetu appearing on page 116, is in *Hearings before the Oversight Committee* at page 29.

The story of Frank Snepp's latest difficulties with CIA on page 117 can be found in the Brief for Appellant, *U.S. v. Frank W. Snepp III,* No. 89–2951, 4th Circuit Court of Appeals, at pages 6–13.

Chapter Eight, *pages 119 to 130*

Gene Lanier's work on behalf of intellectual freedom and some of the incidents of censorship in North Carolina described on pages 119–122 can be found in *The Northhampton News,* Jackson, North Carolina, November 24, 1982, pages 1 and 3.

A Book is Easier to Burn than to Explain on page 121 appears repeatedly in Gene Lanier's public statements, even when he is out of the state of North Carolina. See, for example, the *Bangor (Me.) Daily News,* May 19, 1986, page 1.

"Imagine the thoughts . . ." on page 121 is quoted in *The Northhampton News,* November 24, 1982, page 1.

Mention of Gene Lanier winning the Hugh Heffner First Amendment Award on page 122 appears in the Daily Herald, Roanoke Rapids, North Carolina, May 5, 1982, at page 1.

"When they came and took away the Jews . . ." quoted on page 124 appears in *Texas Library Journal,* Summer, 1989, page 56.

"If you don't have an adversary–hearing process . . ." on page 126 is a quote from Thomas L. Tedford, Professor of Comunication, University of North Carolina at Greensboro, and appears in the *Winston-Salem Sentinel,* August 18, 1982, in Art Eisenstadt's column "Politics and Politicians."

The New York Times article, "Libraries Are Asked by FBI to Report on Foreign Agents," mentioned on page 129 appeared September 18, 1987.

For background on the "Library Awareness Program: described on pages 128–130, see *Hearings Before the Subcommittee on Civil and Constitutional Rights of the Committee on the Judiciary,* House of Representatives, One-Hundreth Congress, 2nd Session, June 20, July 23, 1988.

Chapter Nine, *pages 131–142*

For a description of Judge Hand's attitude on pages 135–136, see "Courtroom Clash Over Textbooks" by Ezra Bowen, *Time Magazine,* October 27, 1986, page 94.

All quotes from the trial are found in the court transcript of *Smith v. Board of School Commissioners of Mobile County, Alabama,* 655 Fed. Supp. 939 (S.D. Alabama, 1987), transcript pages 22, 32–33, 44–45, 48–49, 55, 95, 440, 1359–1360, 1402–1403.

"Just as you make mistakes . . ." on page 133 appears

in *Liberty Denied: The Current Rise of Censorship in America* by Donna Demac (PEN American Center, 1988) at page 16.

Judge Hand's decision and footnote in the case against Ismael Jaffree on page 134 can be found in *Jaffree v. Board of School Commissioners of Mobile County, Alabama,* 554 Fed. Supp. 1104 (S.D. Alabama, 1982) at page 1129; the Supreme Court decision is 472 U.S. 38 (1984).

"A godless religion . . ." quoted on page 134 is from James Kilpatrick's column of February 19, 1986, in the *News and Daily Advance* of Lynchburg, Virginia.

For information on the attorneys appearing on pages 135–136, see "Backgrounds of Humanism Lawyers Tell America's Story" by Michael Jennings in *Birmingham (Ala.) News* of October 21, 1986.

"Do you think . . ." and Pat Robertson's response on pages 137--138; are quoted from the *700 Club* broadcast of March 4, 1986, on the Christian Broadcasting Network.

"Why I Worship" and the quotes from it on page 139 can be found in the *Huntsville (Ala.) Times* of October 5, 1986.

Judge Hand's decision on page 141 is in 655 Fed. Supp. 939 (S.D. Ala. 1987); the appeal can be found in 827 F. 2nd 747 (11th Circuit, 1987).

Chapter Ten, *pages 144 to 157*

The anecdote on pages 144–146 was provided on condition names and locale were changed. The events and the quotes from "Peggy" are real.

"It's not words . . ." on page 146 is found in *The Fear of the Word* by Eli M. Oboler (Metuchen, N.J.: Scarecrow Press, 1974) at page 31.

Gerald Haslam's remembrances and the quotes therefrom appearing on pages 146–148 can be found in "That Filthy Book" in *This World,* April 9, 1989, at pages 10 to 12.

The quotes from Norma Klein (pages 148), Betty Miles (pages 149–150), Daniel Keyes (page 151) appear in *Trust Your Children: Voices Against Censorship in Children's Literature* ed. Mark I. West (New York: Neal Schumann, 1988) at pages 25, 45, 47, 83.

"They are convinced . . ." on page 153 is from *The Schoolbook Protest Movement, 40 Questions and Answers* (Bloomington, Indiana: Phi Delta Kappa Educational Foundation, 1986) at pages 12–13.

Chapter Eleven, *pages 158–175*

The incident at Farmington High School on pages 161–162 is described in "A Plague of Censors," *Progressive Magazine,* July, 1986, at page 9.

For background on bowdlerism and its influence over Shakespearean text appearing on pages 162–164, see *Dr. Bowdler's Legacy* by Noel Perrin (New York: Atheneum, 1969; the excerpt from *Hamlet* on pages 162–163 is from *Battle of the Books* by Lee Burress (Metuchen, N.J.: Scarecrow Press, 1989) at page 94.

"I really did not think . . ." on page 164 is from *Trust Your Children* at page 105.

The statement by Simon and Schuster on page 167 and the publishing background on *Personal Fouls* are found in "Publisher Cancels Book on N.C. State" by Robert McG. Thomas, Jr., *New York Times,* February 23, 1989.

"They were asked to look . . ." on pages 167–168 and the work of the university-wide panel appear in "Panel Broadens Probe of NCSU Basketball Program" by Liz

Clarke and John Day, *Raliegh News and Observer,* April 6, 1989.

"This university over the years . . ." on page 169 appears in "Backing For Valvano," *New York Times,* October 1, 1989.

The story behind *Katherine the Great* and the tale of the Bingham family appearing on pages 169–171 is in *Liberty Denied* at page 69; for more on *Katherine the Great,* see "Censorship in Publishing" by L. Lamb, *Utne Reader,* January/February, 1988, page 17.

For background on Barney Rosset, see "The Bustling Days and Rum-and-Coke Nights of Barney Rosset" in *Seven Days Magazine,* September, 1989, at page 18.

Chapter Twelve, *pages 176 to 191*

The remark by Beverly LaHay on page 176 was made November 4, 1989, to a closed circuit television feed and was part of Concerned Women for America's 10th Anniversary Celebration Conference in Washington D.C.

Robert Simonds quote on pages 176–177 is from a radio show, "Point of View," hosted by Marlin Maddoux and produced by International Christian Media and aired August 29, 1989.

The dialogue between Pat Robertson and Billy Falling on page 177 is from the *700 Club* television show of April 9, 1986, aired by the Christian Broadcasting Network.

"Nearly all of the schoolbook protests . . ." on page 178 is from *The Schoolbook Protest Movement: 40 Questions and Answers,* pages 12–13.

For background on Mel and Norma Gabler, see *The Schoolbook Protest Movement: 40 Questions and Answers,* pages 55–60. Note, too, the Gablers' influence in the 1982 bookbanning furor in Tell City, Indiana, at pages 89–90; the Gablers' quotes on page 181 are at pages 55–57.

"The list is endless . . ." on page 183 is from "The Phyllis Schlafly Report," February, 1983.

The *Stop Textbook Censorship Committee* mentioned on page 184 has had several chairpersons and addresses, but it can be contacted through the Eagle Forum, Box 618, Alton, Illinois 62002.

For background on Beverly LaHay and Concerned Women for America on pages 184–188, see "A Spokeslady of the Right," by Mary T. Schimich, *Chicago Tribune,* March 23, 1986.

"The sad fact is . . ." on page 185 is from *Concerned Women for America Magazine,* October, 1989, page 3.

"This reminded me once again . . ." on page 186 is from *Concerned Women for America Magazine,* July, 1989, page 3.

The trial court's opinion and the appeal in the Tennessee case on pages 187–188 is *Mozert v. Hawkins County School System,* 579 Fed. Supp. 1051 (E.D. Tenn. 1984), *reversed* 765 F. 2nd 75 (6th Circuit, 1986).

For a thorough background on Robert Simonds and his National Association of Christian Educators on pages 188–190 see "Holy Wars in Education" by James C. Schott, *Educational Leadership,* October, 1989, pages 61–66; the quote "the children of our nation . . ." appears on page 61.

"There is a great war being waged . . ." and "The combatants are . . ." on page 189 can be found in the teacher's manual, *Communicating a Christian World View in the Classroom,* National Association of Christian Educators, Costa Mesa, California, 1983, at page 6.

The quotes and descriptions on pages 189–190 from the booklet, *How to Elect Christians to Public Office,* were published by the National Association of Christian Educators, 1985.

Jo Ann Britt's quotes on pages 190–191 and the story are found in "Censorship Feels the Heat of Battle" by Marilyn Milloy, *Newsday,* June 30, 1987.

Chapter Thirteen, *pages 192 to 207*

The anecdote about Andy Ross on pages 192–193 and his quote on page 193 are found in "The Rushdie Crisis: A Report From the Front Lines" by Maureen J. O'Brien, *Publishers Weekly,* September 29, 1989, pages 45–47.

The Ayatollah's quotes on pages 195–196 appeared in most newspapers around the world, but I found them in "Khomeni: Rushdie Must Die," by Michael Ross, *Burlington Vt. Free Press,* February, 1989.

Lord Hale's quote on page 196 can be found in *Freedom of Speech in the United States* by Thomas Tedford (Carbondale, Illinois: Southern Illinois University Press, 1985) at page 52.

The full text of William Pynchon's pamphlet on page 197 and the history of its burning can be found in "American Book Burnings" by Walter Hart Blumenthal, *American Book Collector,* Summer, 1956, page 13.

The story of Ruggles on pages 197–198 is in "Blasphemy," *Columbia University Law Review,* 1970, pages 702–703.

For a description of the incident in California on page 199, see "In a Small Town, A Battle Over a Book" by Seth Mydone, *New York Times,* September 3, 1989, and an editorial on the incident, September 6, 1989.

Paul Blanshard's description of blasphemy on page 200 is found in his *The Right to Read* (Boston: Beacon Press, 1955) at page 205.

The quotes from the Iranian official on page 201 appeared in "Iran Urges that 'Satanic Verses' Be Burned," *New York Times,* March 11, 1989.

The incident of bookburning on pages 201–202 and the quotes therein can be found in "Satanic Books, Tapes Are Burned" by Schuyler Kropf, *Morgantown Dominion-Post,* September 15, 1986.

"The thing that is most disturbing . . ." on page 202 appears in "A Saddened Rushdie Calls Protests Unjustified" by Michael T. Kaufman, *New York Times,* February 4, 1989, page A14.

The incidents of bookburning in New York and St. Louis on pages 203–204 can be found in "American Bookburnings," page 18; the bookburning incidents in Philadelphia, Seminole, Oklahoma, and Alliance, Nebraska, can be found in *Newsletter on Intellectual Freedom,* January, 1964; November, 1987; and November, 1988; the bookstore burnings in Colorado Springs on page 204 are described in "Bookburnings" by Erwin Knoll, *The Progressive,* December, 1985, page 4.

A description of the decision by Revenue Canada on page 205 is found in "Ducking the Rushdie Challenge" by A. Fotheringham, *MacLeans,* march 6, 1989, at page 64; the "embarrassment" of Canada's Prime Minister on page 205 is described in "Diagnosis" A Severe Case of the Wobblies" by A. Fotheringham, *MacLeans,* March 27, 1986, page 56.

Harry Hoffman's and Leonard Riggio's quotes on page 205 appear in "Retailers Debate to Sell or Not," *Publishers Weekly,* March 3, 1989, page 26.

George Bush's quotes on page 206 are in "Bush Discusses Iranian Incitement," *Publishers Weekly,* March 3, 1989.

The remarks of Cardinal O'Connor's spokesman on page 206 are found in "O'Connor is Critical," *New York Times,* February 20, 1989.

Chapter Fourteen, *pages 208 to 222*

The banning of *Huckleberry Finn* and the quotes on pages 209–210 appear in "Banned in Boston and Elsewhere" by Randy F. Nelson, *The Almanac of American Letters* (Los Altos, CA: William Kaufman Inc., 1981) at pages 132–133.

The story of Mary Boyce Temple on pages 211–212 is set out in *Books and Battles* at pages 55–56.

Max Rafferty's efforts to ban *A Dictionary of American Slang* on pages 213–214 are described in *Banned Books* by Anne Lyon Haight (4th edition), published in New York by R.R. Bowker Co., 1977, at page 113.

The banning of Myra Cohn Livingstone's limerick described on page 216 appears in "An Author Looks at Censorship" by Lee Bennett Hopkins, *North Carolina Libraries Magazine,* Fall, 1987, at page 133.

The *Tarzan* anecdote on pages 217–218 is well-known and described in *Censorship: The Search for the Obscene* at page 235.

The attempt to ban Robin Hood on page 218 is set out in *The Right to Read* at pages 83–84.

Oregon's proposed law on page 219 is described in "The Dumbing of America" by Nat Hentoff, *The Progressive,* February, 1984, at page 31.

The reclassification of *Puzzle Palace* described on pages 221–222 appears in *Keeping America Uninformed: Government*

Secrecy in the 1980s by Donna A. Demac (New York: Pilgrim Press, 1984) at page 3.

Chapter Fifteen, *pages 223 to 238*

The full text of the CIA's Secrecy Agreement quoted on page 227 can be found in *Hearings Before the Subcommittee on Civil and Constitutional Rights of the Committee of the Judiciary,* House of Representatives, 98th Congress, April 21, 1984, pages 93–94.

The quoted testimony on pages 228–230 appears in *Hearings Before the Subcommittee on Oversight of the Permanent Select Committee on Intelligence,* House of Representatives, 96th Congress, 2nd session, April 16, 1980 at pages 51–52, 66–67.

Herbert Hetu's quote on page 230 appears in *Hearings Before the Subcommittee on Oversight* at page 2; for a graphic description of what was censored by CIA in *The CIA and the Cult of Intelligence,* see pages 130–162.

The quotes from Eileen Roach Smith on pages 232–234 and the description of the Publications Review Board are set out in her January, 1989, declaration to the United States District Court, Eastern District of Virginia, filed in connection with *United States v. Frank W. Snepp III*, Civil Action No. 78–92–A.

"It's too bad you didn't work . . ." on page 235 is in *Deadly Deceits* (New York: Sheridan Square Publications, 1983) at page 197; the dialogue on page 235 appears at page 199.

The Stansfield Turner quotes on pages 236–237 appear in the introduciton to his book (Boston: Houghton Mifflin Co., 1985) at pages x–xi.

Turner's testimony on pages 237–238 can be found in

Hearings Before the Committee on Government Operations, House of Representatives, 100th Congress, August 10, 1988, at pages 100, 108, 112.

Chapter Sixteen, *pages 239 to 252*

"Customs officers have legal authority . . ." quoted on page 240 is set forth in "Review, Copying and Editing of Documents," *Customs Directive* 3300–04, issued June 12, 1986, page 2.

The *ad hoc* nature of customs enforcement in the 19th and early 20th centuries on pages 240–244 is described in *Federal Censorship: Obscenity in the Mail* by James C.N. Paul and Murray L. Schwartz (Glencoe, Illinois: Free Press, 1961) pages 39–40.

Reference to America's first *Index* on page 243 appears in *The Right to Know: Censorship in America* by Robert A. Liston (New York: Franklin Watts, 1973) at page 27.

Writers and journalists banned by Immigration and Naturalization Service on pages 245–246 are noted in *Freedom at Risk: Secrecy, Censorship and Repression in the 1980s* by Richard Curry (Philadelphia: Temple University Press, 1988) at pages 58–59 and *Historical Dictionary of Censorship in the United States* by Leon Hurwitz (Westport, Connecticut: Greenwood Press, 1985) pages 169–170.

For background on Huntington Cairns described on pages 246–247, see *Federal Censorship: Obscenity in the Mail,* pages 12, 68–69, 88–91.

The story of Edward Haase described on pages 247–249 is set forth in *Haase v. Webster,* 608 Fed. Supp. 1227 (D.C. D.C. 1985), *affirmed* 807 F 2nd 208 (D.C. Circuit, 1986).

"[You] will recognize seditious matter . . ." quoted on

page 250 appears in "Restriction on Importation of Seditious Matter," *Customs Directive* 2210-01, issued August 29, 1986, page 1.

Background on the "record of nonviolation" on pages 250-251 appears in *Heidy v. U.S. Customs Service et al,* case no: CV 86-2365- JSL (Px), filed May 2, 1986 (C.D. California, 1988). "The mere existence and retention . . ." quoted on page 252 appears on page 17 of the opinion.

Chapter Seventeen, *pages 253-267*

John Garvey's quote on page 253 comes from "Tolerance Limits," *Commonweal,* September 26, 1986, page 487.

The full text of the Alabama loyalty oath mentioned on pages 254-255 and its effect is in *The Right to Read,* pages 97-98.

The biases of the Meese Commission board members mentioned on pages 255-258 are described in "Big Boobs; Ed Meese and His Pornography Commission" by Hendrik Hertzberg, *The New Republic,* July 14, 1986, page 21.

The Meese Commission quotes on pages 256-258 are taken from *The Attorney General's Commission on Pornography, Final Report,* U.S. Department of Justice, 1986, pages 367, 382-383.

Maxwell Lillienstein's quote on page 260 appears in *Publishers Weekly,* July 11, 1986 at page 44.

The quote from Benjamin Disraeli on page 261 appears in Chapter 24 of his well-known novel, *Lothair* (London: Longman's Standard Edition, 1870).

The comments of Dana Rohrabacher on pages 263-264 can be found in the *Congressional Record,* House of

Representatives, July 12, 1989, at page H3637; the comments of Pat Williams can be found on page H3651.

The comments of Jesse Helms on pages 265–266 appear in the *Congressional Record*, U.S. Senate, September 28, 1989, at pages S12110, S12130; the comments of Herb Kohl on page 267 appear on page S12130.

Chapter Eighteen, *pages 268–281*

Ralph Ellison's quote on page 269 appears in "The Censorship of the Adventures of Huckleberry Finn: An Investigation" by Michele Cloonan, *Top of the News*, Winter, 1984, page 193.

Raymond English's story and his quotes on pages 271–273 appear in "Trials of a Textbook Writer," *National Review*, February 24, 1989, page 36.

The banning of *Lord of the Flies* on pages 273–274 is described in *Newsletter on Intellectual Freedom*, September, 1988, page 152, with a further reference to *Toronto Globe and Mail*, June 24, 1988.

The book controversy in Amherst, Massachusetts, described on pages 274–275 is set out in "History is Mush" by Daniel Okrent, *New England Monthly*, February, 1989, at pages 12–13.

Andrea Dworkin's views described on pages 276–278 can be found in her *Letters From a War Zone* (New York: E.P. Dutton, 1989).

For a discussion of the "anti-porn" ordinance on pages 277–278, see "The Dubious Porn War Alliance" by Lisa Duggan, *Washington Post*, September 1, 1985.

"These [banning] laws can be used . . ." on page 278 appears in undated releases of F.A.C.T. (Feminist Anti-Censorship Taskforce), Box 135, 660 Amsterdam Avenue, New York, New York, circa 1985.

Judge Barker's statements on page 279 can be found in *American Bookseller's Association v. Hudnut*, 598 Fed. Supp. 1316 (S.D. Indiana, 1984) at apge 1337.

The survey and the quotes on pages 280–281 appear in "A study of Book-Length Works Taught in High School English Courses: by Arthur N. Applebee. *Center for the Learning and Teaching of Literature.* Albany, NY: State University of New York at Albany, 1989, pages 17–19.

Chapter Nineteen, *pages 282 to 293*

The trial testimony of James T. Farrell on pages 283–284 appears in *The First Freedom* by Robert Downs (Chicago: American Library Association, 1960) at page 294.

Henry Miller's letters to *The New Republic* on page 285 appeared in the "mailbag" column on November 8, 1943, at page 656, and on December 6, 1943, at pages 813–814.

M. Hugh MacLennon's testimony on pages 287–288 can be found in *Obscenité et Liberté* by Jacques Hébert (*Montreal: Editions du Jour Inc.*, 1970). I am indebted to Peggy Eriksson for her translation.

Bibliography

A number of newspaper and newsletter articles were used in research as well as congressional testimony and court opinions, and references to them all can be found in the Source Notes. They are not duplicated here, though references to major magazine articles and books that appeared in the Source Notes will be repeated, together with other unreferenced sources.

Books

Attacks on the Freedom to Learn, 1988–1989, 1987–1988. Washington D.C.: People for the American Way, 1989, 1988.

Bailey, Hugh C. *Hinton Rowan Helper: Abolitionist–Racist.* Tuscaloosa, Alabama: University of Alabama Press, 1965.

Blanshard, Paul. *The Right to Read — The Battle Against Censorship.* Boston: Beacon Press, 1955.

Bleikasten, Andre. *Faulkner's 'As I Lay Dying'.* Bloomington, Indiana: Indiana University Press, 1973.

Boyer, Paul S. *Purity in Print: The Vice-Society Movement and Book Censorship in America.* New York: Scribner's, 1968.

Burress, Lee. *Battle of the Books.* Metuchen, New Jersey: Scarecrow Press, 1989.

Burstyn, Varda. *Women Against Censorship.* Vancouver, Washington: Douglas and MacIntyre, 1985.

Cleaton, Irene and Allen. *Books and Battles.* Boston: Houghton Mifflin Co., 1937.

Cleland, John. *Memoirs of Fanny Hill.* New York: New American Library, 1965.

Corder, John W. *Handbook of Current English.* Glenview, Illinois: Scott, Foresman and Co., 1981.

Curry, Richard O. *Freedom at Risk: Secrecy, Censorship and Repression in the 1980s.* Philadelphia: Temple University Press, 1988.

de Grazia, Edward. *Censorship Landmarks.* New York: R.R. Bowker, 1969.

Demac, Donna A. *Keeping America Uninformed: Government Secrecy in the 1980s.* New York: Pilgrim Press, 1984.

Demac, Donna A. *Liberty Denied: The Current Rise of Censorship in America.* New York: PEN American Center, 1988.

Downs, Robert B. *The First Freedom.* Chicago: American Library Association, 1960.

Dworkin, Andrea. *Letters From a War Zone.* New York: E.P. Dutton, 1989.

Ellman, Richard. *James Joyce.* New York: Oxford University Press, 1959.

Ellman, Richard. *Ulysses on the Liffey*. New York: Oxford University Press, 1972.

Epstein, William H. *John Cleland: Images of a Life*. New York: Columbia University Press, 1974.

Ernst, Morris L., and Schwartz, Alan U. *Censorship: The Search for the Obscene*. New York: MacMillan Co., 1964.

Ernst, Morris L., and Seagle, William. *To the Pure*. . . . New York: Viking, 1928.

Fant, Joseph, and Ashley, Robert, eds. *Faulkner at West Point*. New York: Random House, 1964.

Farrer, James A. *Books Condemned to be Burned*. London: A.C. Armstrong, 1892.

Felsenthel, Carol. *Sweetheart of the Moral Majority*. Garden City, New York: Doubleday and Co., 1981.

Fite, Emerson. *The Presidential Campaign of 1860*. New York: Macmillan and Co., 1911.

Gavin, Clark. *Foul, False and Infamous: Famous Libel and Slander Cases of History*. New York: Abelard Press, 1950.

Gardner, Harold C. *Catholic Viewpoint on Censorship*. New York: Hanover House, 1958.

Geller, Evelyn. *Forbidden Books in American Public Libraries*. Westport, Connecticut: Greenwood Press, 1984.

Gwynn, Frederick L., and Blotner, Joseph L., eds. *Faulkner In the University*. Charlottesville, Virginia: University of Virginia Press, 1959.

Haight, Anne Lyon. *Banned Books — 387 B.C. to 1978 A.D.*. 4th ed. New York: R.R. Bowker, 1978.

Haney, Robert W. *Comstockery in America: Patterns of Censorship and Control*. New York: Da Capo Press, 1974.

Hebert, Jacques. *Obsenité et Liberté*. Montreal: Éditions du Jour, 1970.

Helper, Hinton Rowan. *The Impending Crisis in the South — How to Meet It.* New York: Collier Books, 1963.

Hentoff, Nat. *The First Freedom.* New York: Delacorte, 1980.

Hurwitz, Leon. *Historical Dictionary of Censorship.* Westport, Connecticut: Greenwood Press, 1985.

Hutchinson, E.R. *Tropic of Cancer on Trial: A Case History of Censorship.* New York: Grove Press, 1968.

Jenkinson, Edward B. *Censors in the Classroom: The Mind Benders.* Carbondale, Illinois: Southern Illinois University Press, 1979.

Jenkinson, Edward B. *The Schoolbook Protest Movement: 40 Questions and Answers.* Bloomington, Indiana: Phi Delta Kappa Educational Foundation, 1986.

Lewis, Felice Flanery. *Literature, Obscenity and the Law.* Carbondale, Illinois: Southern Illinois University Press, 1976.

Katz, Stanley Nider, ed. *A Brief Narrative of the Case and Trial of John Peter Zenger.* Cambridge, Massachusetts: Belknap Press of Harvard University, 1963.

Liston, Robert A. *The Right to Know: Censorship in America.* New York: Franklin Watts, 1973.

Marchetti, Victor, and Marks, John D. *The CIA and the Cult of Intelligence.* New York: Alfred Knopf, 1974.

McGeehee, Ralph W. *Deadly Deceits.* New York: Sheridan Square Publications, 1983.

Meriwether, James B. *Essays, Speeches and Public Letters by William Faulkner.* New York: Random House, 1965.

Mitgang, Herbert. *Dangerous Dossiers: Exposing the Secret War Against America's Greatest Authors.* New York: D.I. Fine, 1988.

Nelson, Randy F. *Almanac of American Letters.* Los Altos, California: William Kauffman Inc., 1981.

Oboler, Eli M. *The Fear of the Word*. Metuchen, New Jersey: Scarecrow Press, 1974.

Paine, Albert Bigelow. *Mark Twain: A Biography*. New York: Harper, 1912.

Paul, James C.N., and Schwartz, Murray L., *Federal Censorship: Obscenity in the Mail*. Glencoe, Illinois: Free Press, 1961.

Perrin, Noel. *Dr. Bowdler's Legacy*. New York: Atheneum, 1969.

Pivar, David J. *Purity Crusade, Sexual Morality and Social Control 1868–1900*. Westport, Connecticut: Greenwood Press, 1973.

Reichman, Henry. *Censorship and Selection,* Chicago: American Library Association/American Association of School Administrators, 1988.

Rembar, Charles. *The End of Obscenity*. New York: Random House, 1968.

Rhodes, James F. *History of the United States From The Compromise of 1850*. New York: Macmillan Co., 1910.

Schlafly, Phyllis, ed. *Child Abuse in the Classroom*. Alton, Illinois: Pere Marquette Press, 1984.

Snepp, Frank W. *Decent Interval*. New York: Random House, 1977.

Stevens, John D. *Shaping the First Amendment*. Beverly Hills, California: Sage Publications, 1982.

Tedford, Thomas L. *Freedom of Speech in the United States*. Carbondale, Illinois: Southern Illinois University Press, 1985.

Thomas, Cal. *Book Burning*. Westchester, Illinois: Crossways Books, 1983.

Turner, Stansfield. *Secrecy and Democracy: The CIA in Transition*. Boston: Houghton Mifflin Co., 1985.

Van Alstyne, William. *Interpretations of the First Amendment.* Durham, NC: Duke University Press, 1984.

West, Mark I., ed. *Trust Your Children: Voices Against Censorship in Children's Literature.* New York: Neal-Schumann, 1988.

Zeisel, William, ed. *Censorship: 500 Years of Conflict.* New York: Oxford University Press, 1984.

Articles

Abrams, Floyd. "The New Effort to Control Information." *New York Times Sunday Magazine,* September 25, 1983.

Alter, Jonathan. "Slaying the Message: How the Frank Snepp Case Hurts Us All." *Washington Monthly,* September, 1981.

Aufderheide, Pat. "The Next Voice You Hear." *The Progressive,* September 1985.

Barnett, Lincoln. "The Case of John Peter Zenger." *American Heritage,* December, 1971.

"Blasphemy" (Note). *Columbia University Law Review,* 1970.

Blumenthal, Walter H. "American Book Burnings." *American Book Collector,* Summer 1956.

Bolte, Charles G. "Security Through Book Burning." *Annals of the American Academy of Political and Social Sciences.* Vol. 2, July, 1955.

Bowen, Ezra. "Courtroom Clash Over Textbooks." *Time Magazine,* October 27, 1986.

Boyer, Paul S. "Boston Book Censorship in the Twenties." *American Quarterly,* Vol. 15, Spring, 1963.

Cairns, Huntington. "Freedom of Expression in Literature," in *Annals of the American Academy of Political and Social Science 76,* (1938).

Campbell, C. "BookBanning in America." *New York Times Book Review,* December 20, 1981.

"Books and Schools" (editorial). *Nation,* May, 30, 1987.

Carlin, D.R. Jr. "God's Right Hand." *Commonweal,* May 8, 1987.

Carver, George. "The CIA's Case Against Snepp." *Newsweek,* March 17, 1980.

"Censorship in Children's Books (Symposium)." *Publishers Weekly.* July 24, 1987.

Cloonan, Michele V. "The Censorship of The Adventures of Huckleberry Finn: An Investigation." *Top of the News.* Winter, 1984.

De Voto, Bernard. "The Case of the Censorious Congressman." *Harper's Magazine,* April, 1953.

Dick, Judith. "North of 49: Schools and Controversial Books in Canada." *Phi Delta Kappan,* March, 1982.

Doyle, Kevin, ed. "Sex and Censorship." *MacLeans,* September 1, 1986.

English, Raymond. "Trials of a Textbook Writer." *National Review,* February 24, 1989.

Faulkner, William. "On Privacy." *Harper's Magazine,* July, 1955.

Fields, H. "Senate Unit Hears Testimony on Censorship." *Publishers Weekly,* March 24, 1989.

Florence, Heather G. "Controlling Ideas." *Society,* July/August, 1987.

Fotheringham, A. "Diagnosis: A Severe Case of the Wobblies." *MacLeans,* March 27, 1989.

Fotheringham, A. "Ducking the Rushdie Challenge." *MacLeans,* March 6, 1989.

Garvey, John. "Tolerance Limits." *Commonweal,* September 26, 1986.

Gest, T. "A Bombshell Court Ruling in Tennessee." *U.S. News & World Report,* November 3, 1986.

Glenn, C.L. "Other Sides of the Textbook Controversy." *Christian Century,* July 15–22, 1987.

Grant, Sidney S., and Angoff, Samuel E. "Massachusetts and Censorship." *Boston University Law Review,* January, 1930.

Hentoff, Nat. "The Dumbing of America." *The Progressive,* February, 1984.

Hertzberg, Hendrik. "Big Boobs: Ed Meese and His Pornography Commission." *The New Republic,* July 14/21, 1986.

Holbrook, Stewart H. "Hinton Helper and His Crisis." *American Mercury,* January, 1945.

Hopkins, Lee Bennett. "An Author Looks at Censorship." *North Carolina Libraries Magazine,* Fall, 1987.

Janigan, Mary. "Confronting Pornography." *MacLean's,* October 29, 1984.

Jorstad, E. "What Johnny Can't Read." *Commonweal,* June 17, 1988.

Kilodney, Crad. "Kill the Censor!" *Harper's Magazine,* September, 1986.

Knoll, Erwin. "Bookburners." *The Progressive,* December, 1985.

Krug, Judith F. "Intellectual Freedom in the 1980s." *North Carolina Libraries Magazine,* Fall, 1987.

Lamb, L. "Censorship in Publishing." *Utne Reader,* January/February, 1988.

Lanier, Gene D. "Intellectual Freedom — That Neglected Topic. An Introduction." *North Carolina Libraries Magazine,* Fall, 1987.

Lawton, K.A. "Striking Down the Textbook Rulings." *Christianity Today,* October 2, 1987.

Lettis, R. "Book is Not For Burning." *Journal of Reading,* November, 1977.

Lewin, Nathan. "The High Court Hexes Free Speech." *The New Republic,* March 22, 1980.

Lyach, B.P. "Freedom to Choose. *Society,* July/August, 1987.

Marchese, John. "The Bustling Days and Rum-and-Coke Nights of Barney Rosset." *Seven Days,* September, 1989.

Miller, Henry (letters). "From the New Republic Mailbag." *The New Republic,* November 8, 1943; December 6, 1943.

Miller, Holly G. "Concerned Women for America: Soft Voices With Clout." *Saturday Evening Post,* October, 1985.

Mitgang, Herbert. "Royalties to the Treasury." *New York Times Book Review,* August 31, 1980.

Muck, T.C. "Unrighteous Indignation." *Christianity Today.* April 7, 1989.

Nelson, Jack. "Censors and Their Tactics." *Library Journal,* December 15, 1963.

O'Brien, Maureen J. "The Rushdie Crisis: A Report From the Frontlines." *Publishers Weekly,* September 29, 1989.

Okrent, Daniel. "History is Mush." *New England Monthly,* February, 1989.

"A Plague of Censors" (Comment). *The Progressive,* July, 1986.

Poppel, Norman, and Ashley, Edwin M. "Toward an Understanding of the Censor." *Library Journal,* July, 1986.

Reuter, Madalynne, ed. "Book World Reacts to Khomeni's Threats." *Publishers Weekly,* March 3, 1989.

Scales, Peter. "Sex, Psychology and Censorship: Preserving the Freedom of the Mind." *Humanist,* September/October, 1987.

Schott, James C. "Holy Wars in Education." *Educational Leadership,* October, 1989.

Snepp, Frank. "The CIA vs. Me." *Newsweek,* July 31, 1978.

"Special Report on Censorship" (Symposium). *Publishers Weekly,* July 11, 1986.

Sumner, John. "Effective Action Against Salacious Plays." *American City,* November, 1925.

Sumner, John. "Obscene Literature—Its Suppression." *Publishers Weekly,* July 8, 1916.

Sumner, John. "The Truth About 'Literary Lynching'." *Dial,* July, 1921.

Swan, John. "Untruth or Consequences." *Library Journal,* July, 1986.

Teachout, T. "The Pornography Report That Never Was." *Commentary,* August, 1987.

Wall, J.M. "A New Right Tool Distorts Regulations." *Christian Century.* April 24, 1985.

Wall, J.M. "Scopes Trial II: A Narrow God Defended." *Christian Century,* July 30–August 8, 1986.

West, M.I. "What Is Fit For Children?" *New York Times Book Review,* August 24, 1986.

White, Howard D. "Majorities for Censorship." *Library Journal,* July, 1986.

Williams, J.A. "Prior Restraints [discrimination against Blacks in publishing decisions acts as censorship]." *Nation,* April 23, 1988.

Woodward, K.L. "Secular Humanism in the Dock." *Newsweek,* October 27, 1986.

Books Challenged or Banned

Authors Challenged
or Banned

Index

332